AF726123

COLLECTED WRITINGS OF W. D. GANN

VOLUME 5

# INTRODUCTORY STOCK MARKET COURSES

## *MECHANICAL METHODS*

## *AND*

## *TREND FOLLOWING SYSTEMS*

BY

**WILLIAM D. GANN**

*COSMOLOGICAL ECONOMICS*
*WWW.COSMOECONOMICS.COM*

This Edition © Copyright 2015
Cosmological Economics
www.CosmoEconomics.com

This Series is Published by the:
Institute of Cosmological Economics

Cosmological Economics
is an imprint of:
Sacred Science Institute
www.SacredScience.com
institute@sacredscience.com
US: 800-756-6141 θ Intl: 951-659-8181

## *COSMOLOGICAL ECONOMICS*

# THE MASTERS OF TECHNICAL ANALYSIS SERIES

The Masters of Technical Analysis Series brings together a collection of the most important classical and modern works on technical analysis and financial market forecasting. These classic works from the Golden Age of Technical Analysis were carefully selected by the late Dr. Jerome Baumring of the Investment Centre Bookstore in the 1980's, as representing the most valuable and important works in technical analysis ever written. They were included as the foundational source texts for his program in advanced financial market analysis and forecasting, and serve as the ideal foundation for any analyst seeking a thorough education in market theory and technical trading.

The Golden Age of technical analysis was a period from the early 1900's through the 1960's where the foundational theories of modern financial analysis were initially developed. The ideas and technologies developed during this fruitful period have formed the basis for most modern technical market theory, which is considered to be mostly a repetition or reworking of these past ideas and techniques developed by the Old Masters of the Golden Age. In these historical works can be found the timeless trading wisdom which has laid the foundation for all modern investment theory and literature. These techniques are as useful in today's markets as they were in the past, providing rare and valuable insights, tools and strategies that give the modern trader an edge over traders and investors that are unaware of these time honored tools.

Each quality reprint of these classical texts has been reproduced as an exact facsimile of the original text, maintaining the original layout, typeset, charts, and style of the author and time period, helping to preserve and communicate a sense of the feeling of the original work that a reproduction in modern format does not capture. Many of these rare works and courses were originally printed in only very small private editions or as correspondence courses, so that the originals were easily lost or destroyed over time. Our reproductions of these important source works have been printed on acid free paper and bound in a quality hardcover format that will compliment any trading library and help to preserve this important resource for generations to come.

The series is also currently being digitized and archived for permanent digital preservation by the Institute of Cosmological Economics, creating a searchable reference library of market wisdom accessible globally and available in new digital formats to keep the knowledge fresh and accessible through new devices and technology as we advance further into the information revolution. To see our full catalog of hardcover reprints, new publications, and digital editions please visit our website at www.CosmoEconomics.com.

# Introductory Stock Market Courses
# Mechanical Methods & Trend Indicators

## W. D. Gann

# Chapter 1

## *Speculation As A Profitable Profession*

## *A Course Of Instructions On Stocks*

# SPECULATION A PROFITABLE PROFESSION

A Course of Instructions
on Stocks

by

W.D.GANN

# SPECULATION A PROFITABLE PROFESSION

A Course of Instructions With Rules for Trading in Stocks

## FOREWORD

Be ready for opportunities. Knowledge more important than capital. To succeed in any business you must be prepared, and in preparing for a speculative or investment business you must look up the greatest advance or the greatest decline a stock has ever had and the greatest time period from the high or low. Most profits are made in active fast moving markets. Examples: Stocks 1924-1929- September 29th to November 15th, 1929; November 13, 1929 to April 17, 1930.

## FAST ADVANCES

You will find these from June 1949 to June 1950; June 13, 1950 to July 14, 1950 this was a fast decline.
1952 and 1953 - September 1953 to April 1954, fast advance.

## SLOW TRADING MARKET

You should keep out of slow trading markets or watch until you get a definite indication of a change in trend. There was a slow trading market from November 1946 to November 1949, that is the range in most stocks was narrow because the market was going through a period of consolidation or accumulation and getting ready for the big bull market which followed later.

## CROSS CURRENTS

You must learn to know that some stocks sometimes are declining while others are advancing, and that there are cross currents, and you must know about these. Example: 1952 to 1954 Studebaker, Chrysler, Celanese declined while Vanadium, Steel, DuPont and Aircraft stocks advanced. Only by a study of the individual stocks and the different groups can you determine what stock is supposed to decline at the time when another stock is going to advance.

## HOW TO SELECT THE GROUP OF STOCKS WHICH WILL LEAD AN ADVANCE OR A DECLINE

During 1953 - 1954 the Aircrafts were big leaders. You can see from the chart and the group of the averages on Aircrafts where they broke into new high levels. Example: Douglass Aircraft, Boeing Aircraft, United, Glenn Martin and Lockheed all indicated that they were in a position to advance when the average price or average value of the group of stocks indicated a strong position. Without a knowledge of these things y could not make a success.

LOW PRICE STOCKS DISAPPOINTING

A study past history proves that buying low price stocks often ties up capital for a long period of time. You wait, and if you do not lose money you lose your patience and when your patience is exhausted in advance of the start you get out. Many low price stocks have held in a narrow trading for 5, 10 years or more before they started to advance or to decline and some, after remaining in a narrow trading range for a long period of time, declined to new low levels. The best way to make money is to take higher price stocks and buy them after they have broken into new high ground and show activity as outlined under the rules below.

NEW INDUSTRIES AND GROWTH STOCKS

Select stocks to buy in new industries but make careful study of their prospects and make up charts on stocks that you intend to trade in, and if they are part of a group that you can get a record of, study this group and then pick the individual stock to buy that shows indication of leading the group.

STOCKS OF THE FUTURE

When considering what stocks to buy in the future, you must make up charts and study the companies which are producing Uranium and are developing Atomic Energy machinery for commercial purposes. Among this group of stocks are Babcock & Wilcox Co., Bendix Aviation Corp., Dow Chemical Co., DuPont , General Dynamics Corp., General Electric (which is one of the largest in the business and has orders from the U. S. Government as well as a few commercial concerns), Newport News Shipbuilding, Phillips Petroleum, Sylvania Electric Products, Inc., Union Carbide and Carbon Corp., Vanadium Corp. of America and Westinghouse Electric Corp.

Among the very best of these stocks for the future we consider Vanadium, Molybedeum, General Dynamics Corp., which has now consolidated with Consolidated Vultee.

Among the low priced stocks with future possibilities of enhancement in value due to Uranium deposits is New Park Mining listed on the American Exchange. Fairchilds Engine and Aircraft Corp. also has possibilities of becoming a future leader.

You must, of course, buy any of these stocks at the time the total value of all stocks on the N. Y. Stock Exchange show up-trend and buy the best of the individual stocks when the individual groups show up-trend, selecting the one you buy that is in the strongest position.

You would not buy any of these higher priced stocks at the present time because the total value of all stocks on the N. Y. Stock Exchange is at the highest levels in history and because the trend of stocks has been up in a general way since 1932 and the last extreme low was April 1942 and the present swing in the bull market started in June, 1949. Therefore it is natural to expect a decline in stocks during the last half of 1954 and you must be cautious on the buying side.

## HOW TO MAKE SPECULATION A PROFITABLE PROFESSION

Speculation or investment is the best business in the world if you make a business of it. But in order to make a success of it you must study and be prepared and not guess, follow inside information or depend on hope or fear. If you do you will fail. Your success depends on knowing the right kind of rules and following them.

## FUNDAMENTAL RULES

Keep this well in mind. For stocks to show up-trend and continue to advance they must make higher bottoms and higher tops. When the trend is down they must make lower tops and lower bottoms and continue on down to lower levels. But remember, prices can move in a narrow trading range for weeks or months or even years and not make a new high or a new low. But after a long period of time when the stocks break into new lows they indicate lower prices and after a long period of time when they advance above old highs or old tops they are in a stronger position and indicate higher prices. This is the reason why you must have a chart a long way back in order to see just what position the stock is in and at what stage it is between extreme high and extreme low.

## THE KIND OF CHARTS TO KEEP UP

Remember the old Chinese proverb, "One good picture is worth 10,000 words". You should make up charts and study the picture of a stock before you make a trade. You should have a weekly high and low chart, a monthly high and low chart, and a yearly high and low chart. A yearly high and low chart should run back 5, 10 or 20 years, if you can get records that far. Monthly high and low chart should run back for at least 10 years and the weekly high and low chart should run back for 2 or 3 years. When stocks are very active you should have a daily high and low chart. This need not go back more than a few months, especially start the daily chart after the stock breaks into great activity.

## FOLLOW THE MAIN TREND

You will always make money by following the main trend of stocks up or down. Remember that stocks are never too high to buy as long as the trend is up and they are never too low to sell as long as the trend is down. Never sell short just because the stock is high or because you think it is too high. Never sell out and take profits just because the price is high. Buy and sell according to definite rules and not on hope, fear or guesswork. Never buy a stock just because the stock is low. There is usually a good reason why it is low and it can go lower.

## RULES FOR BUYING AND SELLING

The first thing to remember before you start to apply any rules is that you must always use a STOP LOSS order to protect your capital. When making a trade remember that you can be wrong or that the market may change its trend and the STOP LOSS order will protect you and limit your loss. A small loss or several small losses can easily be made back with one large profit but when you let large losses run against you it is hard to make them back.

## PROVE ALL THINGS AND HOLD FAST TO THAT WHICH IS GOOD

The Bible tells us this and it is well worth remembering. Many people believe that it is wrong to buy at new high levels or to sell at new low levels but it is most profitable and you must prove this to yourself because when you do buy at new high levels or sell at new low levels you are going with the trend of the market and your chances for making profits are much better than any guesswork or buying or selling on hope or fear.

## PROLONGED ADVANCES

After stocks have had a prolonged advance and wind up with a fast, active, runaway market in most cases they come down very quickly and much faster or in a shorter period of time than when they go up. That is why you must keep up some daily charts at the end of a fast move and keep up the weekly charts to determine the first change in trend and be able to go with it.

## SHARP DECLINE IN A SHORT PERIOD OF TIME

This usually follows a rapid advance and the first sharp declines which may last from one month to as much as seven weeks usually corrects an overbought position and leaves the market in position for a secondary advance.

When you are able to catch extremes at the end of any great time cycle you can make a large amount of money in one year's time trading in fast active markets. It makes no difference whether you catch the extreme low or the extreme high; the opportunities are great for making money providing you select the stocks that will lead.

LARGE PROFITS ON SMALL RISKS

You can make large profits on small risks provided you use a STOP LOSS order and apply all the rules, then wait for a definite indication of a change in trend up or down before you make a trade.

FIXED IDEAS AND FIXED PRICES

Never get a fixed idea of just how high any price is going to go or just how low they are going. Never buy or sell on a price that you fix because you may be trading on hope or fear and not following the trend of the market and applying rules which will determine when the trend is changing.

HOW TO PROTECT PROFITS

After you have accumulated profits it is just as important to protect them with STOP LOSS orders as it is to protect your original capital because once you have made profits it is your capital and STOP LOSS orders must be used to protect it. The most dangerous thing that you can do is to let a trade start going against you. You lose back your profits. A STOP LOSS order will protect the profits and you can always get in again when you are out with capital. Remember when you are out of the market, the only thing you can lose or miss is an opportunity.

My 52 years' experience has taught me that thousands of people have gone broke trying to hold on until the trend turned. Avoid getting out of the market too soon after move starts when you have a small profit. This can be a great mistake. Get out of the market quickly as soon as you see that you have made a mistake. If you place a STOP LOSS order this will put you out of the market automatically.

TOO LATE OR TOO SOON

You can lose money or miss opportunity by getting into the market too soon or getting out too late. That is, not waiting until a definite change in trend is indicated or failing to act in time when you see a definite change in trend. Wait until you have a well defined indication that the trend has changed, then buy or sell. Follow all the rules in my book "45 YEARS IN WALL STREET". There are many rules in my book "45 YEARS IN WALL STREET" which are not in this course of instruction and by using all the rules you will make a greater success.

HOPE AND FEAR

I repeat this because I have seen so many people go broke trading on hope or fear. You will never succeed buying or selling when you hope the market is going up or down. You will never succeed by making a trade because you fear the market is going up or down. Hope will ruin you because it is nothing more than wishful thinking and provides no basis for action. Fear will often save you if you act quickly when you see that you are wrong. "The fear of the market is the beginning of wisdom". Knowledge which you can only obtain by deep study will help you to make a success. The more you study past records the surer you are to be able to detect the trend of the future.

MAKE THE MARKET MOVE YOUR WAY

You must learn to realize that you cannot make the market go your way, you must go the market's way and must follow the trend. Many successful business men who are accustomed to giving orders to others and have them carried out will often, when they get into the market, especially for the first time, expect the market to follow their orders or move their way. They must learn that they cannot make the market trend go their way. They must follow the market trend as is indicated by fixed rules and protect their capital and profits by the use of STOP LOSS orders. There is no harm in making a few mistakes and a few small losses because small losses are the expense of a successful speculator.

NEVER AVERAGE A LOSS

This is the surest way to lose all or a great part of your capital. If you have bought a stock and it shows you a loss, the trend is moving against you, and it is very foolish to buy more, which will only increase your losses. The time to increase buying is when the market is moving in your favor, and you have a profit. If you intend to make speculation a profitable profession, you must learn all the rules and apply all of them to determine the trend. Professional men, such as lawyers, doctors, accountants and engineers spend years in training and a large amount of money to learn how to succeed in their chosen profession. You must spend time and money to learn the profession and become a successful speculator or investor.

RULE 1. Buy at new high prices or old top levels.

RULE 2. Buy when prices advance above old low price levels.

RULE 3. Sell when prices decline below old top levels or high prices.

RULE 4. Sell at new low price levels. As a general rule it is safer to wait until prices advance at least 1 to 2 points above high levels and still more important to wait until they close above these levels before buying and at the same time it is safer to wait until prices decline 1 to 2 points below old levels and still safer to wait until they close below these old levels before making a trade.

RULE 5. Closing Prices. Wait to buy or sell until prices close above old highs or below old lows on the daily or weekly charts when markets are very active and moving fast; it is important to use the daily high and low chart and the closing price above highs or below lows. Prices may advance rapidly during the day but when it comes to closing time they may run off several points and close lower than the previous day, and at the same time when there is a sharp decline, prices may go below the low of the previous day but when they close they close near the high levels; therefore, it is the closing price that is always important to keep up on the daily, weekly or monthly high or low charts. The longer the time period in days, weeks, months or years when prices exceed old highs or break old lows, the greater the importance of the change in trend and the move up or down. Remember the general rule, when prices advance to new high levels they generally react back to the old tops which is a safe place to buy and when they decline below old lows, as a rule they rally back to the old lows which is a safe place to sell. Always, of course, protect with STOP LOSS orders.

RULE 6. STOP LOSS ORDERS. Your capital and your profits must be protected at all times with STOP LOSS orders which must be placed when you make the trade and not later.

RULE 7. Amount of capital required. It is very important to know exactly how much of your capital you can risk on any one trade and never lose all of your capital. When you make a trade you should never risk more than 10% of the capital you have to trade with, and if you have one or two losses, reduce your units of trading.

THE BEST BUYING POINT. This point is when prices decline to 50% of the highest price at which a stock has ever sold; the next strongest and best buying price is 50% between the extreme low and the extreme high (See example on Chrysler Motors).

SELLING LEVEL: When prices advance after they have been considerably below the 50% point and advance for the FIRST TIME, it is a selling level and a price to sell short, protected with STOP LOSS orders 3 points above the 50% level. The first time a stock reaches these levels, if the indications on the daily chart and the weekly chart show it is making tops, you should sell out long stocks and sell short.

The next important selling level is 50% between the extreme low and the extreme high.

CHRYSLER MOTORS: Example of 50% price.

1946, February high 141½, divide by two and get 50% of the highest selling price. This gives 70 3/4. After Chrysler was split up and sold ex-stock dividend in 1947, it declined to 44 in June 1949; from this level, which was a buying point, the trend started up.

1953, January high 98½; we always expect selling just under 100 and Chrysler made top at this level. We figure the range being 44 and 98½ which gives a 50% price at 71¼.

1953, June Chrysler low 70, just below the 50% price. It rallied to 73 in August which was a very feeble rally and closed at 71 indicating lower and was a short sale.

1932, Chrysler extreme low $5 per share; 1953 high 141½. 50% of these extremes is 73¼; when Chrysler can advance and close above 73¼ it will indicate higher prices.

1954, February, Chrysler declined to 57 and has shown very little rallying power. At the time of this writing the main trend is down and when it closes below 57 it will indicate lower. The next price to watch is the old low of 44 made in June 1949.

Look up the extreme highs and lows and figure all other stocks in the same way to get buying and selling points and resistance levels.

When you start trading be sure that you know all of the rules and that you follow them, and be sure that you place a STOP LOSS order.

WHERE TO PLACE STOP LOSS ORDERS: You must place STOP LOSS orders below the lows of swings and not just below the lows on the daily chart. STOPS must be above old tops or below old bottoms on a weekly or monthly chart.

STOP LOSS orders should be placed below closing prices on the daily, weekly or monthly chart. They are much safer under closing prices and less likely to be caught, because you are trading with the trend. STOP LOSS orders placed above closing prices on the daily or weekly chart are caught a smaller number of times than if you place them below the daily bottoms or daily tops.

The swings or reversals in the market are the prices to place STOP LOSS orders below the price of the swing or above the price of the swing. It is of great importance to know where to place STOP LOSS orders properly.

For stocks selling around $10 a STOP LOSS order is usually safe if you place it 1-point below closing price.

For stocks selling between 20 and 30, STOPS should be placed 2-points below bottoms or below closing prices.

Stocks selling between 90 and 150; in this range of prices STOPS should be 3-points under the lows or closing prices, and 3-points above the high or low closing prices.

When stocks are very active and selling at these extreme high prices, you must depend upon the daily high and low chart to give you the first indication of a change in trend which will later be confirmed on the weekly high and low charts.

When stocks are selling at extreme high levels, follow all the rules in my book, "45 YEARS IN WALL STREET", and if you have taken my Master Forecasting Course apply the rules on Great Time Cycles as well as the minor time periods.

Remember you can never have too much knowledge. Continue to study and learn more for the knowledge can always be turned into profits later.

WHAT TO DO BEFORE YOU MAKE A TRADE. Check all records of prices, daily, weekly, monthly and yearly and note all time periods. Note when the prices are near some old high levels or nearsome old low levels of recent weeks or years. Then calculate just what your risk will be before you make the trade and after you make it, place the STOP LOSS order for your protection in case you are wrong.

WEEKLY HIGH AND LOW CHART: The weekly high and low chart is a very important trend indicator. When prices get above a series of weekly highs or lows, or decline below a series of weekly lows, it is of greater importance and indicates a greater change in trend which may last for many weeks.

MONTHLY HIGHS AND LOWS: When prices advance above or decline below prices which have occurred for many months past, it means a greater change in trend which can last for several months.

YEARLY HIGHS AND LOWS: When prices advance above or decline below the prices made several years in the past, it is nearly always a sure sign of big moves which will last for a long period of time or at least have a greater advance or decline in a short period of time, and when these old highs are crossed, or lows broken, always watch for a reaction to come back to around the old highs or slightly lower and after they are broken, expect the rally to advance back to around the old highs or slightly below.

Study the yearly highs and lows and you will see the proof. Remember the greater the time period when it is exceeded, the greater the move up or down.

RULES FOR STOCKS:

A. How much decline to expect in a bull market and how much rally to expect in a bear market.

After a bull market gets under way and stocks are moving up fast, the reactions are likely to be quick and sharp but they will never last more than 3 to 4 weeks as a general rule and then the upward trend will be resumed, so you can always figure that stocks are a buy on a reaction of about 1 month in a bull market. In a bear market after the main trend has been established downward, the rallies will run three weeks to four weeks and seldom ever more than one month, but in some cases after sharp, severe declines in a short period of time rallies will last as much as 2 months - just the same there is a possibility of a reaction in a bull market running 2 months after extremes. By keeping theserules in mind you will have a guide as to when the main trend is changing up or down.

B. How to make the most money in the shortest period of time.

People want to get rich quick, that is why they lose their money because they try to get rich quick without first preparing themselves for getting ready or having the knowledge to know how and when to make the most money in the shortest period of time. I am going to prove to you, by examples, and you can also prove to yourself, when you can make the most money in the shortest period of time. Do not try to lead the market or make the market. Follow the big men with big money and you will make big money. Buy when the big market makers are ready for prices to move up fast and you will make the most money in a short period of time. Sell when the big market money makers have distributed stocks and are ready for them to go down and there is indication of a definite trend downward. Then sell short and you will make the most money in the shortest period of time.

It requires time for a market to get ready, time for stocks to be absorbed or accumulated but once we have passed from weak into strong hands, then they move up fast because the offerings are smaller and the big people just have to let the market roll and do a little buying and it goes up easy.

It also requires a long period of time to sell out stocks or distribute them once they have reached the high levels and let the stocks pass from strong hands into weak hands. When this period is over and the market is ready, then it declines fast and if you trade this way and wait until there is a definite indication that the trend has changed, you really can make the most money in the shortest period of time.

Below I am giving you some examples to prove that these rules work and that the market goes up the fastest after a long period of time and down fastest in the last stages after a long period of declining market.

BOEING AIRCRAFT 1949, June low 17½; 1950, May high 31½, UP 14 points in 11 months.

1950, September. Buy at 37 in new highs; 1951, February high 56, up 19 points in 5 months. This is making the most profits in the quickest and shortest period of time.

1954, February. Buy at 57 at new highs. 1954, April Sell at 83, UP 26 points in 2 months. It takes nerve to buy at new highs but that is what big people do and you are only following them when you buy at new high levels and then you make the most money in the shortest period of time.

DOUGLAS AIRCRAFT: 1951, June low 43½; October 1951 high 66½, UP 23 points in 4 months.

GLENN L. MARTIN: 1949, June low 7; 1951 high 22; 1952, July low 9. Therefore, the low of 9 in July 1952 was a higher bottom, a support and buying level. The trend was up until February 1953, high 18½. Note last previous high 19½ in September 1951; from this lower top the trend started down.

1953, June to September low 12 at the old tops of April to September 1952, remaining for four months in a range of 2 points and indicated good support and a buying level and you should buy.

1954, February crossed 18⅞, the high of February 1953. Here you would follow the rule and buy at new high levels.

1954, high is 25½ on a volume of 384 thousand shares for the week ending April 3, 1954. The large volume indicated public buying at high levels and short covering and a reaction was due.

Note April 1948 high 22½ and January 1951 high 22; the price of 25½ was 3½ points above these old high levels indicating a possibility of higher prices.

Later. The reaction during the week ending May 8 brought prices down to 21 3/4 which was at the old high levels of 1948-1951 and a rally started up from 21 3/4.

UNITED AIRCRAFT: 1951, May high 41½; 1951, July low 26; 1951, October high 33; 1951, December low 28½; 1952, February high 33½, same high as October 1951 and a selling level.

1952, May low 27½, about the same low as December 1951 and higher than June 1951 low.

1952, September crossed 33, the old high. Buy at new highs.

1953, April high 40½, just below 41½, the high of May 1951, making this a selling level.

1953, April and May low 32 to 31½, just below the old tops of 33, a buying level, then the advance was resumed.

1953, October prices crossed 41½, the high of May 1951. Follow the rule and buy at new high levels as the trend was up and continued up with very small reactions.

1954, April high 59½, the highest price since September 1930 when the last high was 65 and the two previous highs were 64; therefore, 64-65 is the next resistance level to watch for tops. The price is now up more than 100% from May 1952 and a natural reaction often comes when stocks have advanced 100%.

Analyze any other Aircraft stock in the same way in which we have analyzed these stocks and in fact any other stock of any other group. First you should keep a chart of the total value of the group as published by the New York Stock Exchange Statistical Bureau and then keep up weekly, monthly and yearly highs and lows on the different individual stocks so that you will have a record far enough back that you will know where the important tops and bottoms are and know when change in trend comes by prices advancing above old highs or breaking below old lows. You cannot have too much information or too many records when you are going to risk your capital. You must be fully prepared and ready, then you can take advantage of opportunities when they come based on scientific mathematical deductions and not hope, fear or guesswork.

DOUGLAS AIRCRAFT: 1953, October buy at new high 74. 1954, April sell at 133. UP 59 points in 6 months. This was making the most money in a short period of time after you bought it at very high levels. Why? Because the big people had absorbed all the stock offered below and offerings were very small, so when buyers come in the market advanced rapidly and profits to the buyers who bought at high levels made profits fast in a short period of time.

LOCKHEED AIRCRAFT: 1943, November low 12½; 1944, August high 24, 11½ points profit in 21 months.

1945, August low 25; 1946, May high 45½, up 21½ points in 5 months. Here you were making nearly as much in 5 months as you made in 21 months previously.

1951, July low 17½; 1953, March 26½, UP 9 points in 20 months. A small profit in a long period of time.

1953, October. Buy at 24 above old highs; 1954, March high 37 profit, 13 points in 5 months. This is making a quick profit and a large profit based on the capital in a short period of time.

GLEN L. MARTIN: 1943, December low 14½; 1944, December high 24½, up 10 points in 12 months.

1945, August Buy at 22; 1945, December sell at 46½, UP 24½ points in 4 months. This is again making the most profits in the shortest period of time.

1952, June low 9; 1953, March 18½, UP 9½ points in 8 months.

1953, June to September low 12. This is a buying level; 1953, October, Buy at 15 after it crossed 5 months tops. 1954, April, sell at 26. Profit 9 points in 6 months.

SOUTHERN RAILWAY: 1951, July low 46½. September high 56½, UP 10 points in 2 months.

1952, February low 48; 1952, March buy at 53 after it crossed old tops. 1953, May sell at 99, UP 46 points in 12 months. This is making the most profits in the short period of time.

UNITED AIRCRAFT: 1951, July low 26; 1953, March high 40, UP 14 points in 20 months. 1953, October buy at 40 at a newhigh. 1952, April sell at 59. Profit 19 points in 6 months.

VANADIUM STEEL: 1950, December low 28½; 1952 August high 45½, up 17 points in 20 months.

1953, September. Buy at 32 against a series of old bottoms. 1952, April sell at 59, making 27 points profit in 7 months.

1954, March. Buy at 47 at a new high; 1954, April high 59 3/4. UP 12 3/4 points in 1 month. Here you would make the most profits in the shortest period of time after buying at a new high level. Why was this move so fast? Because after a long period of time the insiders or people who were in the know had bought all the Vanadium that was offered and when it all was absorbed and bidding started to come into the market, it advanced very rapidly. In this way, when you buy you are going with the trend and following people who make the market. Therefore, you make the <u>most money</u> in the <u>shortest period</u> of <u>time</u>.

These examples of seven stocks are not exceptions. You can go over the list of stocks and pick out hundreds of them that make moves of a similar nature and you should always have the average of the different groups, and when the average of the groups show up or down, then pick out the stocks in strong or weak position and watch them and buy when they make new highs, or sell them at new lows; in the first and last stage of the market you make the most money in the shortest period of time.

You cannot make money without getting ready to make it and in doing this you have to spend some money for charts, records, books and course of instruction. In this way you are ready to follow the big men who make the market and make big money.

STOCKS NOT MANIPULATED: Before the Stock Exchange started regulating brokers and the control of markets; there was manipulation and pools often were organized that could advance low priced stocks that had very little merit to extreme high levels. This does not happen under present conditions; therefore, most of the buying is by investors and long term speculators and there is practically no manipulation; for this reason it is more necessary to study the market carefully and study individual stocks and get definite indications that they are going to move up, because they will not be put up just by manipulation, as they were years in the past. Under present conditions more traders and investors buy stocks on the prospects of dividends and an increase in their investment. This you can do by a careful study of all the rules.

NEW INDUSTRIES AND GROWTH OF STOCKS: In the future, stocks connected with the atomic energy will naturally be leaders because like all new discoveries and inventions, it will prove to be very valuable and a lot of companies will make a lot of money. These companies with prospects on the atomic stocks will be covered later. In selecting stocks to buy under new industries, you should make a careful study of their prospects and make up charts on the individual stocks that you intend to trade in, and if they are part of the group, you can get a record of the group average, study this group average and then pick the individual stock to buy that shows an indication of leading the group.

URANIUM STOCKS: Uranium is now one of the most valuable of all precious metals. It is much more valuable than gold and the stocks that have made discoveries and have Uranium deposits, such stocks as Vanadium have better prospects to be leaders in the future. We will cover the other stocks later under the Uranium Stocks.

VALUE OF ALL STOCKS LISTED ON THE NEW YORK STOCK EXCHANGE: The Department of Research and Statistics of the New York Stock Exchange has done a most valuable work for investors and they deserve great credit for it. At the end of each month they publish a total value of all stocks listed on the N. Y. Stock Exchange, the average value of all stocks, the total number of stocks listed and the total number of shares and the total value, that is, the market value of each group of stocks and the average of 39 or more different groups. This is of great value to any investor and trader who will study these records and use them, as I will show how to do later with the charts covering these averages and total value of stocks. The number of stocks listed on the N. Y. Stock Exchange is 1536. The total number of shares listed is 2 billion 936 million, nearly 3 billion shares. The market value of all stocks listed on the N. Y. Stock Exchange at the end of March 1934 was nearly 125 billion dollars and the average price of all stocks was 42.53, this is the highest price in recent years.

1932, June - the total value of all stocks was a little less than 18 billion dollars.

1928, November - the flat average price was 97.80 and in March 1929 the average price was 96.67. August 31, 1929 the total value of all stocks on the N. Y. Stock Exchange was 89 billion, 668 hundred million dollars.

1932, July 1 - the total number of companies on the N. Y. Stock Exchange was 831; the total number of issues was 1233, and the number of shares was 1 billion, 315,334,428 and at the present time the total number of shares listed is nearly 3 billion. From this you can see that while the value of stocks increases, the number of shares is increasing all of the time.

1941, June was the last extreme low in stocks. At that time the average price was 40.74 and the total value of all stocks was$63,921,054,342.

1950, May. The value of all stocks $85,624,559,669. The average price 38.48. When prices crossed the high of May 1946, they indicated much higher prices but of course, you have to learn to pick the stocks in the strong groups to buy.

THE AVERAGE VALUE OF ALL STOCKS ON THE NEW YORK STOCK EXCHANGE AND HOW THEY INDICATE THE TREND OF PRICES:

THE DOLLAR TREND: Please refer to Chart; it which shows the total market value of all stocks at the end of each month. Refer to chart on which shows the total market value in dollars of Aircraft stocks. Refer to chart on which shows the total market value of 39 steel and iron stocks at the end of each month.

HOW TO USE VALUE CHART AS A GUIDE TO THE TREND INDICATOR (The scale on this chart shows 16.20 and up to 135, this means billions of dollars).

EXAMPLE: 1932, June 30 lows show just the low of 16 this means at the extreme low in 1932 the total value of all stocks was 15 billion, 633 million, 633 thousand dollars. We will refer to 26, 36, and 40, etc., which is on the scale and means billions of dollars.

1932, February high just below 28; June low 16; August high 28, 1933, February low 20 billion dollars - this was a secondary decline and made a higher bottom than June 1932. 1933, in April the value line crossed the high of February 1932 and August 1932 this indicated that the main trend was up. 1933, June and August high just above 36 billion dollars. October low just above 30 billion dollars.

1934, January high 37 billion dollars. February, March and April the value held just above 36 billion and when prices broke below 36 it indicated lower.

1934, July low just below 31 and above the low of October 1933.

1935, March - low slightly below 31 billion. This made three lows of supports near the same level making it a buying level.

1935, June - the value crossed 37 the high of January 1934. Here is where we use the rule and buy at new high levels.

The advance continued. February and March 1936 high just under 52 billion. April 1936 a one month's decline to 48, less than 4 billions decline.

The upward trend was resumed and on July 1936 the averages crossed 52, the high of March 1936, indicating higher. Again we follow the rule and buy at new high levels.

1937, February and March high, 62½ million dollars. For 3 months the value was in a range of one billion dollars which indicates resistance and good selling as the total volume of sales was very large.

1936, December low 58. 1937, April this low was broken indicating lower prices. Here we follow the rule and <u>sell</u> at <u>lower levels</u>.

1937, June low 55; a rally followed to July high 59, a lower top then broke below 55; the low in June showing down trend. You would remain short and sell more and should be out of all long stocks. The main trend continued down.

1937, December low 39; 1938, February high 41½, a small rally; 1938, March low, just below 32 billion and above the lows of October 1933. July 1934 and March 1938 the decline was 50% of the high of February and March 1937. Therefore, March 1938 was a buying level.

1938, June the dollar trend crossed 41½, the hig... of February 1938 indicating to buy more.

1938, October and December high 47 to 47½. Under the low of April 1936 where prices broke below 45 indicated lower. 1939, March and April low just above 40. June and August higher bottoms indicating support and good buying.

1939, September Hitler started the war and the value advanced to just below 41-48, a double top against December 1938, a selling level or place to watch indicating a change in trend. 1940, May the price was just above 36, a rally followed to October high 42. 1941, July 41, higher than October 1940. November prices broke the bottom of April 1941 and later went below May 1940 indicating lower prices.

WHEN TO WATCH FOR SUPPORT AND BUYING LEVEL.

1948, March low just under 32. 1942, April low 31½. The average value was 32½ in March and May 1944. Then started to move up showing strong up-trend.

1943 crossed the high of October 1940 and July 1941. Follow the rule, buy more at new highs. 1943, June high just below 49 and above December 1938 and September 1938, indicating higher prices.

1943, September high 49, same high as May and June 1943 indicating good selling.

1943, November low 45½, a decline of less than 5 billion dollars in value and a recovery started. 1944, May prices crossed the highs of June and September 1932. Here we again follow the rule and buy when prices moved up to new highs. August 1945, when the Japanese war ended, prices crossed 62½, the high of February 1937, a sure indication of higher prices. You would buy the stocks in strong groups.

1946, January high 78½; February declined to 74, about the same decline as November 1943, not enough to show a change in the main trend.

1946, May high 85 billion dollars up 55 billion from April 1942 low and 22 billions above the highs of February 1937. This was the time to watch for a change in trend.

The high in May 1946 was about 5 billion below the high of August 31, 1929 which is just under 90 billion dollars.

1946, April high was 80 billion dollars; June 80 billion dollars; July low 79 indicating lower. The trend continued down to November 1946 low 65 billion. 1947 January high 68¼, a small rally. May low 63½ billion. July high 69¼ same high as January 1947. The trend continued down.

1948, February low 63 billion 158 million dollars. Slightly lower than May 1947 but still above the highs of February 1937 making this a buying level.

1948, May and June high 74½ under the low of February 1946. 1948 July low indicated lower prices. September 65½, October high 72¼, the decline was resumed. 1949 June low just below 64 billion. Same low as May 1947 and February 1948, a buying level at old lows. 1949, August prices crossed the highs of January and March 1949, indicating higher. Buy more. 1949, December the value was 76 billion above the high of May and June 1948. Follow rule and buy at new high levels. A rapid advance followed.

1950, May high 85 billion 624 million dollars, above May 1946 high, an indication of higher prices.

1950, June 25 the Korean War started and heavy selling followed because stocks were at very high levels. July low just below 81 billion, a 1 month's decline from new highs.

1950, August; the averages crossed the 1946 highs made in May 1950 - follow the rule and buy at new high levels. 1950, December - average value above the high of August 1929. Follow the rule and buy at new high levels.

1951, April high 103 billions. June low 97 billion. An average decline of about the same as June 1950.

July high 104 billions near the high buy at new high levels. 1952, January high 112. February low 108, March a new high at 113 billions. April low 108 billions, a decline of 5 billions. A normal decline based on previous reaction. From this level the advance was resumed.

1952 July high 116 billions. September and October low just below 113 billion, a smaller decline than April 1952.

1952, December and January 1953 high 120½ billions. This was 33 1/3% more than 1929 high.

1953, February low just below 119 billions. This was 3 months with no gain, an indication that a reaction was due, since June 1949 no reaction had been more than 5 billions and a greater reaction was due, possibly 10 billions.

1953, August and September low slightly below 10 billions or 2 times the previous reaction.

1953, October Average 116 billions above July 1953 high, an indication of higher prices.

1954, January the prices crossed 120 billions, the high of December 1952. Again we would follow the rule and buy at new high levels, selecting the stocks in the groups which showed strong up trend. (See charts on U.S.Steel, Vanadium Steel, and the Aircrafts and the average value of these). You can see by the charts on Boeing, Douglas Aircraft, Glen Martin and Vanadium Steel why we would select these stocks to buy and the price of these stocks moved up fast in March and April 1954.

1954, March 31 the average value of all stocks in the New York Stock Exchange was just above 129 billion dollars. We now come to the problem of estimating when the average will meet resistance and good selling. We use 1929 high of 90 billion dollars and add 50% of this which would give 135 billion.

If we add or use approximately 325% on the high of April 1944, we get close to 135 billions as a selling level.

April 30, 1954 is 12 years from the low of April 30, 1942 and from June 30, 1932 low to April 30, 1954 is 262 months. The Dow Jones Industrial Averages made secondary highs at 297½ in April 1930. By going back over the past history you find many changes in trend in April and May, therefore, the time is near to watch for a change in trend in Stocks and groups like Aircrafts and Steels which have led the 1954 advance.

HOW MUCH DECLINE TO EXPECT: The greatest decline since 1942 lows was from February 1937 to March and April 1938. The decline was 31 billion 168 million dollars. The decline from May 1946 to February 1948 and June 1949 was 21 billion 785 million dollars. This gives you a guide as to how much the first decline may amount to.

The advance from June 1949 to date has already exceeded 100% gain in value of all stocks and this would indicate that the time is near for at least a substantial corrective decline but groups and individual stocks must be studied to indicate their strength and weakness in relation to the average value of all stocks.

WHEN STOCKS ARE IN THE STRONGEST AND WEAKEST POSITION. When a stock has sold at very high levels declines and remains for a very long time at low levels and then finally crosses 50% of the highest prices at which it ever sold, or 50% between the extreme low and the extreme high, it is then in a very strong position and indicates higher prices.

When a stock declines and breaks 50% of the highest prices ever sold, it is in a very weak position and as a general rule when the stocks reach this point they have a moderate rally and sometimes it is a final bottom for a big advance. The next important point is 50% between the extreme high and the extreme low when stocks cannot hold this level and break below it they are in the weakest possible position and indicate much lower prices. In many cases a decline tothese points or a rally to these important 50% points remains for weeks or months without advancing above the halfway point of 50% or breaking below it, but when once these points are exceeded, you should reverse the position. If you are short cover shorts and buy. If you are long, sell out longs and sell short. In this way you will make money because you will be going with the trend buying the stocks in the strongest position and selling the stocks in the weakest position. You must remember if it is time to sell out a stock you are doing it because in a weak position the trend is down and it is also equally good then to sell short following, of course, all rules given in this book and all rules given in my book, "45 YEARS IN WALL STREET".

You must give the market time to show a change in trend. Suppose people in the last two years have bought Studebaker too high, Chrysler at high levels or Celanese. When they saw that the main trend had changed, if they had a 5 point loss or even a 10 point loss if they sold out, took the loss and went short, they would not only make back the loss they had but make big profits on the short side. This is how money is made by going with the trend. Example: Celanese high 58 in 1951, 50% of this is 29 in April 1953. Celanese broke 29 and never sold 2 points higher before it declined to 16 in April 1954. This is the proof of how weak stocks get when once they have lost 50% of their value.

In 1953 Studebaker high 43½. 50% of this high price is 21 3/4; after it broke this level in December 1953 it never rallied 2 points before it sold at 15 in April 1954, another proof of why it pays to sell stocks short when they are down 50% from the high level, because when you do this you are going with the trend.

WHY IT IS PROFITABLE TO BUY AT NEW HIGH PRICES AND SELL AT NEW LOW LEVELS:

When the stock is in a strong enough position to advance to new highs after several months, weeks or years it has remained below these highs, it is strong as a result of good demand and because powerful interests are buying; therefore, when you buy you are going with the main trend and that's the right way to make profits.

Never buck the trend, go with the trend always and you'll make money.

When stocks decline to new low levels they are in a weak position because the supply is greater than the demand and the selling is better than the buying, and for this good reason you will be right 90% of the time if you sell stocks when they are weak but always protecting with a STOP LOSS order based upon the rules.

MORE PROFITS IN SWINGS: If you will go over any active stock over a period of 5, 10 or 20 years and note all moves of 10 points or more, you will see that there is more profit trading for these swings than there is trading for dividends or holding for big increase in capital.

From 1925, where Chrysler has started around 28, it moved up to 141 and after having many swings up and down, running 10 to 50 and 75 points, it finally declined to 5 in 1932. From 1932 up to 1954 Chrysler has made a range from $5 a share to 141, a total of 136 points which would give a profit of $13,600 on 100 shares. During this same time, Chrysler, figuring 10 point moves or more has made a total move of 1458 points. Just suppose you could catch 1/2 or 50% of these moves which would give 729 points profit against the range of 136 points. This is proof that it pays to trade for the swings. That is, get out of the market when it shows an indication that prices have reached high and go short and then get in again when there is a definite indication that they have made low trading in and out and not holding and letting the market go up and down over a period of years and receiving nothing but dividends, finally winding up with a smallreturn on your capital counting interest from the time you bought up to the time you sold out. Go over any active stocks and you can prove this to yourself.

CHANGE WHEN THE TREND CHANGES: Conditions change from time to time and trends change after a period of time, and to make profits you must change with the trend and with the time. Do not hold too long or hold just because you are receiving dividends; trade to increase your capital and do not worry too much about dividends. The value of any rules is, "Will it stand the test of time in actual trading?". I offer proof of all my rules such as buying at new highs and selling at new lows by actual practice and prove to you that it does pay to go with the trend and buy when stocks are reaching new high levels and sell when they break into new low levels. Go over the charts in the Course, Celanese, Douglas Aircraft, Boeing, Lockheed, Glen Martin, Studebaker, United Aircraft and Vanadium Steel and in this way you can prove to yourself how the rules work.

BUYING ONE STOCK AND SELLING ANOTHER SHORT AT THE SAME TIME: To prove this rule, I show the chart on Celanese and Douglas Aircraft and Studebaker and Vanadium Steel.

BUYING AND SELLING A DIFFERENT GROUP OF STOCKS AT THE SAME TIME: 1951, July bought 100 Douglas at 48, August sold 100 Celanese at 52 when both stocks were selling at around the same levels. Suppose you placed a STOP LOSS order on Douglas at 45 and when you sold Celanese at 52 you placed a STOP at 59, 1 point above the high of 58 in August. Suppose you do not buy more Douglas which you should many times, based on the rules and should have sold short more Celanese based on the rules, and could have made a larger amount of money on a very small risk.

Suppose in April 1954 when Douglas made the final grand rush and was advanced crossing the high of 110, you finally soldthe Douglas at 130; you would make 72 points on the Douglas or $7,200 less interest and commission and at the same time you buy in 100 short Celanese at 16 making 34 points at $3,400 profit, less commission, or a total on the two trades of $10,600 on a capital of $5,200, more than 100% in less than 3 years. Refer to the chart on Studebaker and Vanadium Steel where we show why, by buying Vanadium and selling Studebaker short, big profits were made.

1951, March sell 100 Studebaker at 34 short because there were twotops at 36 and the third top was 35, a lower top, place STOP at 37.

1951, August bought 100 Studebaker at 26 because 3 lows around this same level and bought 100 Studebaker for long account.

1951, March bought 100 Vanadium at 32 because it was 6 months around this low level at 31. Place STOP at 29.

1953, March sell 100 Vanadium at 44½ because the highs previously were 45 and 45½ in August 1952 and March 1952, making this a double top.

1953, March sell 100 Vanadium short at 44½, place STOP at 47.

1953, February Studebaker high at 43½ near the same level as Vanadium.

1953, March sold 100 Studebaker short at 38½ and sold 100 Studebaker that we had for long account at 38½. When it broke under the low ofFebruary and the low of 39½ made in May 1952. Place a STOP LOSS order on Studebaker, sold short at 45½.

1953, June Studebaker broke 34, the low of October-November 1952 and you should sell more at 31.

1953, June make STOP on 200 short at 34. Studebaker continues to go down and in September 1953 broke below 21 3/4, a decline of 50% from 43½, rallied to only 26 and then broke 21 3/4 which indicated much lower.

1954, January and February high 21 3/4, a very weak rally, remain short of the 200 shares with STOP 22 3/4.

1954, April 30 Studebaker low 15 main trend down. Profits, if you close all the Studebaker, is 60 points or $6,000.

1951 March bought 100 Vanadium at 32; 1953 sold 100 at 44½ and sold short 100 at 44½.

1953 bought 100 to cover shorts of 31 because it was at the low of April and May 1951 and at the same time we bought 100 Vanadium for long account at 31 and placed a STOP LOSS order at 29.

1954, February bought 100 Vanadium at 41 because it was at the new high above 2 tops of 39½ in July and August 1953, and above 2 tops of 39½ in December 1953 and January 1954.

1954, March bought 100 Vanadium at 47 because it was at new high levels above the high of August & December 1952 & March 1953 showing main trend up and at the highest level since 1931, indicating a very strong position.

1954, April Vanadium reached a high of 59 3/4. Note September 1953 low of 30½, add 50% gives 61 and a possible high. The volume of sales was the largest for years indicating that it might be reaching a possible top for reaction anyway. So we sell 300 shares that were long at 59½ but would not go short because the main trend is still up. These shares which we sold were bought at 31, 41, and 47. This gives a total of 57 points profit or $5,700 less interest and commission. Add this to $6,000. profit on Studebaker gives $11,500. in 3 years time on a capital of about $3,500. or over 300% on the capital, or 100% profit for each year by following rules and not guessing.

I have not picked these stocks because they were exceptions. There are many more in different groups that would have made a showing equally as good.

1953, Vanadium low 30½ and Studebaker 28, just 4 points apart.

1954, April Vanadium was approximately 45 points higher than Studebaker, a spread of 45 points in 7 months time. This proves that it pays to buy the stocks in strong position and sell the ones in weak position, which indicates main trend down.

WHY LOW PRICED STOCKS DO NOT MOVE UP:

Changed conditions are the cause why low price stocks or so called "cats and dogs" have not followed the advance from September 1953 to April 1954. With the Dow Jones Stocks up 66 points in 7 months and the total value of all stocks listed on the N Y Stock Exchange up about 24 billion dollars, there must be some reason why the low priced stocks have not followed this advance.

In the old days when pools operated and manipulation and watched sales were permitted, the low priced stocks nearly always advanced in the last stage of a bull market but it is not the case now because no pools are operating. The Investment Trusts, and the people with large amounts of money for investment buy into the strong companies where the earnings are good and the dividend prospects are good. They buy good stocks like General Motors, Standard of New Jersey, American Tel. & Tel., Dupont, General Electric, Westinghouse, Douglas, U.S. Steel, Bethlehem Steel and Vanadium Steel.

The public buys and holds the low priced stocks hoping they will follow the high priced stocks and go up, but hope will not put these low priced stocks up. The big people don't want them and the result will be many low priced stocks will decline faster in the next bear market than the high priced stocks. Of course, the day will come when the great time cycle indicates a great depression, that large and small investors will lose confidence and sell the blue chips when they are at very low levels.

AIR CRAFT STOCKS ON THE NEW YORK STOCK EXCHANGE.

The New York Stock Exchange, Department of Research, publishes at the end of each month the total value of all aircraft stocks listed on the Exchange, and this chart is very valuable as a guide in selecting the best aircraft stocks to buy or sell. The chart which we have made up on these averages we call the Dollar Trend because it is not the average price of stocks but the value in dollars of the entire group, and this is a more important trend indicator than the average price. However, the Research Department does publish the average value of all aircraft stocks at the end of each month as well as all other groups.

1951, September total value 1 billion, 135 million dollars. November low 955 million dollars.

1952, January 1 billion 10 million dollars. April low 892 million dollars. This was the extreme low. At this time you would look up the monthly high and low, and weekly high and low chart on the individual aircraft stocks to decide which is the best buy.

BELL AIRCRAFT.

April 1952, in a slow trading range, had been split up and was not one of the best to buy at that time.

1953, September - it was making higher bottoms and was better to buy.

BOEING AIRCRAFT.

April 1952. Made low in June after the stock was split up and was good to buy, but was better to buy in September 1953 because the average value of all Aircraft Stocks had made a new low, and were higher in September indicating that the trend was turning up.

1954, February was the time to buy Boeing for quick profits in a short period of time because it had crossed old high levels.

DOUGLASS AIRCRAFT.

April 1952 was the very best buy among the Aircrafts because it had declined from 66½ to 52, and 50% of the range from 43½ to 66½ was 55 and it closed in April 1952 at 57, making it a good buy with STOP at 51.

1953, September Douglass made low of 62. It had been making higher bottoms since April 1952 and it was one of the very best stocks to buy, protected with STOP at 60. In December 1953 it crossed 74, the old high level, and was one of the best stocks to buy for a fast move up and large profits in a short period of time.

LOCKHEED AIRCRAFT.

In April 1952 it made higher bottoms but was slow because it had been split up. It was a much better stock to buy in October 1953 when it crossed old tops.

GLEN L. MARTIN.

April 1952 was good to buy because it had held for four months making higher bottoms than 1949 low. It was a still better buy in September 1953 when it was crossing old tops.

UNITED AIRCRAFT.

April 1953 was a good stock to buy because it was making higher bottoms but the big profits in a short period of time could have been made by buying in September 1953.

ALL AIRCRAFT STOCK AVERAGES.

1953, February the average was 1 billion 180 million dollars.

1954, January the averages made a new high and in February 1954 they were higher, and if you bought Douglass or almost any other Aircraft Stock at that time you could have made large profits in a short period of time.

1954, March 31 the average of all Aircraft Stocks was 1 billion 504 million dollars, the highest for many years, and at the end of April 1954 they had probably advanced 100% from the extreme low of April 1952. (At this writing we do not have the figures for the end of April 1954).

39 STEEL AND IRON STOCKS AVERAGE VALUE.

These figures are for the average price on the last day of each month. Study the chart in back of the book of instructions and it will help you to determine the trend of the entire group of steel stocks and when you want to select the best stock to buy or sell, study the chart of the individual steel stocks.

1951, September high 3 billion 805 million dollars. From this level the trend turned down and made lower tops and lower bottoms each month with no gain of more than 100 million dollars in one month until April 1952 when the low was 3 billion 350 million dollars. The trend turned up from this low level and July high 3 billion 635 million dollars.

1952, September and October low 3 billion 384 million dollars, a higher bottom and a buying level. At this time you would look up the individual steel stocks in order to select the best stocks to buy.

BETHLEHEM STEEL.

September 1952 low 47, higher than May 1952 and good to buy with a STOP at 45, but it was a much better buy in September 1953 when the average of all steel stocks was 3 billion 105 million dollars. At this time Bethlehem Steel was selling at 44½, not 3-points below the old bottoms and good to buy with STOP at 43.

VANADIUM STEEL.

April 1952 low 35½, good to buy because it was making higher bottoms and you would have made fair profits buying it at this time.

1952, September low 30½, higher than the lows of 1950 and 1951, a good buy with a STOP at 29, especially because it had such good prospects for increased profits through its Uranium mines.

1954, February Vanadium was a safe and best buy at 41 because it crossed the old high and you could buy more in March 1954 when it crossed 47, the old highs, and the average value of all steel stocks was up at that time. Vanadium advanced to 59 3/4 in April 1954, and the volume of sales was very large. If you were keeping up the daily and weekly high and low chart, you would sell out at this time. It reacted to 54 and then advanced to 59 again. It will have to decline below 54 to indicate lower prices and when it crosses 60 and closes above this level, the next resistance level is 67 - 68; after this price is crossed, the next price to watch is 76½, the old high in March 1931.

It will pay you to keep up the average value of each group of stocks monthly and the average price of the group, as well as the total value of all stocks listed on the N Y Stock Exchange each month. These averages of value give you the dollar trend which is much more accurate and valuable than the Dow-Jones 30 Industrial Averages which cover only a small percentage of the total stocks listed.

Remember that the harder you work, the more knowledge you will get, and the more profits you will make. King Solomon, the wisest man who ever lived, shows wisdom and understanding above everything else. You will do well to follow his example. "Happy is the man who findeth Wisdom, and the man who getteth understanding". (Proverbs).

The rules which I have laid down in this course are practical. I have followed them and made money, and you can follow them and make money. My greatest pleasure in life comes from helping others.

"If I can throw a single ray of light,
Across the darkened pathway of another;
If I can aid some soul to clearer sight,
Of life and duty, and thus bless my brother;
If I can wipe from any human cheek a tear,
I shall not then have lived in vain while here."

I am nearing my 76th birthday and I have realized happiness and success. I feel that I have not lived in vain, because thousands of people have benefited through my books and my course of instructions and I feel confident they will benefit through the rules in this course, SPECULATION - A PROFITABLE PROFESSION.

W. D. GANN

May 18, 1954.

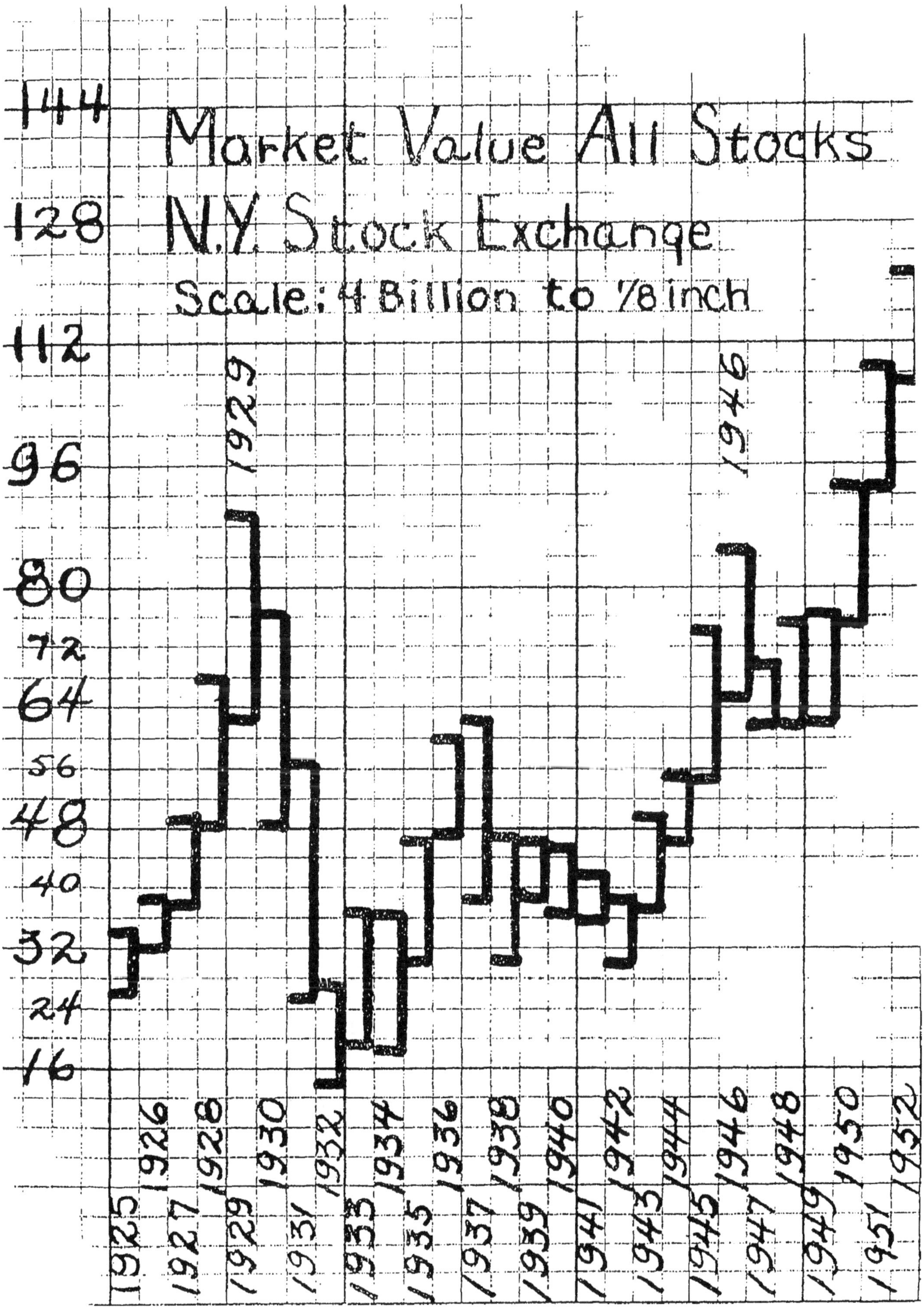

Market Value All Stocks
N.Y. Stock Exchange
Scale: 4 Billion to 7/8 inch
144
128
112
96
80
72
64
56
48
40
32
24
16
1929
1946
1925
1926
1927
1928
1929
1930
1931
1932
1933
1934
1935
1936
1937
1938
1939
1940
1941
1942
1943
1944
1945
1946
1947
1948
1949
1950
1951
1952

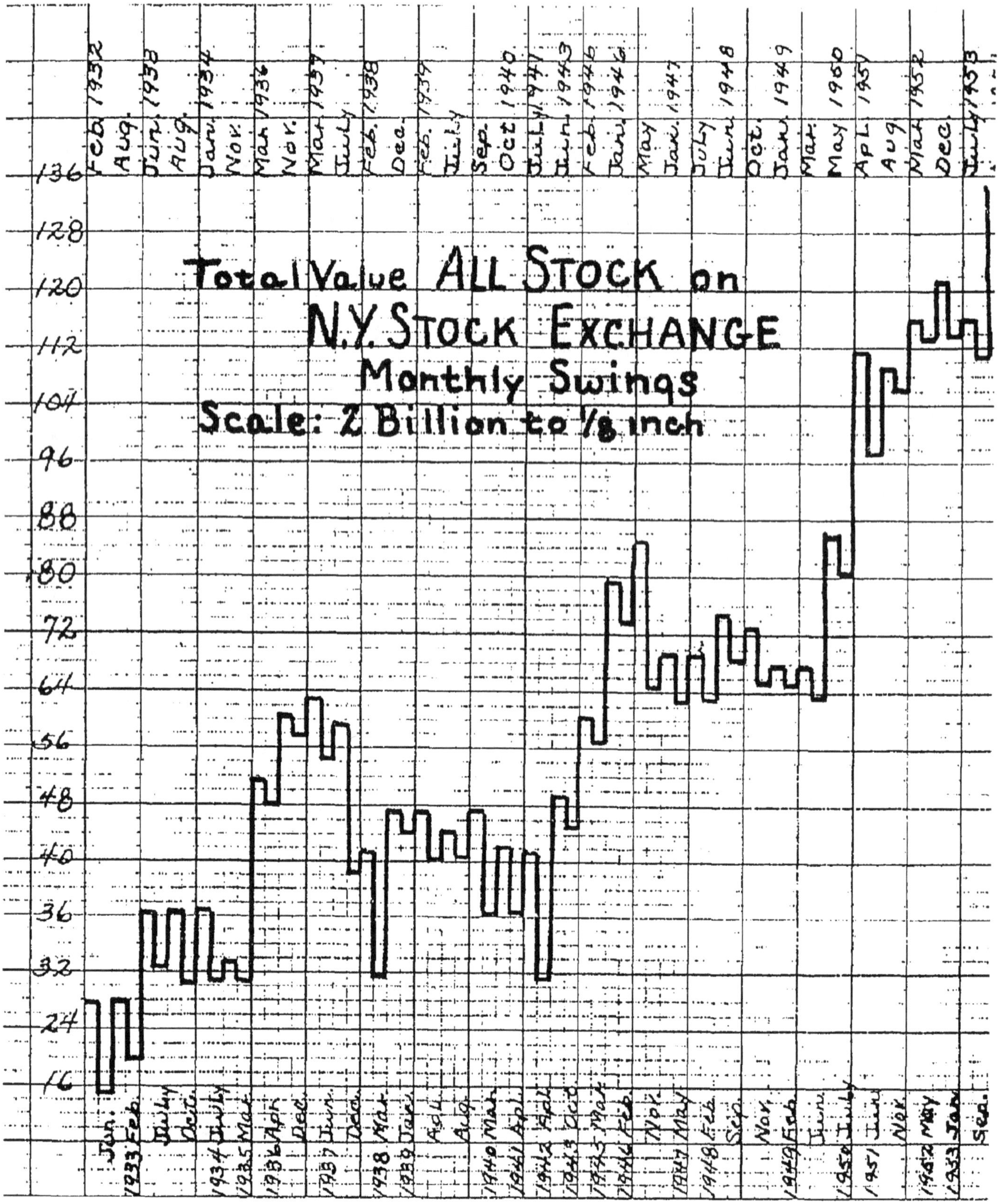
Total Value ALL STOCK on
N.Y. STOCK EXCHANGE
Monthly Swings
Scale: 2 Billion to 1/8 inch

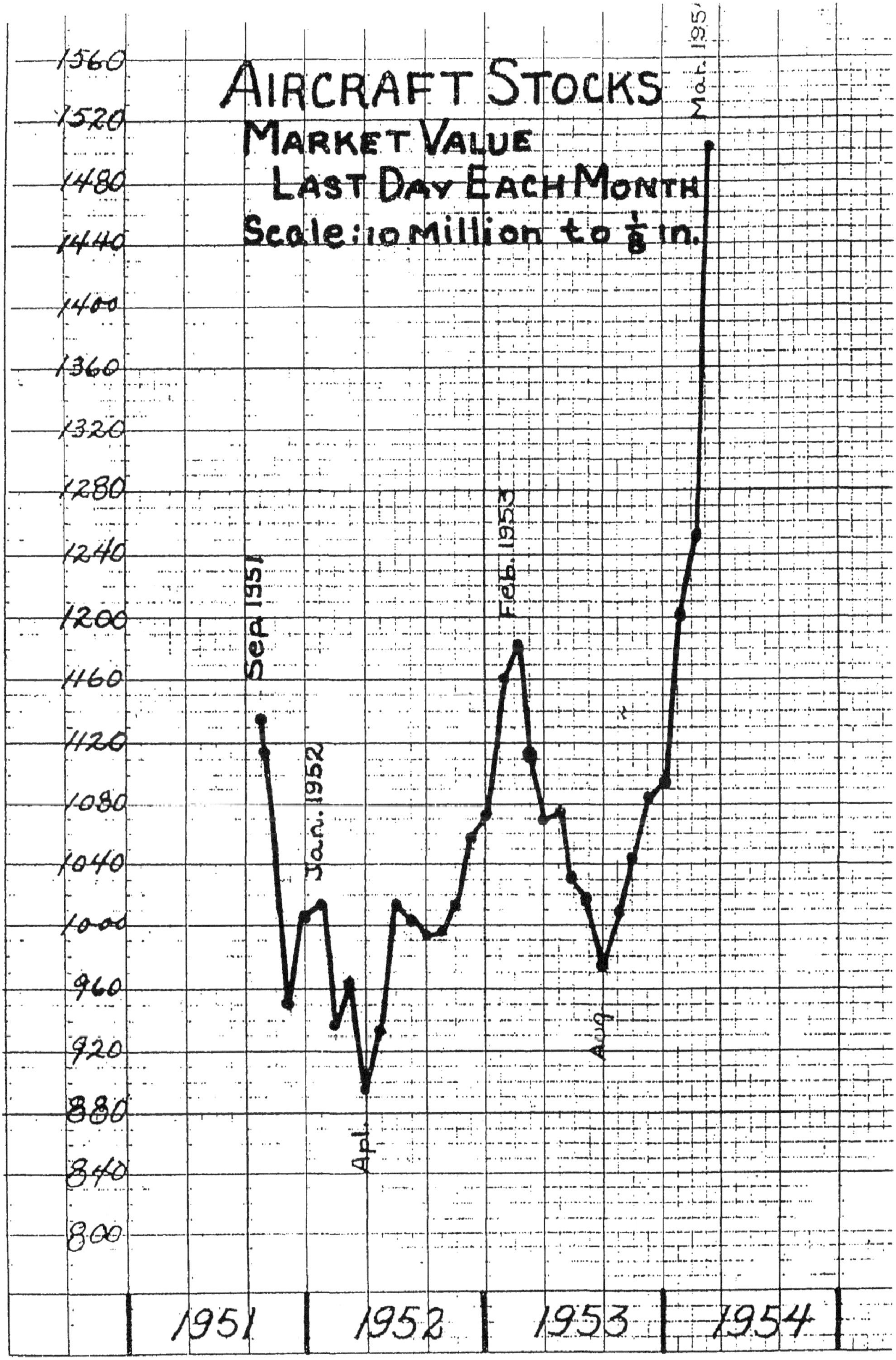
AIRCRAFT STOCKS
MARKET VALUE
LAST DAY EACH MONTH
Scale: 10 Million to 1/8 in.
1560
1520
1480
1440
1400
1360
1320
1280
1240
1200
1160
1120
1080
1040
1000
960
920
880
840
800
Sep 1951
Jan. 1952
Apl.
Feb. 1953
Aug
Mar. 195
1951
1952
1953
1954

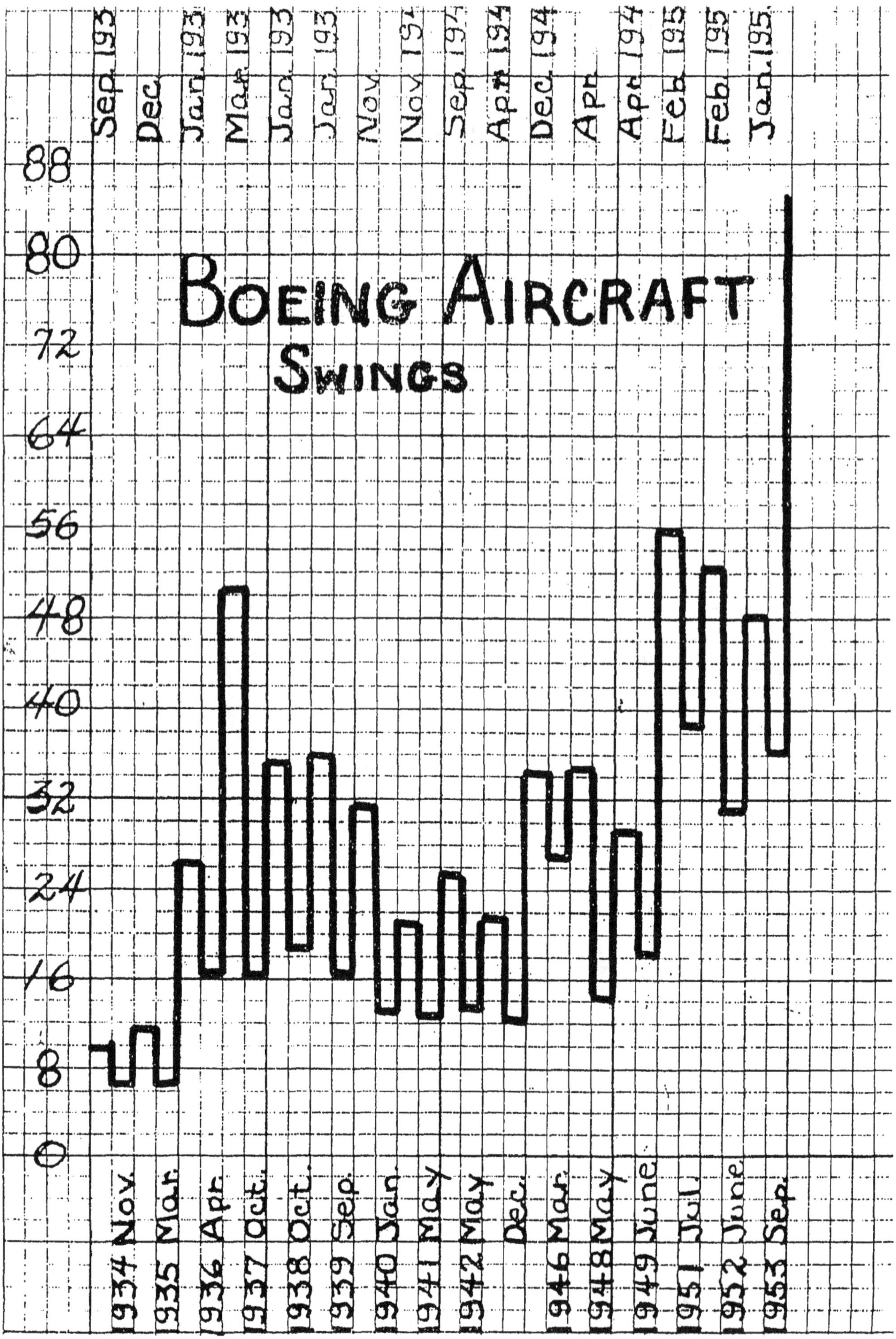

BOEING AIRCRAFT
SWINGS
88
80
72
64
56
48
40
32
24
16
8
0
Sep. 193
Dec.
Jan. 193
Mar. 193
Jan. 193
Jan. 193
Nov.
Nov. 19
Sep. 194
Apr. 194
Dec. 194
Apr.
Apr. 194
Feb. 195
Feb. 195
Jan. 195
1934 Nov.
1935 Mar.
1936 Apr.
1937 Oct.
1938 Oct.
1939 Sep.
1940 Jan.
1941 May
1942 May
Dec.
1946 Mar.
1948 May
1949 June
1951 Jul.
1952 June
1953 Sep.

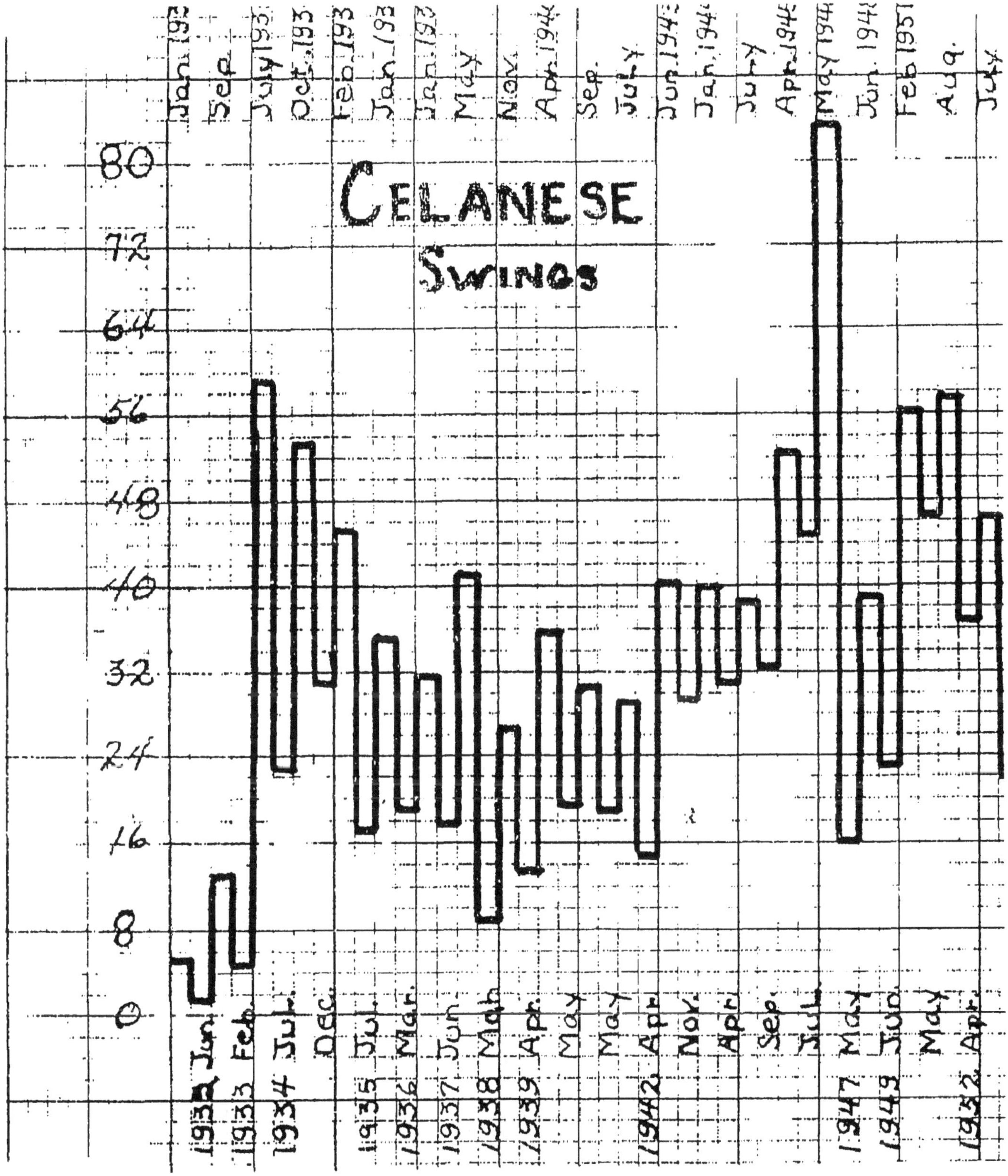
CELANESE
SWINGS
80
72
64
56
48
40
32
24
16
8
0

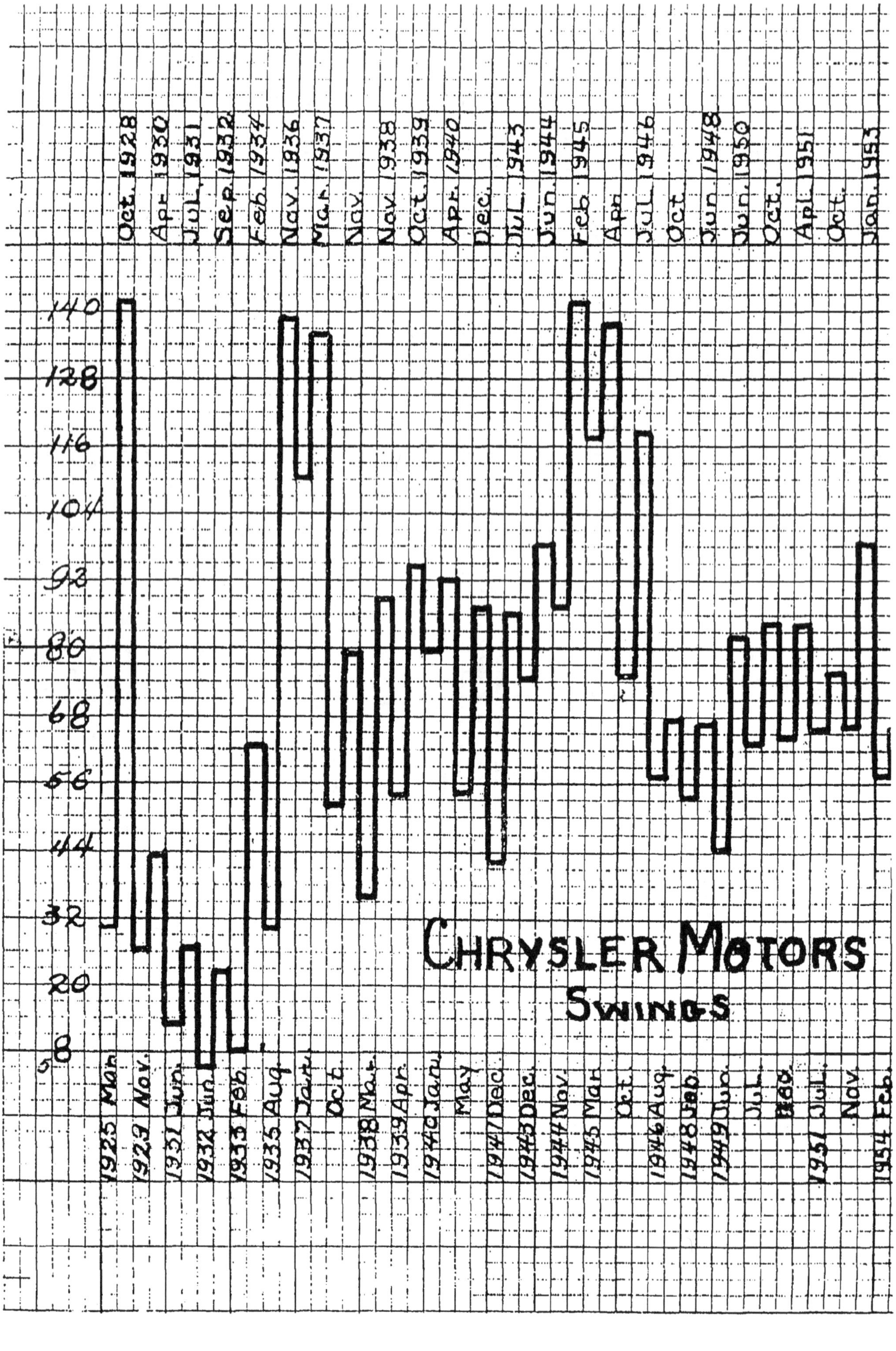
CHRYSLER MOTORS
SWINGS
140
128
116
104
92
80
68
56
44
32
20
8
Oct. 1928
Apr. 1930
Jul. 1931
Sep. 1932
Feb. 1934
Nov. 1936
Mar. 1937
Nov.
Nov. 1938
Oct. 1939
Apr. 1940
Dec.
Jul. 1943
Jun. 1944
Feb. 1945
Apr.
Jul. 1946
Oct.
Jun. 1948
Jun. 1950
Oct.
Apr. 1951
Oct.
Jan. 1953
1925 Mar.
1929 Nov.
1931 Jun.
1932 Jun.
1933 Feb.
1935 Aug.
1937 Jan.
Oct.
1938 Mar.
1939 Apr.
1940 Jan.
May
1941 Dec.
1943 Dec.
1944 Nov.
1945 Mar.
Oct.
1946 Aug.
1948 Feb.
1949 Jun.
Jul.
Feb.
1951 Jul.
Nov.
1954 Feb.

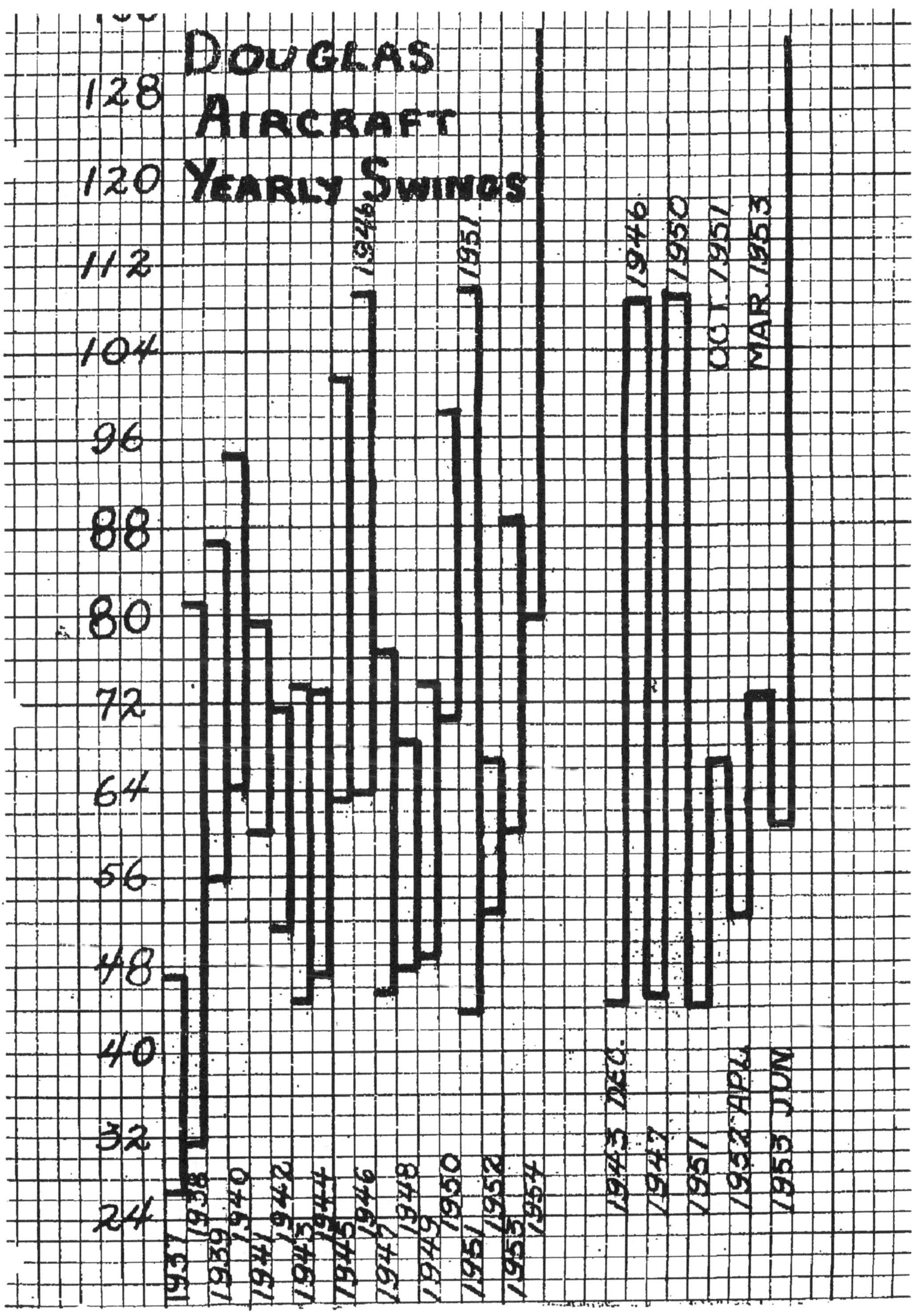

DOUGLAS
AIRCRAFT
YEARLY SWINGS
128
120
112
104
96
88
80
72
64
56
48
40
32
24
1946
1951
1946
1950
OCT 1951
MAR 1953
1937
1938
1939
1940
1941
1942
1943
1944
1945
1946
1947
1948
1949
1950
1951
1952
1953
1954
1943 DEC.
1947
1951
1952 APL
1953 JUN

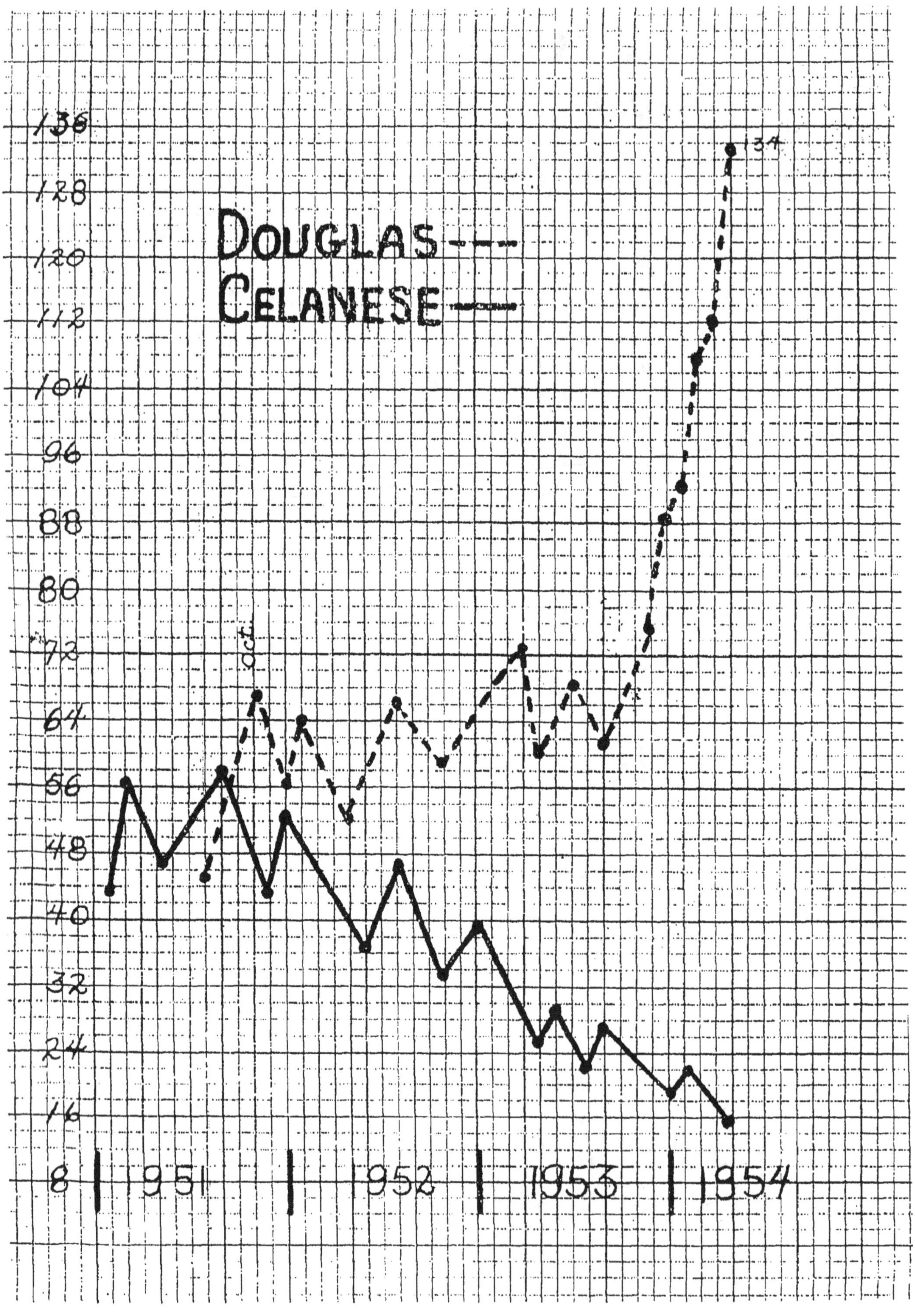

DOUGLAS---
CELANESE—
136
128
120
112
104
96
88
80
72
64
56
48
40
32
24
16
8
1951
1952
1953
1954
134
Oct.

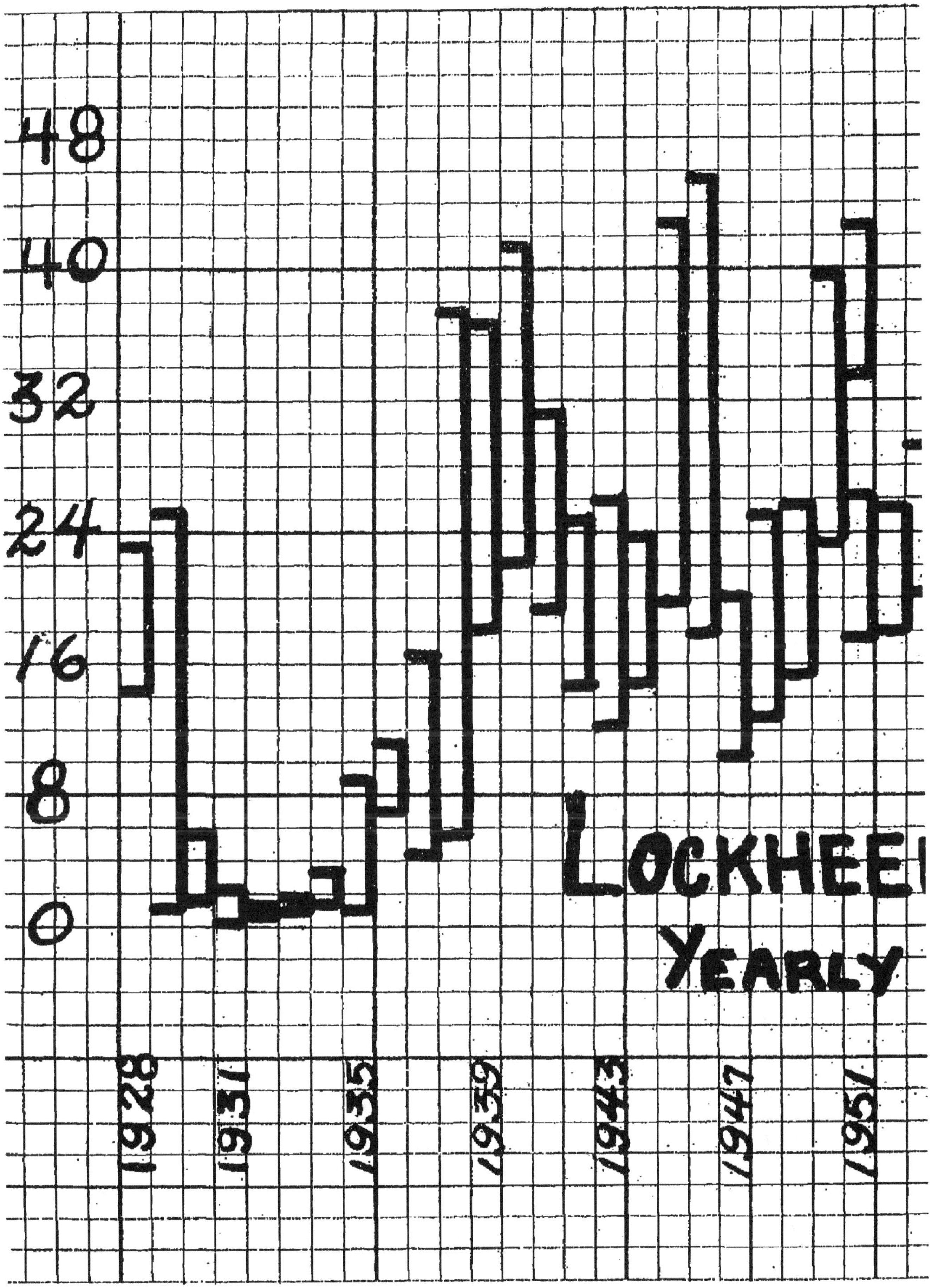
48
40
32
24
16
8
0
LOCKHEE
YEARLY
1928
1931
1935
1939
1943
1947
1951

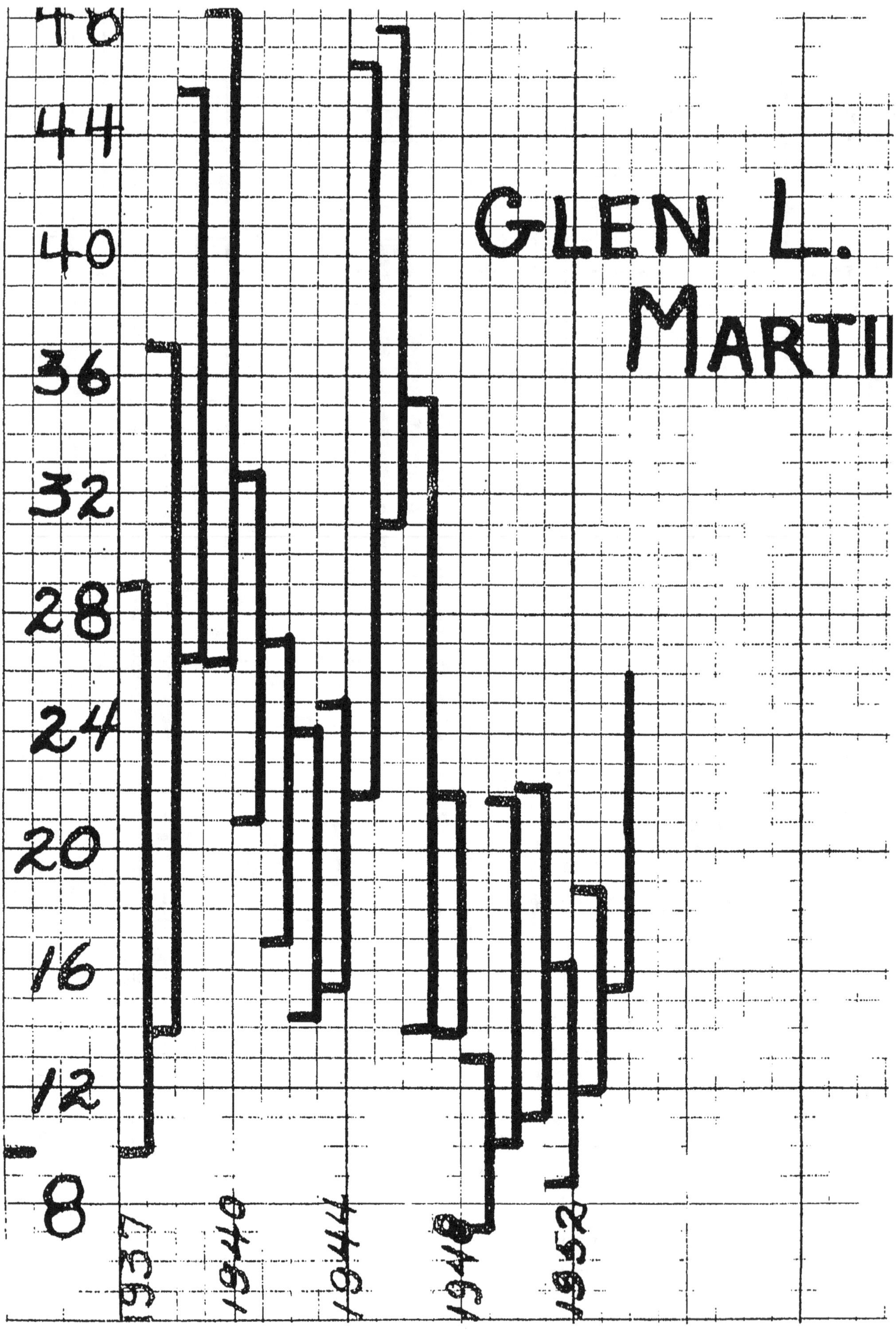

GLEN L.
MARTI
44
40
36
32
28
24
20
16
12
8
1940
1944
1948
1952

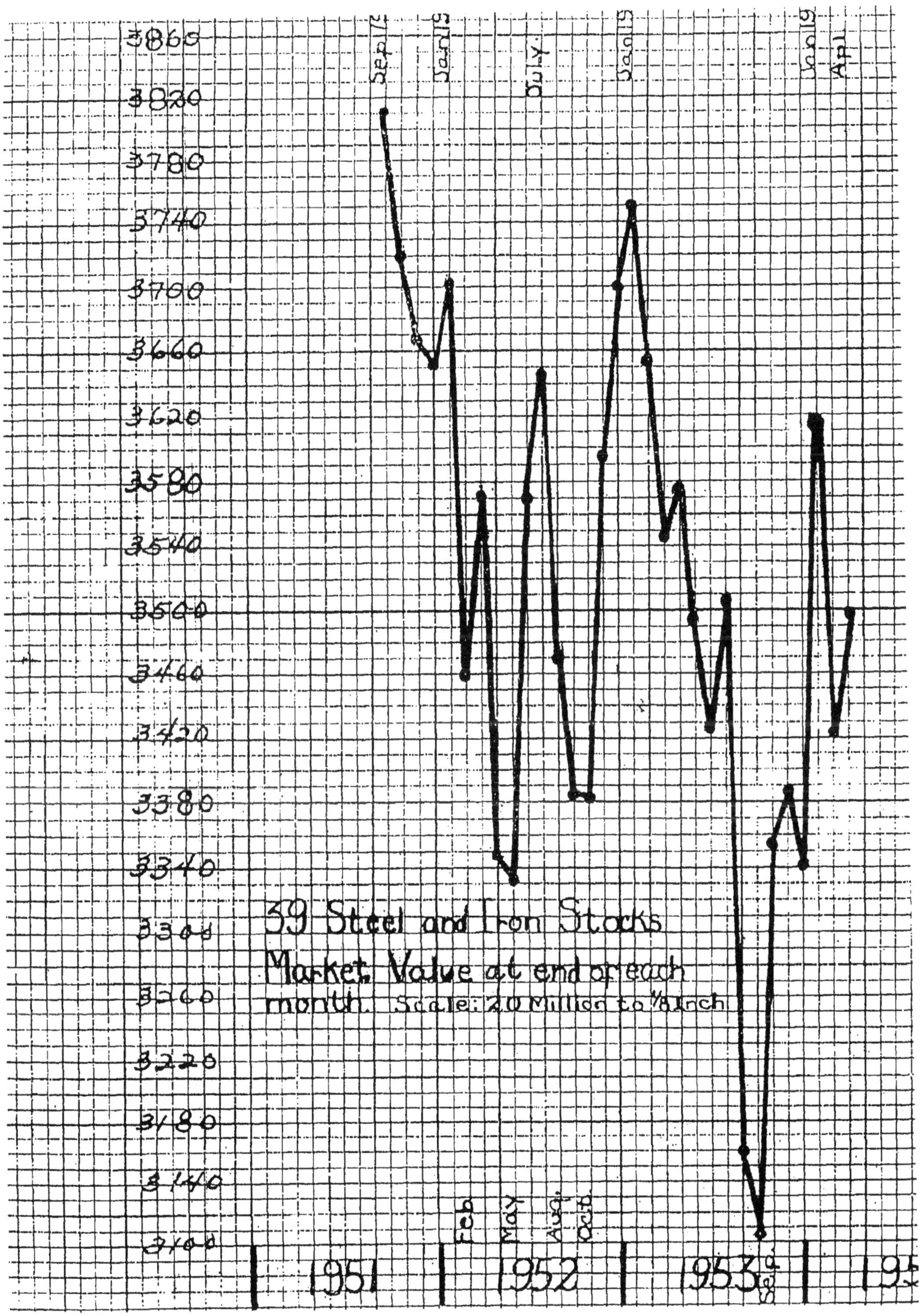
39 Steel and Iron Stocks
Market Value at end of each month. Scale: 20 Million to 1/8 Inch
3860
3820
3780
3740
3700
3660
3620
3580
3540
3500
3460
3420
3380
3340
3300
3260
3220
3180
3140
3100
Sep/
Jan/
July
Jan/
Jan/
Apl
Feb
May
Aug
Oct
Sep
1951
1952
1953

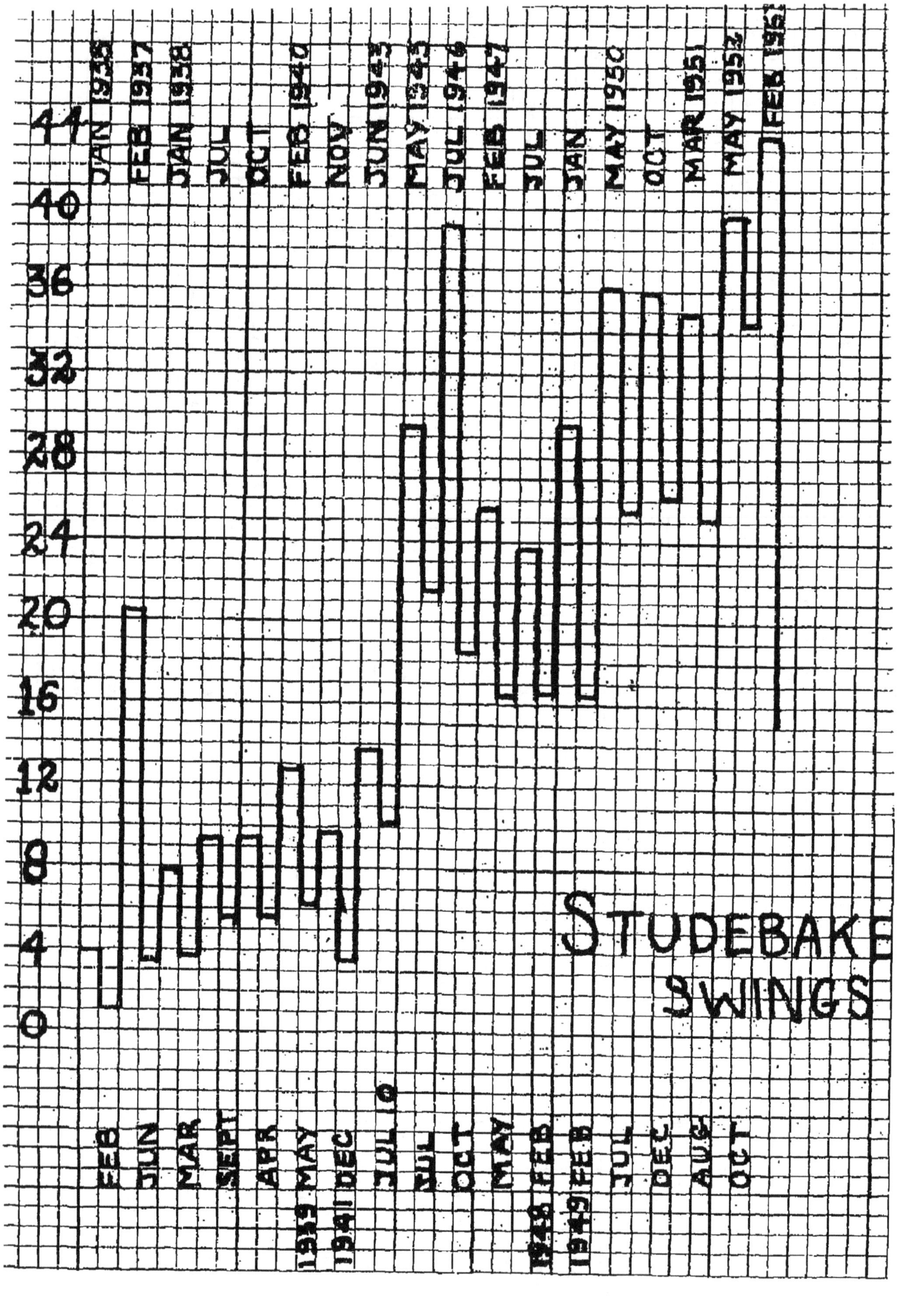
STUDEBAKER
SWINGS
0
4
8
12
16
20
24
28
32
36
40
44
FEB 1937
JAN 1938
JUL
OCT
FEB 1940
NOV
JUN 1943
MAY 1945
JUL 1946
FEB 1947
JUL
JAN
MAY 1950
OCT
MAR 1951
MAY 1952
FEB
JUN
MAR
SEPT
APR
1939 MAY
1941 DEC
JUL
JUL
OCT
MAY
1948 FEB
1949 FEB
JUL
DEC
AUG
OCT

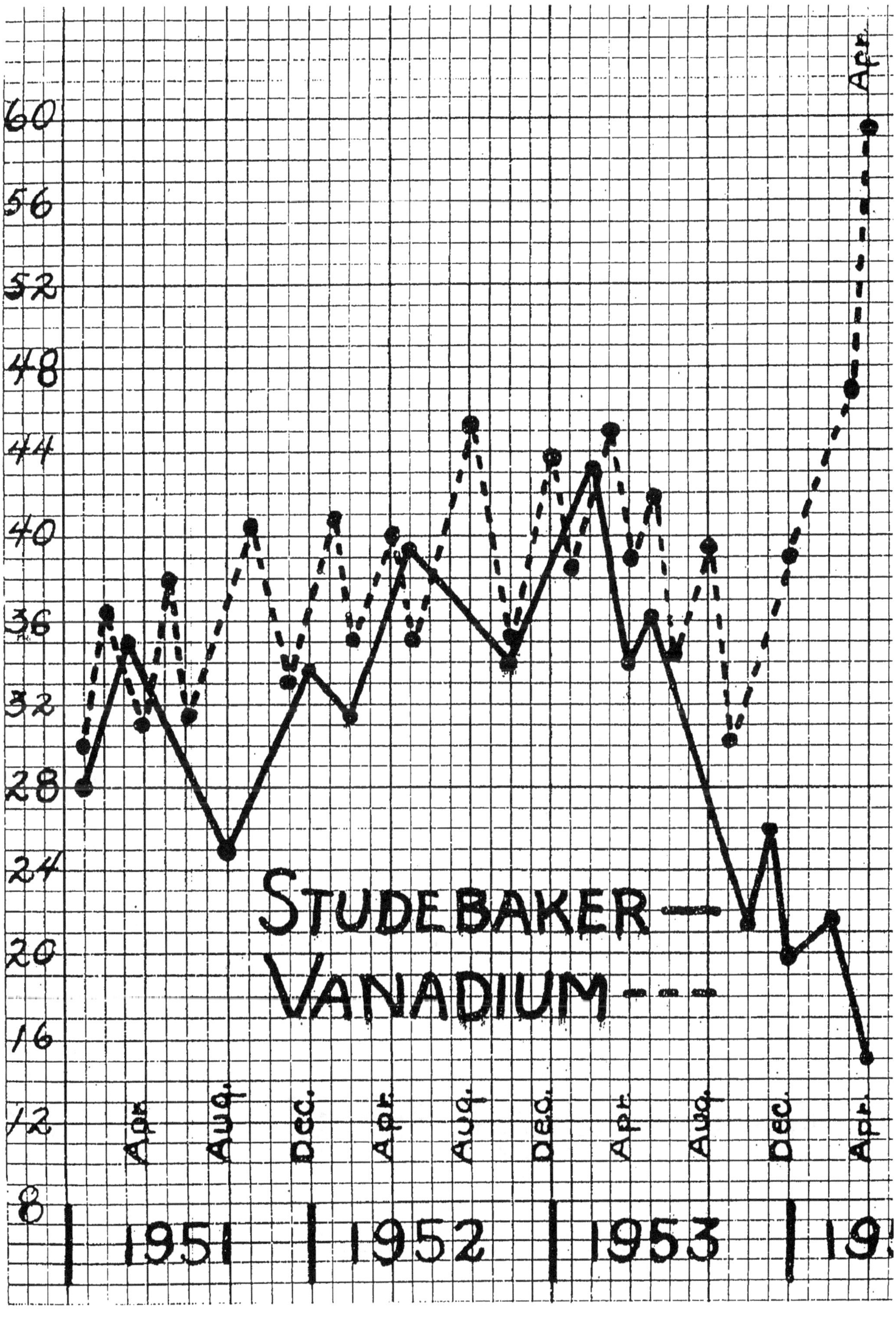

60
56
52
48
44
40
36
32
28
24
20
16
12
8
STUDEBAKER —
VANADIUM - - -
Apr.
Aug.
Dec.
Apr.
Aug.
Dec.
Apr.
Aug.
Dec.
Apr.
1951
1952
1953

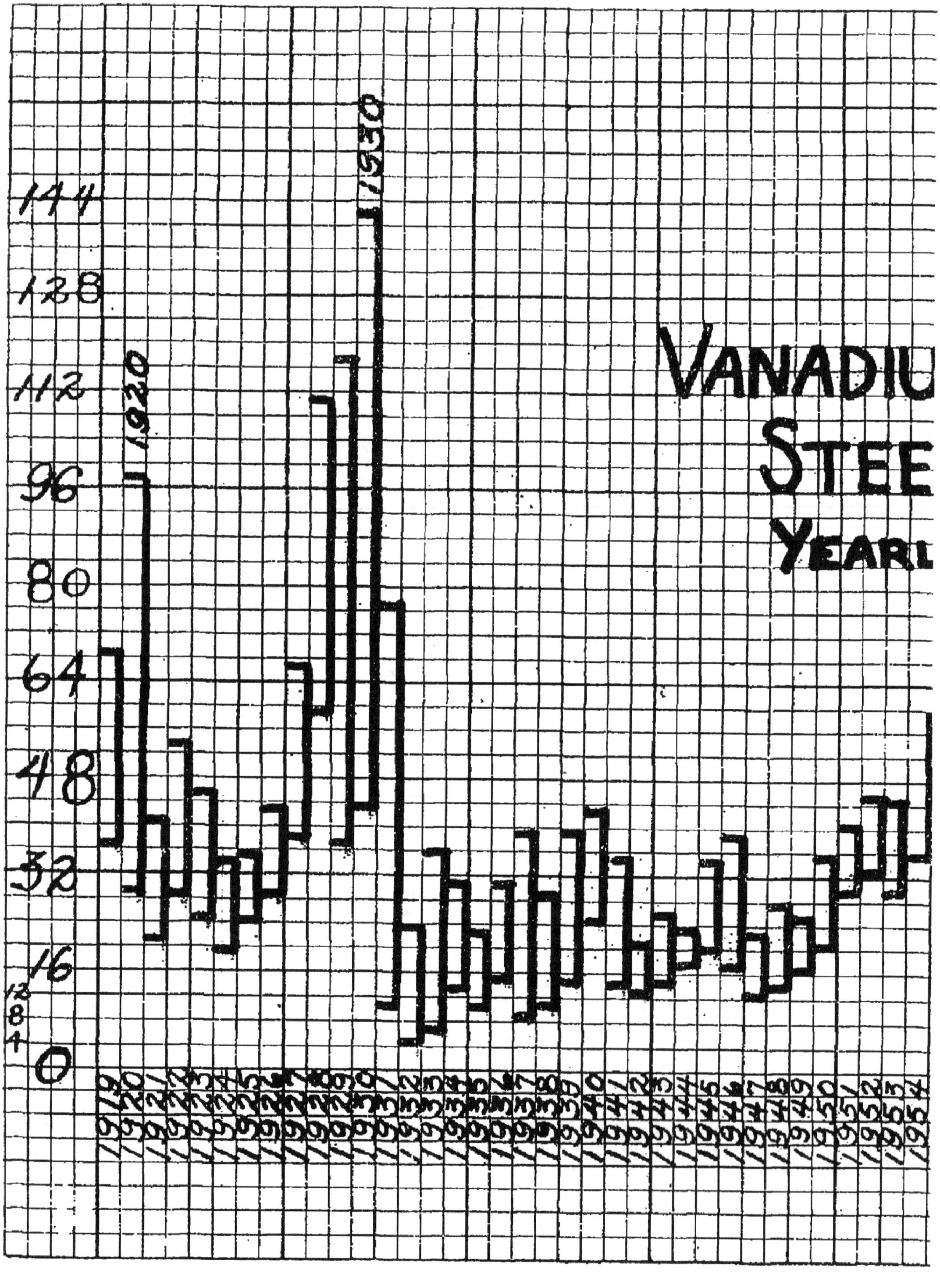

VANADIU
STEE
YEARL
144
128
112
96
80
64
48
32
16
0

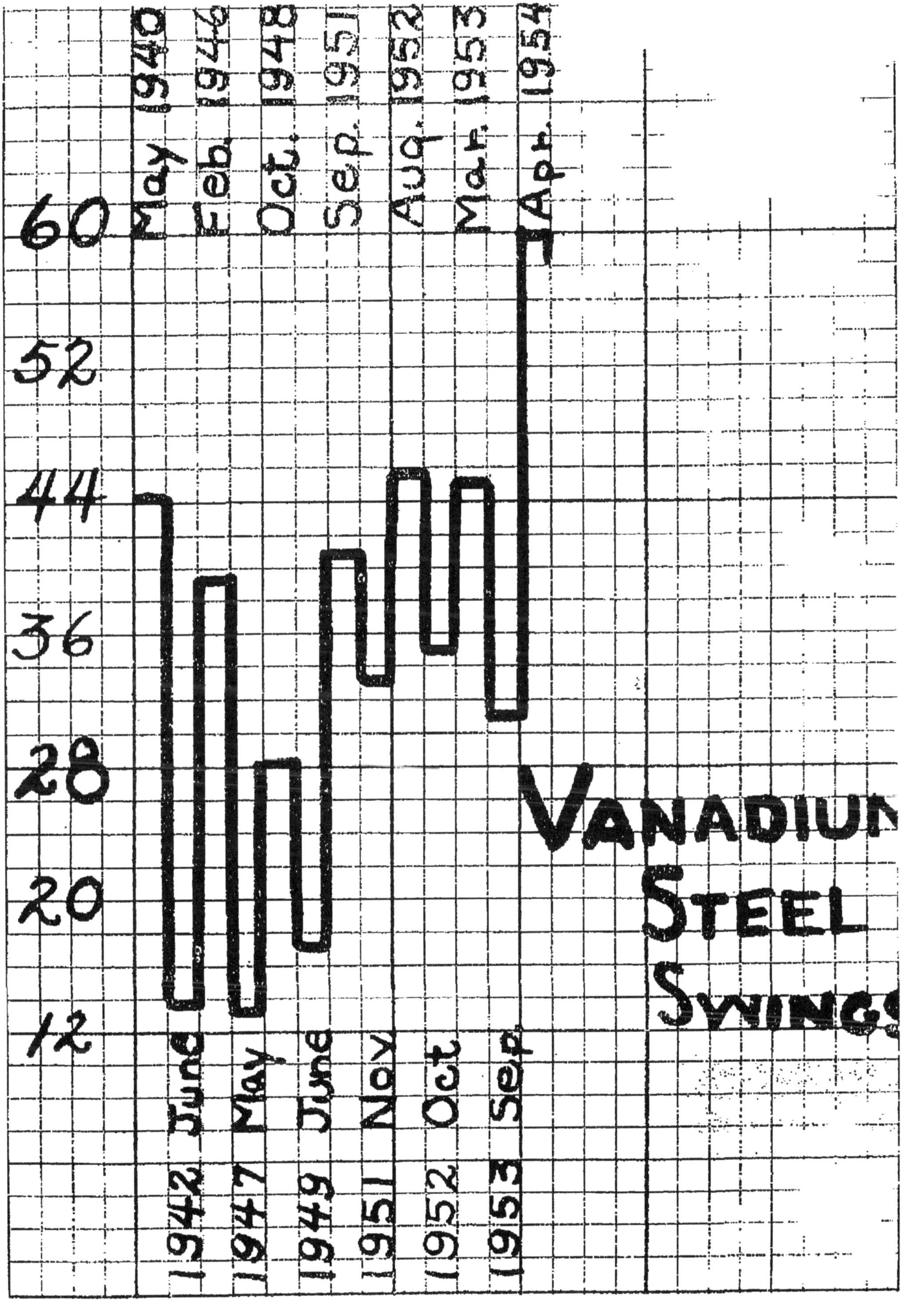
May 1940
Feb. 1946
Oct. 1948
Sep. 1951
Aug. 1952
Mar. 1953
Apr. 1954
60
52
44
36
28
20
12
VANADIU
STEEL
SWING
1942 June
1947 May
1949 June
1951 Nov
1952 Oct
1953 Sep.

# Chapter 2

## *Method For Trading With The Overnight Chart*

## *The W. D. Gann Mechanical Stock Trading Method*

W. D. GANN
91 WALL STREET
NEW YORK

SCIENTIFIC ADVICE
AND ANALYTICAL REPORTS
ON STOCKS AND COMMODITIES
AUTHOR OF "TRUTH OF THE STOCK TAPE"
AND "THE TUNNEL THRU THE AIR"

MEMBER
AMERICAN ECONOMIC ASS'N
ROYAL ECONOMIC SOCIETY
CABLE ADDRESS
"GANWADE NEW YORK"

## METHOD FOR TRADING WITH THE OVERNIGHT CHART

The Overnight Chart and the method for operating it is purely mechanical. You use no judgment but simply follow rules and reverse your position when the Overnight Chart indicates it. If you buy and sell and use stop loss orders according to rules, this Method will make a large amount of profits over a long period of time.

The Overnight Chart is taken from the daily high and low chart and the rule for keeping it is as follows:

As long as a stock makes higher bottoms each day, you move the Overnight Chart up, but the first day it makes ½ point or more under a previous day's bottom, you move the Overnight Chart down to this level, but always recording the highest top reached before the Overnight Chart turns. Then as long as the Overnight Chart makes lower bottoms, you continue to move it down. Should it make a higher bottom and a lower top the same day, you would move it up to the top of that day because the Overnight Chart is based on bottoms. When there is a wide swing and the market runs up early in the day and makes a higher top than the previous day and then runs down later in the day and makes a lower bottom, you first move your chart up to the top, or highest point reached during the day, and then bring it down to the lowest level. Then suppose next day it makes a higher bottom, you move it up to the top of that day.

You can use the Resistance Levels in connection with the Overnight Chart, but the only rule that I use in connection with the trading record on U. S. Steel, which will follow, is the half-way point, taking extreme low and extreme high of the last move and dividing it by two to get the gravity center or half-way point. Then buy or sell when this point is reached and protect it with a 1 point stop loss order. The other trading indications are according to the Overnight Chart.

When a stock reaches a new high where you have no Resistance Levels between a previous high and a previous low, you simply follow the Overnight Chart and reverse position when the rule indicates it.

You should watch the daily highs and lows on your daily chart around Permanent Resistance Levels as they will help you to determine a change in the major or minor trend on the Overnight Chart.

RULE I: Buy or sell on double or triple tops or bottoms with a stop-loss order 1 point above the top or 1 point under the bottom. This is the rule that I use. However, many times you will make more money if you use a 3-point stop loss order but by using a 1-point stop loss order most of the time, the stop will not be caught very often and when it is, it will be time to reverse. The greatest advances and declines usually start from triple tops or bottoms, but remember that these triple tops or bottoms must be several weeks or several months apart to be of great importance. Triple tops or bottoms which are only a limited number of days apart do not mean such big moves as those that occur weeks or months apart.

RULE 2: When a stock reaches the same top or bottom the 4th time, especially if it is several weeks or months apart, it nearly always goes through. Therefore, when you buy or sell the 4th time at a bottom or a top, you must always use a 1-point stop loss order over the top or under the bottom.

RULE 3: When the Overnight Chart makes tops or bottoms on Resistance Levels like the 1/2, 2/3 and 3/4 points, you should buy or sell with a stop loss order 1 or 2 points under these exact Resistance Levels. As a general rule, the stop should be 1 point.

RULE 4: When your stop loss order is caught, it indicates that the Overnight Chart has reversed, so you should reverse position and double up every time it is caught. You will make a great deal more money trading in this way, as will be shown by the trading operations which follow on U. S. Steel. In my trading, the only place where I do not reverse position, that is, double up when the stop loss order is caught, or the trend changes, is where there is no second top or bottom close enough for me to place a stop loss order if I reverse position. As a general rule, I place the stop loss order 1 point above a previous top or 1 point under a previous bottom.

RULE 5: The rule for pyramiding is to sell or buy half as much as your trading unit every 3 to 5 points apart, determining the distance according to the activity of the stock and according to previous Resistance Levels which are broken. Your 3rd trade in a pyramid should be one-half the amount of your 2nd trade, your 4th one-half of the 3rd, and so on. In this way, you take your greatest risk first, then when you make the 2nd, 3rd and 4th trades, you are reducing your trading units, therefore when a stop loss order is caught your loss will be small on the last trade in the pyramid and large on the ones that you bought or sold the most of first. Suppose you are pyramiding a stock when it has declined or advanced 20 or 30 points and has a fast move up or down without making any change on the Overnight Chart. In nearly every case before the trend changes, the Overnight Chart will make a reverse move and allow you to place your stop loss order at least 3 to 5 points away from the bottom or top, but when you have a very large profit and the market has a sharp move one way or the other, and you have a pyramid, you do not want to lose any more of your profits than you can help. In this case, I usually pull my stop loss order down 5 points from the low level each day or, if on the up side, place it up 5 points under the high level, then when the market makes the first reverse move of 5 points, I am out on stops on all of the pyramiding trades.

RULE 6: For very active, fast moving stocks, especially when they are at high levels, you should wait for a change in trend on the

Overnight Chart before reversing position. By a change in the Overnight Chart, I mean wait until it breaks a previous low level, or crosses a previous high level, in case you are operating on the down side

RULE 7: After any big advance or decline, reverse position when Overnight Chart shows a change in trend, that is, double up on changes and go with the trend. The big money is made by going with the trend. That is why every time the trend changes or a stop loss order is caught, we reverse position. If the trend has changed and it is time to sell out longs, it is also time to go short, and vice versa.

For example: In fast moving markets, like the panic of October and November, 1929, when you pyramid on active stocks and make a large amount of money, if you have very large profits, you should follow down with a stop loss order about 10 points away from the market. Then, after a severe decline reduce stop loss order, placing it about 5 points above the low level, because when a market is moving so fast as this, you should not wait for the Overnight Chart to show a change in trend by crossing a previous top before changing position. In fast moving markets you would also watch for the market to stop around important half-way points. For example: U. S. Steel at 150 had reached the half-way point from 38 to 261¾. You would not wait until the Overnight Chart showed a change but when Steel got around 150, you would cover shorts and buy with a stop at 149, or if you use the 3-point rule, place stop at 147. Suppose Steel had broken this 150 level. When your stop loss order was caught at 149 or 147, whichever was used, you would have gone short.

RULE 8: Watch the daily, weekly, and monthly closing prices. When a stock is active and closes for 3 days, 3 weeks or 3 months around the same price, then the trend changes, it will usually go a considerable distance in the direction in which it starts. However, it is not necessary to depend on this rule at all in connection with the Overnight Chart. I am only giving it to help those who study the daily, weekly and monthly charts.

RULE 9: In very weak or very strong markets watch for the first advance of 3 full points from any low level. By 3 full points I mean, for example, from 100 low, a rally to 103 would be 3 full points. Suppose the low was 99½. We would not count 3 full points until the stock rallied to 103. Reverse this rule for a stock when it is advancing. Suppose it advances to 150 7/8 and has not had a 3 full point reaction for some time. Then if it declined to 147, I would consider it a 3 full point reaction and an indication that the minor trend was reversing. In this case, suppose the stock only declined to 147½ or even to 147¼. We would not count it a full 3 point reaction, because full points are based on even figures.

No matter at what point or at what price you begin trading according to this Method, you must follow the rules and not risk more than 3 points on any one trade, then after that use the Overnight Chart and make your stop loss orders 1 point away from the top or bottom which I always do in my trading example which follows on U. S steel. Then when the stop loss order is caught, buy or sell double the amount, reversing your position. When you cover shorts on a stop loss order, you buy and go with the trend. In the same way when you sell out longs on a stop loss order, you reverse position and go short the same amount which keeps you with the trend.

In my trading, I do not use or take advantage of other rules which I know which might help me at points. I make many trades when I know there is going to be a loss just to demonstrate that the Method will work over a long period of years and make money by reversing position every time and using stop loss orders and, at the same time, following the capital rule and not overtrading, always allowing $3000 capital for each 100 shares traded in. If you start with $300 capital, then trade in 10-share lots and never risk more than 3 points, or $30, on each of your initial trades. Do not increase your trading unit on initial trades until your capital has increased so that the loss will be only 10% of your capital, if the loss comes.

In pyramiding, it is different. When you make the 2nd or 3rd trade, you have a profit already and are risking part of your profits, but always keep these risks protected with stop loss orders according to the Overnight Chart, so that if your stop loss orders on a pyramid are caught, your total loss will not exceed 10% of your capital. A man who will follow this rule over a long period of years will not only keep his capital, but will make a fortune. This can be demonstrated on any active stock. Use as little human judgment as possible and you will make better success in trading. The Mechanical Method beats human guesswork, because it reverses at the time the trend reverses and doubles up and goes with the trend, while the man who is guessing or using human judgment will wait. You must have machine-like action in order to succeed, and must buy or sell according to the rules, regardless of what you think or hope. This is exactly what I always do in the trading operations which follow on U. S. Steel.

# U. S. STEEL TRADES ACCORDING TO OVERNIGHT CHART

## 1915 - 1930

This trading plan requires $3,000 to start with, to trade in 100-share lots. My rule is never to risk more than 3 points or $300 on any one trade. I protect all trades with stop loss orders. Follow the rules for Resistance Levels and the rules for using the Overnight Chart. When I pyramid, or buy or sell a second lot, I limit my risk so that I will not lose more than 10% of my original capital. In other words, when I buy or sell a second lot, I place stop so that my loss will not exceed $300.

The following operations are based on trading according to the Overnight Chart and the use of Resistance Levels to determine buying and selling points:

## 1915

February 1, low 38, February 3, high 41½— a 3 point rally indicated a buying point. Either buy at market or on a reaction. We buy 100 shares at 41. On February 5 it declined to 38¾, then crossed 41½, the top of February 3, and turned Overnight trend up. Stop would now be at 36½ or 3 points under 39½. Trend continued up to 45 on February 13, then declined to 40¼ on February 24, making a higher bottom than February 5. Raise stop to 38½ or 2 points under 2 bottoms close together.

March 8th high 46, then made 3 bottoms around 43½ to 44¼ on March 5, 13 and 18. Here raise stop to 42½ or one point under three bottoms. Then we buy more at 47 when it goes one point above top at 46. Trend continues up to 49¾ on March 29; again made three bottoms around 47¾ to 48½; raise stop to 46¾. Then we buy more at 51 and raise stop on three lots to 48. The advance continued to 58 on April 10, reacted to 55¼ on April 13. We raise stop to 52¼ or three points under.

April 19 made top 60¾, reacted to 56¾ on April 24. Raise stop to 55¼, last bottom. April 26 high 59¼, April 27 low 57, a third higher bottom. Raise stop to 56 on all three lots. April 29 high 60-5/8, just 1/8 under top of April 19, April 30 low 58½. Raise stop to 57½.

May 3rd advanced to $60\frac{3}{4}$, the third top around same level, where we should either sell out and go short with stop at $63\frac{3}{4}$ or leave stop at $57\frac{1}{2}$. We sold on stop at $57\frac{1}{2}$

1st purchase 100 at 41, sold at $57\frac{1}{2}$ - profit $16\frac{1}{2}$ points
2nd purchase 100 at 47, sold at $57\frac{1}{2}$ - profit $10\frac{1}{2}$ points
3rd purchase 100 at 51, sold at $57\frac{1}{2}$ - profit $6\frac{1}{2}$ points

or a total of. . $33\frac{1}{2}$ points on 100 shares,

gives.......................................... $3,350
Deduct $100 for commission, Tax and Interest... . 100

Net Gain............... $3,250

Then we increase trading to 200 shares but loss must be limited to $600, or 3 points on each 100 shares. This would give us 200 short at $57\frac{1}{2}$ with stop at $60\frac{1}{2}$.

Decline followed, broke three bottoms made April 24, 27 and 30. We sell 200 shares more at $54\frac{1}{4}$. Decline continued to $48\frac{1}{4}$ where there were three bottoms March 26, 31 and April 1st. Rule says, buy the fourth time with one point stop. We covered 300 shares short at $48\frac{1}{2}$ and bought 200 at $48\frac{1}{2}$ with stop at $46\frac{3}{4}$, which was one point under bottom of March 26th and April 1st. The profits are as follows:

Sold 200 at $57\frac{1}{2}$, closed at $48\frac{1}{2}$ - profits $1,800.00
" 200 " $54\frac{1}{4}$ " " $48\frac{1}{2}$ - " 1,150.00

Total - 2,950.00

Commission and Taxes...................... 116.00

Net Profit 2,834.00

Previous Capital & Profits............... 6,250.00

Gives a Capital of.............. $9,084.00

which will allow 300 shares as a trading unit with risk limited to $900 on each trade. We bought 200 at $48\frac{1}{2}$ when we covered shorts, then we would have 100 more to buy later.

The stock advanced to $55\frac{1}{4}$ on May 12th. If we were watching the resistance level of $54\frac{1}{2}$ or 1/2 from $60\frac{3}{4}$ to $48\frac{1}{4}$, we would expect top and a reaction and could have sold out longs and gone short at $54\frac{1}{2}$ with stop at $57\frac{1}{2}$, but we waited for a change on the Overnight Chart.

May 14th, low $49\frac{3}{4}$. Here we buy 100 more at $50\frac{1}{2}$, then make stop on 300 at 48. The advance was resumed and on May 17th made $53\frac{1}{2}$, then reacted to $51\frac{3}{4}$, then turned trend up again. We would now raise stop to $49\frac{3}{4}$, the last bottom.

May 24th high 56¼ and crossing 54½, the 1/2 point, the second time indicated higher.

May 26th and June 1st reacted to 53¼ and made double bottom. Raise stop to 50¾ or one point under previous low level and when it crossed 56¼, last top, buy 200 more at 56½ and raise stop on all trades to 52¼, one point under last double bottom. June 4th the stock advanced to 64-1/8. June 9th declined to 56¾. Holding above 56¼, the 1/2 point from last low of 48¼ to high of 64-1/8, was a sign of strong support and showed that the main trend was up because the stock had gone three points above the triple tops made April 19, 29 and May 3rd.

From June 9th a rally followed to June 12th, when the high was 61¼. We now raise stops to 55¾ or one point under low of June 9th.

June 14th declined to 59, then raise stop on all trades to 58. This stop was never caught. The stock advanced to 61¾ on June 22nd, then after a series of lower tops and bottoms, declined to 58¼ on July 7th, then rallied to 59½ on July 9th and declined same day to 58¼, making a double bottom from which advance was resumed and on July 17th reached 65-1/8, reacted to 62-1/2 on July 20th, rallied to 62-1/8 on the 26th and declined same day to 62¾, making a double bottom again, then went to new high and crossed 66-3/8, the 1/2 point from 94-7/8 to 38. We bought more at 67 and raised stop on all trades to 61¾ or one point under last low of July 26th. Buy 200 more at 72.

August 10th high 76¾; 11th declined to 73-5/8;
12th advanced to 75½; 14th declined to 73-3/8;
18th advanced to 77-5/8.

We now raise stop on all trades to 72-3/8 or one point under the last bottom at 73-3/8. The stop was caught and we sold short 400 shares at 72-3/8.

The account now stands as follows:

| | | | | | | | | |
|---|---|---|---|---|---|---|---|---|
| Bought | 200 | at | 48½ | closed | at | 72 3/8 | profit | $6,725.00 |
| " | 100 | " | 50½ | " | " | 72 3/8 | " | 2,162.50 |
| " | 200 | " | 56½ | " | " | 72 3/8 | " | 3,125.00 |
| " | 200 | " | 67 | " | " | 72 3/8 | " | 1,075.00 |
| | | | | | | | | 13,087.50 |
| | 200 | " | 72 | | | 72 3/8 | | |
| | Less loss of 3/8 on 200 | | | | | | 75.00 | |
| | Commissions | | | | | | 225.00 | 300.00 |
| | Net Gain | | | | | | | 12,787.50 |
| | Previous Capital and Profits | | | | | | | 9,084.00 |
| | Gives an Operating Capital of | | | | | | | $21,871 50 |

This would give a limit of 700 shares as a trading unit.

We sold 400 short at 72-3/8
Sold 300 " " 69-3/8

Always calculate the 1/2 point of a previous move.

Last low 58-1/8 July 9th to 77-5/8 high August 18th, making 1/2 point at 67-7/8. August 23rd, declined to 67-3/4. Here we cover shorts and buy 700 longs at 68½, stop 64-7/8. However, a stop at 66-7/8, just one point under 1/2 point, would have held, as low of 67-3/4 was not reached again.

Here our account stands as follows:

| | |
|---|---|
| Sold 400 at 72-3/8 closed at 68½ profit | $1,750.00 |
| " 300 " 69-3/8 " " 68½ " | 252.50 |
| | 2,002.50 |
| Less Taxes and Commissions | 175.00 |
| | 1,827.50 |
| Previous Capital | 21,871.50 |
| Operating Capital | $23,698.00 |

We continue with 700 shares as trading unit. We are now long of 700 shares bought at 68½ with stop 64-7/8. Buy 300 at 72.

Aug. 27th, advanced to 77; Sept. 1st, declined to 73-3/4; Sept. 2nd, rallied to 76-3/4.

Here we raise stop to 72-3/4, just one point under September 1st low.

Sept. 10th advanced to 76¼; Sept. 11th declined to 73¾; Sept. 14th rallied to 76; Sept. 17th declined to 74¼;

making five bottoms around 74¼ to 73-3/4, a sure indication that stop should be at 72-3/4.

September 27th, advanced to 79-3/4, getting above all tops since August 27th. We bought 300 at 78½, stop 75½.

October 1st high 81-3/4; 6th low 76-3/4, advance resumed; 19th high 87¼; 20th low 85½; 21st high 87-5/8, stop 84½; 26th low 85¼: 26th high 87¼, the third top around same level.

We could have sold out but we assume stop was caught at 84½, and we went short 700 at 84½.

Our account now reads as follows:

| | |
|---|---:|
| Bought 700 at 68½, sold at 84½ profit | $11,200.00 |
| " 300 " 72, " " 84½. " | 3,750.00 |
| " 300 " 78½, " " 84½. " | 1,800.00 |
| Profit | 16,750.00 |
| Less Tax and Coms. | 325.00 |
| | 16,425.00 |
| Previous Capital | 23,698.00 |
| Operating Capital | $40,123.00 |

We can now raise trading unit to 1000 shares. We are short 700 at 84½. The last low, October 6th, was 76-3/4, high October 21st, 87-5/8. Makes 1/2 point 82-1/8. October 29th, the stock declines to 82¼. Note October 16th low 82¼. Here we would cover shorts and buy with stop at 81¼. Our account now stands, sold 700 at 84½, closed at 82½, profit $1,400.00

| | | |
|---|---:|---:|
| Less Com. | 175.00 | |
| | 1,225.00 | $1,225.00 |
| Previous Capital | | 40,123.00 |
| Operating Capital | | $41,308.00 |

We now have 1000 shares bought at 82½.

November 1st, advances to 88-3/8; 3rd, low 86; 4th, high 88.

Raise stop to 85, one point under November 3rd low. The stop was caught, and we sold short 1000 at 85. Our account now stands:

| | |
|---|---:|
| Bought 1000 at 82½, sold at 85, profit | $2,500. |
| Less Tax and Commissions | 250. |
| | 2,250. |
| Previous capital | 41,308. |
| Operating Capital | $43,558. |

Short 1000 at 85, stop 88-3/8. The stock declines to 83-5/8 on November 9th; then rallies on November 12th to 88-3/8; declines on November 16th and 20th to 86¼; November 26th high 88¼, December 2nd low 84½. December 7th high 88¼, making the same level five times. Our stop should be 89¼. December 13th, 17th, 21st made lows 85¼ to 84-7/8, higher than previous bottoms, and our stop should have been reduced to 87¼, one point above December 20th high. This stop was caught, and we would reverse position and buy 1000 at 87¼. Account now stands:

| | |
|---|---:|
| Sold 1000 at 85, closed at 87¼, loss | $2,250.00 |
| Commissions | 250.00 |
| Net loss | $2,500.00 |
| Capital of | 43,558.00 |
| | 2,500.00 |
| Net Operating Capital | $41,058.00 |

We have 1000 bought at 87¼. December 27th, advanced to 89½; December 29th, low 86-3/4; December 31st high 89½, a double top - raise stop to 85-3/4. This double top near 90, a strong resistance level, would be the place to sell out and go short, but we stay to see if overnight trend turns down. Stop is caught at 85-3/4, and we sell 1000 short at 85-3/4. Account now stands as follows:

| | |
|---|---|
| Bought 1000 at 87¼, sold at 85-3/4, loss | $1,500.00 |
| Commissions | 250.00 |
| | $1,750.00 |

from capital of $41,058.00 leaves a balance of $39,308.00, and 1000 short at 85-3/4.

## 1916

January 24th, declined to 82½, same low as October 16th and 29th, 1915. We cover shorts at 82½ and buy 1000 82½.

Account now stands:

| | |
|---|---|
| Sold 1000 at 85-3/4 closed at 82½ profit | $3,250.00 |
| Less commissions | 250.00 |
| | 3,000.00 |
| Capital | 39,308.00 |
| Operating balance | $42,308.00 |

Bought 1000 at 82½, stop 81½.

January 26th high 86; 27th low 82-3/4; 28th high 84¼.

Raise stop to 81-3/4, one point under January 27th low. This stop was caught and we go short 1000 at 81-3/4. Account now stands:

Bought 1000 at 81½, sold at 81-3/4, even, counting commissions.

Capital $42,308.00

Short 1000 at 81-3/4, stop 85¼.

January 31st low 79-7/8; February 4th high 84-3/4; 5th low 82¼; 10th high 85-5/8.

Stop caught and we buy 1000 at 85-5/8. Account now stands:

Sold 1000 at 81-3/4, closed at 85-5/8, loss $3,787.50

From $42,308.00 leaves $38,520.50, with 1000 bought at 85-5/8, stop 81-1/4.

February 17th and 24th, made lows at 82⅛ and 82-3/8. Raised stop to 81½. Stop caught and we go short 1000 at 81½. Account stands:

> Bought 1000 85-5/8, sold at 81½, loss $4,125.
> Less commissions 250.
> $4,375.
> from capital $38,530.00, leaves $34,145, with 1000 short at 81½.

March 1st declines to 79-3/4, same low as January 31st. We cover shorts and buy 1000 at 80¼. Account now stands:

| | |
|---|---|
| Sold 1000 at 81½, closed 80¼, profit | $1,250.00 |
| Less commissions | 250.00 |
| Net | $1,000.00 |
| Added to Capital gives | 39,520.00, |

with 1000 bought at 80¼, stop 79¼. March 17th high 87¼, March 22nd low 84. We raise stop to 83. April 4th high 86. April 8th and March 31st lows 83-3/4. April 10th high 85¼. Decline follows Stop is caught at 83 and we go short 1000. Account now stands:

> Bought 1000 at 80¼, sold at 83, profit $2,750., less commissions of $250.00, leaves $2,500. net profit. Added to capital gives $42,020.00 with 1000 short at 83.

April 22nd declines to 80 and we cover at 80¼ and buy 1000 because this is same bottom as January 31st and March 1st. We protect with stop 79¼, this being a triple bottom.

April 25th high 84, April 26th low 80-3/8, a higher bottom. May 1st high 84¼, May 5th low 80½, a slightly higher bottom. From high of 89½ on December 31, 1915 to low of 79-3/4 March 1st, 1916, makes 1/2 point 84-5/8, and making 85-5/8 would indicate higher.

May 25th high 86-5/8 and last low on 17th was 84. Therefore we raise stop to 83. The stock declines to 83-5/8 on June 2nd, June 12th advances to 87¼. June 12th low 86. June 14th high 87. We raise stop to 85, which is caught, and we go short 1000 at 85. Account stands:

> Bought 1000 at 80¼, sold at 85, profit $4,750.00, less $250.00 commission, gives net $4,500.00. Added to capital gives $46,520.00 and 1000 short at 85, stop 88.

June 27th declines to 82-3/4 and as top on June 26th was 84¼ we reduce stop to 85¼, which is caught, and we buy 1,000 at 85¼. The account now stands:

> Sold 1000 at 85, closed 85¼, loss of 1/4 point and commission, makes $500. from $46,520.00, leaves $46,020.00 and 1000 bought at 85¼, stop 81-3/4.

July 6th high 87¼, July 14th low 83¼, we raise stop to 82¼. June 24th high 87¼, July 25th low 85¼, we raise stop to 84¼. July 27, August 2nd and 5th, makes low 85-3/4 and 86, and we raise stop to 84-3/4. A big advance follows and at 90½ we buy 300 more because the stock has gone one point into new high after holding for nine months between 89½ and 79-3/4. August 17th high 92-5/8, August 18th low 91. We raise stop on all trades to 90 and at 94 buy 300 more, August 23rd high 99½, the highest in its histoty. August 24th low 96-3/4. We raise stop to 95-3/4. August 25th high 99¼. August 28th low 95-3/4. Catches stop and we go short 1000 at 95-3/4. The account now stands:

| | | | | | |
|---|---|---|---|---|---|
| Bought 1000 at | 85¼, | sold | 95-3/4, | profit | $10,500. |
| " 300 " | 90½, | " | 95-3/4, | " | 1,575. |
| " 300 " | 94 | " | 95-3/4, | " | 525. |
| | | | | | 12,600. |
| Less commissions | | | | | 400. |
| Net profit | | | | | $12,200. |
| Capital | | | | | 46,030. |
| | | | | | $58,220. |

with 1000 shares short at 95-3/4. We can now increase trading unit to 1200 shares. August 30th low 95¼. The high on 29th was 97, so we make stop to 97. August 31st stop is caught and we buy 1,200 at 97. Account now stands:

Sold 1000 at 95-3/4, closed at 97, loss $1,500.
from capital leaves $56,720 and 1200 bought at 97.

August 31st advances to 99-3/8 for third time and can't go thru 100, so we sell out at 99 and go short 1200 at 99. Account now stands:

Bought 1200 at 97, sold at 99, net profit $2,100.
Added to capital gives $58,820.00 and 1200 short at 99.

September 1st declines to 95, getting only 1/4 under low of August 30th. We reduce stop to 99, which is caught, but we wait to buy until stock can make new high and go through 100 - a very important Resistance Level. Account now stands:

Sold 1200 at 99, closed at 98, profit $900.00.
Added to capital gives $59,720.

The advance continues and at 100½ we buy 1200 with stop 99½, and at 105½ we buy 600 more, and at 110½ - 600 more. The lows on September 19th and 20th were 107, so we raise stop to 106 on all trades. At 115½ we buy 300 more. September 25th high 120, a Resis-tance Level. September 26th low 113-3/4. We raise stop on all trades to 112-3/4. September 29th high 120½. September 30th low 116¼. We raise stop to 115¼. October 2nd, 4th, 5th, makes tops at 118-5/8 to 118-3/4 and low on October 4th was 117, so we raise stop to 116, which is caught, and we go short 1200. Account now stands:

| | | | | |
|---|---|---|---|---|
| Bought 1200 at 100½, | sold at 116, | profit | $18,600. |
| " 600 " 105½ | " " 116 | " | 6,300. |
| " 600 " 110½ | " " 116 | " | 3,300. |
| 300 " 115½ | " 116 | | 150. |
| | | | 28,350. |
| Less commissions | | | 675. |
| | | | 27,675. |
| Previous Capital | | | 59,720. |
| Operating Capital | | | $87,395. |

and short 1200 at 116, with stop 119. We can now increase trading to 1500 shares.

Decline follows and we sell 600 more at 111. October 9th low 108; October 10th high 113. Reduce stop to 113. October 14th low 108, same as October 9th, a double bottom. We figure from last low September 1st at 95 to high 120½ September 29th and find 1/2 point is 107-3/4, so we cover shorts at 108½ and buy 1500 with stop 106-3/4. The account now stands:

| | | | |
|---|---|---|---|
| Sold 1200 at 116, | closed at 108½, | profit | $9,000. |
| " 600 " 111, | " at 108½, | " | 1,500. |
| | | | 10,500. |
| Less Commission | | | 950. |
| Net profit | | | 9,550. |
| Capital Added | | | 87,395. |
| Operating Capital | | | $97,045. |

with 1500 bought at 108½. Bought 700 more at 114. October 23rd high 121-3/4. Bought 400 more at 121½, because it was a new high. October 26th low 117¼. Raised stop on all trades to 116¼. November 2nd high 122¼. November 4th low 119-3/4. Raised stop to 118-3/4. November 5th high 126. November 9th low 122½. Raised stop to 121½. Stops were caught, and we go short 1500 at 121½. The account now stands:

| | | | |
|---|---|---|---|
| Bought 1500 at 108½, | sold 121½, | profit | $9,500. |
| " 700 " 114 | " 121½, | " | 5,250. |
| " 400 " 121½ | " 121½, | " | --- |
| | | | 24,750. |
| Less Commissions | | | 650. |
| | | | 24,100. |
| Capital | | | 97,045. |
| Operating Capital | | | $121,145. |

with 1500 short at 121½. We can now be very conservative and increase trading to 2000 shares and should we have ten consecutive losses of 3 points each, we would still have half our capital left to operate with, and ten consecutive losses are highly improbable.

November 14th, declined to 120¼, failing to make low of November 4th, which was 119-3/4. We reduce stop to 123¼, which is caught and we buy 2000 at 123¼ with stop at 120. November 27th, high 129-3/4, November 28th low 125-3/4. We raise stop to 124-3/4. This stop was caught, and we go short 2000 shares. The account now stands:

1500 sold at 121½, closed at 123¼, loss $3,000
2000 " " 123¼ " " 124-3/4 profit $3,000
Leaves a loss of commissions on 3500 shares, which is $875 from capital $121,145, leaves $120,270.00.

with 2000 short at 124-3/4. December 4th high 120½, and we make stop 127½. Decline follows. We sell 1000 more at 119-3/4. December 13th high 120½ and we reduce stop to 121½ on all trades. We sell 500 more at 115½. December 15th low 109¼. December 16th high 114-5/8. We reduce stops to 115-5/8, which are caught, and we go long 2000 at 115-5/8. The account now stands:

| | | | | |
|---|---|---|---|---|
| Sold 2000 at 124-3/4, | closed | 115-5/8, | profit | $18,250.00 |
| " 1000 " 119-3/4 | " | 115-5/8 | " | 4,112.50 |
| " 500 " 115-1/2 | " | 115-5/8 | " | 22,362.50 |
| Less loss of 1/8 on 500 and commission | | | | 937.50 |
| Profit | | | | 21,425.00 |
| Capital | | | | 120,270.00 |
| | | | | $141,695.00 |

with 2000 bought at 115-5/8. December 19th high 116¼. The low on 18th was 112½, so we raise stop to 111½, which is caught and we go short 2000 at 111½. Account stands:

| | |
|---|---|
| Bought 2000 at 115-5/8, sold at 112½, loss | $6,250 |
| Commissions | 500. |
| | $6,750. |

from capital of $141,695 leaves $134,945, with 2000 short at 111½. The decline continues, and we sell 1000 more at 106½. December 21st panicky decline. Stock sells at 100, a Resistance Level, where we should cover, but we reduce stop to 105, which is caught, and we buy 2000 at 105. Account now stands:

| | | | | |
|---|---|---|---|---|
| Sold 2000 at 111½, | closed | 105, | profit | $13,000. |
| " 1000 " 105½ | " | 105 | " | 1,500. |
| | | | | 14,500. |
| Less Commissions | | | | 750. |
| Profit | | | | 13,750. |
| Capital | | | | 134,945. |
| Total Capital | | | | $148,695. |

with 2000 bought at 105, and we buy 1000 more at 110.

1917

January 4th high 115-3/4. We figure high 129-3/4 to 110 low and get 1/2 point 114-7/8, and looking back to December 19th, we see last high was 116¼. Therefore, we sell out longs at 114½ and go short with stop 117½. The account now stands:

| | |
|---|---|
| Bought 2000 at 105, sold at 114½, profit | $19,000 |
| " 1000 " 110 " " 114½ " | 4,500 |
| | 23,500 |
| Less Commissions | 750 |
| Net Profit | $22,750 |
| Capital | 148,695 |
| | $171,445 |

with 200 short at 114½. The stock declines to 109¾ on January 5th; then advances to 113-7/8 on January 9th, and on 11th makes 109¼, same low as January 5th. We cover shorts and buy 2000, because 108 is 1/2 point from 100 to 115-7/8. The account now stands:

| | |
|---|---|
| Sold 2000 at 114½ closed at 110 profit | $9,000 |
| Less commissions | 500 |
| Profit | $8,500 |
| Capital | 171,445 |
| Total capital | $179,945. |

with 2000 bought at 110, stop 107. January 19th and 26th advances to 115½. We sell out at 114½ and sell short with stop 116½; because it is 1/2 point and strong Resistance Level. The account stands:

| | |
|---|---|
| Bought 2000 at 110, sold 114½, profit | $9,000 |
| Less Commissions | 500 |
| | $8,500 |
| Capital | 179,945 |
| Total | $188,445. |

with 2000 short at 114½. We sell 1000 more at 109½. February 1st, just two years from the low of 38 on February 1, 1915, U.S.Steel declines to 99. We cover shorts and buy 2000 at 100, because 100 was low on December 21, 1916. We protect with stop at 99 and stop is caught, and we go short 2000 at 99. The account now stands:

| | |
|---|---|
| Sold 2000 at 114½, closed at 100, profit | $29,000 |
| " 1000 " 109½ " " 100 " | 9,500 |
| Profit | $38,500 |
| Loss one point on 2000 and Commissions on 5000 | 3,250 |
| Net Profit | 35,250 |
| Capital | 188,445 |
| | $223,695. |

with 2000 short at 99. February 2nd high 104-1/8. We place stop 105-1/8. February 3rd low 99¼, a higher bottom than February 1st, and counting December 21st, three bottoms around the same level. We reduce stop to 102¼ and stop is caught. We reverse and buy 2000 at 102¼. The account now stands:

| | |
|---|---|
| Sold 2000 at 99, closed at 102¼, loss | $6,500 |
| Commissions | 500 |
| | $7,000 |

Deducted from capital leaves $216,695. and 2000 bought at 102¼. The stock advances, making higher bottoms until February 20th and 25th, when it makes double top at 109½ with bottom at 106¼ on February 23rd. We raise stop to 105¼. This stop was caught and we sell 2000 short at 105¼. The account now stands:

| | |
|---|---|
| Bought 2000 at 102¼, sold at 105¼, profit | $6,000 |
| Commissions | 500 |
| Profit | 5,500 |
| Capital | 216,695 |
| Total | $222,195. |

with 2000 short at 105¼. March 1st low 103½ same low as March 9th. Figuring 1/2 point from 99 to 109½ high makes the 1/2 point at 104¼ a buying level. We cover shorts and buy 2000 at 104½. The account now stands:

| | |
|---|---|
| Sold 2000 at 105¼, closed at 104½, profit | $1,500 |
| Commissions | 500 |
| Net Gain | $1,000 |
| Capital | 222,195 |
| Total | $223,195. |

with 2000 bought at 104½, stop 102½. The stock advanced and we bought 1000 more at 110½, when it crossed the last two tops. March 6th high 111½; March 7th low 109½. We raise stop on all trades to 108½. Then buy 500 more at 114½. March 21st high 118; March 22nd declined to 115¼. We raise stop to 114¼ which was caught and we go short 2000 at 114¼. The account now stands:

| | |
|---|---|
| Bought 2000 at 104½, sold at 114¼, profit | $19,500 |
| " 1000 " 110½ " " 114¼ " | 3,750 |
| Profit | 23,250 |
| Less loss of ¼ on 500 and commissions | 1,000 |
| Net Profit | $22,250 |
| Capital | 223,195 |
| Total | $245,445. |

with 2000 short 114$\frac{1}{4}$. March 31st declines to 113-3/4. Last tops on March 28th and 30th were at 116. We make stop 117, which is caught, and we buy 2000 at 117. The account now stands:

| | |
|---|---|
| Sold 2000 at 114$\frac{1}{4}$, closed at 117, loss | \$5,500. |
| Commissions | 500. |
| Net Loss | \$6,000. |
| from capital leaves balance of | \$239,445. |

with 2000 bought at 117. April 3rd advances to 118-3/4. We raise stop to 116-3/4, which is caught, and we go short 2000 at 116-3/4. The account now stands:

| | |
|---|---|
| Bought 2000 at 117, sold at 116-3/4, loss | \$500 |
| Commissions | 500 |
| Net Loss | \$1,000 |
| Subtract from capital leaves | \$238,445.00 |

with 2000 short at 116-3/4. The decline follows and we sell 1000 at 112-3/4, because it is under the last three bottoms. March 10th low 108-3/4. From 99 low to 118-3/4 high makes the 1/2 point 108-7/8. We cover shorts at 109$\frac{1}{4}$ and buy 2000 at 109$\frac{1}{4}$, stop 107-7/8. The account now stands:

| | |
|---|---|
| Sold 2000 at 116-3/4, closed at 109$\frac{1}{4}$, profit | \$15,000 |
| " 1000 " 112-3/4 " " 109$\frac{1}{4}$ " | 3,500 |
| | 18,500 |
| Less Commissions | 750 |
| Net Profit | \$17,250. |

Added to capital gives \$245,695.00

with 2000 bought at 109$\frac{1}{4}$. April 20th last low 110$\frac{1}{2}$. We raise stop to 109$\frac{1}{2}$. We buy 1000 more at 113$\frac{1}{2}$. April 26th and May 1st high 117-3/4, and May 28th low 115$\frac{1}{4}$. We raise stop on all trades to 114$\frac{1}{4}$. The stop was caught, and we go short 2000 at 114$\frac{1}{4}$. The account now stands:

| | |
|---|---|
| Bought 2000 at 109$\frac{1}{4}$, sold at 114$\frac{1}{4}$, profit | \$10,000 |
| " 1000 " 113$\frac{1}{2}$ " " 114$\frac{1}{4}$ " | 750 |
| Net Profit | \$10,750 |
| Less Commissions | 750 |
| | \$10,000 |
| Capital | 245,695 |
| Total | \$255,695 |

with 2000 short at 114¼, stop 117¼; May 9th low 112½; May 8th last high 116¼; May 11th high 116-3/4; May 11th low 114-3/4. Stop was caught at 117-1/4, and we buy 2000 at 117-1/4. The account now stands:

Sold 2000 at 114¼, closed at 117¼, loss $6,000
Commissions 500

Net Loss $6,500
Deducted from capital leaves balance of $249,695.00

with 2000 bought at 117¼. The advance gets under way, and we buy 1000 more at 119-3/4, because it is one point above high of April 3rd. We buy 500 at 124-3/4; we buy 300 at 129-3/4 May 31st high 136-5/8. Last low on May 28th was 131¼. We raise stop on all trades to 130¼. This stop was caught, and we sell 2000 short at 130-1/4. The account now stands:

| | |
|---|---|
| Bought 2000 at 117¼, sold at 128-3/4, profit | $23,000 |
| Bought 1000 at 119-3/4 " " 128-3/4, profit | 9,000 |
| Bought 500 at 124-3/4 " " 128-3/4, profit | 2,000 |
| | $34,000 |
| Bought 300 at 129-3/4, sold 128-3/4, loss | 300 |
| | $33,700 |
| Less Commissions | 950 |
| Net | 32,750 |
| Capital | 249,695 |
| Total | 282,445. |

with 2000 short at 128-3/4. June 1st low 126-3/4. June 2nd high 131¼. We make stop 132¼. Stop was caught, and we bought 2000 at 132¼. Account now stands:

Sold 2000 at 128-3/4, closed at 132¼, loss $7,000
Commissions 500

Net Loss $7,500

Deducted from $282,445.00 leaves $274,945.00.

with 2000 bought at 132¼. May 14th high 134-5/8. May 15th low 130¼. We make stop 129¼, which was caught, and we go short 2000 at 129¼. The account now stands:

Bought 000 at 132¼, sold 129¼, loss $6,000
Commissions 500
Net Loss $6,500

Deducted from Capital leaves $268,445.00

with 2000 short at 129¼. June 20 low 125½. We reduce stop to 129½, which was caught, and we buy 2000 at 129½. Account now stands:

| | |
|---|---|
| Sold 2000 at 129¼, closed at 129½, loss | $500 |
| Commissions | 500 |
| Net | $1,000 |

Deducted from Capital leaves $267,445.00

with 2000 bought at 129½. June 27th high 132-3/4. Last low was 128-3/4 on June 26th. We raise stop to 127-3/4, which was caught, and go short 2000 at 127-3/4. Account now stands:

| | |
|---|---|
| Bought 2000 at 129½, sold at 125-3/4, loss | $6,750 |
| Commissions | 500 |
| Net | $7,250 |

Deducted from capital leaves $260,245.00

with 2,000 short at 127-3/4; sold 1000 more at 123-3/4. July 19th low 118-3/4. Last high was 122½, on July 18th. We reduced stop to 123¼, which was caught, and we buy 2000 at 123¼. The account now stands:

| | |
|---|---|
| Sold 2000 at 125-3/4, closed at 123¼, profit | $4,500 |
| " 1000 " 123-3/4 " " 123¼, " | 500 |
| | $5,000 |
| Less Commissions | 750 |
| Net | 4,250 |
| Capital | 260,245 |
| | 264,495. |

with 2000 bought at 123¼. The advance follows, and we calculate from the high 136-5/8 to the low 118-3/4 and find the 1/2 point is 127-5/8. The stock advances to 127-7/8 on August 7th, and we sell out longs and go short 2000 at 127½. The account now stands:

| | |
|---|---|
| Bought 2000 at 123¼, sold at 127½, profit | $8,000 |
| Less Commissions | 500 |
| Net | 7,500 |
| Capital | 264,491 |
| | $271,995 |

with 2000 sold at 127½. We sell 1000 more at 122, because it has broken three bottoms. We sell 500 more at 117½ after it has broken four other bottoms. September 4th low 104½. September 6th high 109½. We reduce stop on all trades to 110½. September 17th low 103-3/4, and the last high was 108-3/4 on September 14th. We reduce stops to 109-3/4. The stops were caught, and we bought 2000 at 109-3/4. The account now stands:

| | |
|---|---:|
| Sold 2000 at 127½, closed at 109-3/4, profit | $17,500 |
| Sold 1000 at 122 " " 109-3/4 " | 12,250 |
| Sold 500 at 117½ " " 109-3/4 " | 4,575 |
| Total | $34,325 |
| Less Commissions | 875 |
| Net | $33,450 |
| Capital | 271,995 |
| Total | $305,445. |

with 2000 bought at 109-3/4. September 25th high 113-7/8. The last lowwas 109-1/2 on September 24th. We raise stop to 108½. The stop was caught, and we sell short 2000 at 108½. The account now stands:

| | |
|---|---:|
| Bought 2000 at 109-3/4, sold at 108½, loss | $2,500 |
| Commissions | 500 |
| Net Loss | $3,000 |

Deducted from capital, leaves $302,445.00

with 2000 short at 108½. Sold 1000 more at 103½. October 15th it declines to 99, and we reduce stop to 104, which was caught, and we buy 2000 at 104. The account now stands:

| | |
|---|---:|
| Sold 2000 at 108½, closed at 104, profit | $9,000 |
| " 1000 at 103½ " " 104, loss | 500 |
| | $8,500 |
| Less Commissions | 750 |
| Net Profit | $7,750 |
| Capital | 302,445 |
| Total | $310,195 |

with 2000 bought at 104. October 22nd high 107-3/8. October 26th low 103-7/8. We raise stop to 102-7/8. The stop was caught, and we go short 2000 at 102-7/8. The account now stands.

| | |
|---|---:|
| Bought 2000 at 104, sold at 102-7/8, loss | $2,250 |
| Commissions | 500 |
| | $2,750 |

Deducted from capital leaves $307,445.

with 2000 short at 101-7/8. Sold 1000 more at 98. Sold 500 more at 93. November 8th low 88-3/4. November 12th high 94-3/4. Reduced stop to 95-3/4. November 14th low 89¼. Reduced stop to 94-3/4. The stop was caught, and we buy 2000 at 94-3/4. The account now stands:

| | | | |
|---|---|---|---|
| Sold 2000 at 101-7/8, | closed at 94-3/4, | profit | $14,250 |
| " 1000 " 98 | " " 94-3/4 | " | 3,250 |
| | | | 17,500 |
| Sold 500 93 | closed at 94-3/4, | loss | 875 |
| | | | 16,625 |
| Less Commissions | | | 875 |
| Net | | | $15,750 |
| Capital | | | 307,445 |
| Total | | | $323,195 |

with 2000 bought at 94-3/4. November 26th high 99¼. Last low on November 22nd at 96. We raise stop to 95, and it was caught. We go short 2000 at 95. The account now stands:

Bought 2000 at 94-3/4, sold at 95 makes it even allowing 1/4 for commissions, Balance $323,195.00.

with 2000 short at 95. Sold 1000 more at 90. Sold 500 more at 85. December 13th low 79-7/8. December 14th high 84½. December 17th low 80⅓. December 18th high 83-3/4. December 20th low 79½. As 79-3/4 was last low March 1, 1916, we cover shorts at 80 and buy 2000 with stop at 79. The account now stands.

| | | |
|---|---|---|
| Sold 2000 at 95, | closed at 80, profit | $30,000 |
| " 1000 " 90, | " " 80, " | 10,000 |
| " 500 " 85, | " " 80, " | 2,500 |
| | | $42,500 |
| Less Commissions | | 875 |
| Net | | $ 41,625 |
| Capital | | 323,195 |
| Total | | $364,820 |

with 2000 bought at 80, stop 79. Bought 1000 more at 85 and raised stop to 82. Bought 500 more at 90 and bought 300 more at 95.

## 1918

January 3, 1918 high 98 and January 5th low 82½. Raised stop on all trades to 91¼. January 8th high 97¼. January 9th low 93½. Raised stop to 92½. The stop was caught, and we went short 2000 at 92½. Account now stands:

| | | |
|---|---|---|
| Bought 2000 at 80, | sold 92½, profit | $25,000 |
| " 1000 " 85, | " 92½ " | 7,500 |
| " 500 " 90, | " 92½ " | 1,250 |
| | | $33,750 |

| | |
|---|---|
| Brought Forward | $33,750 |
| Bought 300 at 95, sold at 92½, loss | 750 |
| | $33,000 |
| Less Commissions | 950 |
| Net | $32,050 |
| Capital | 364,820 |
| Total | $406,870. |

with 2000 short at 92½. January 15th low 88½. January 16th high 91¼. Reduced stop to 92¼. We figure last low 79½ on Dec. 20th to high 98 on January 3, 1918, and find 1/2 point - 88-5/8. On January 18th low 88-3/4. We cover shorts at 89 and buy 2000 at 89, with stop 87-5/8. February 1st, 19th and 27th highs at 98½ to 98, failing to cross top of January 3rd. We sell out at 98 and go short 2000 at 98, with stop 99.

The decline follows. Sold 1000 more at 93-3/4, because it is one point under February 21st. March low 89½. March 6th high 91-7/8 . We reduce stop to 92-7/8. March 25th low 86-1/2. April 1st high 90-5/8. We reduce stop to 91-5/8. The stop was caught, and we buy 2000 at 91-5/8. April 2nd and 5th low 89-3/4. We raise stop to 88-3/4. Stop was caught and we sell 2000 short 88-3/4. Last top was 91-5/8 on April 5th. We place stop at 92-5/8. The stop was caught. We buy 2 000 at 92-5/8. April 22nd high 96-1/4. April 23rd, 26th, 27th and 30th lows at 93-3/4. We raise stop to 93-3/4. May 5th, we buy 1000 more at 99, because the stock has crossed all tops made early in the year. We raise stop to 96-3/8. We buy 500 more at 104 and raise stop to 101, which was one point under May 9th low.

We buy 200 more at 109. May 16th high 113-3/4. May 14th low 109-3/8. We raise stop to 108-3/8. Stop was caught, and we sell short 2000 at 108-3/8. May 22nd high 110½. We make stop 111½. We sell 1000 more at 105½. June 1st low 96¼. We figure from low of 79½ to high 113-3/4 and find 96-5/8 the 1/2 point. We cover shorts and buy 2000 at 97 with stop 95-5/8. After June 10th, we raise stop to 96½. We buy 1000 more at 104½. June 27th high 110½. Last low June 25th 107¼ so we raise stop to 106¼. The stop was caught, and we sell short 2000 at 106¼. July 15 low 101½. Last top July 12th was 104-3/4. We make stop 105-3/4. Stop was caught, and we buy 2000 at 105-3/4. We buy 1000 more at 110-3/4. August 28th high 116½. Last low 110-3/4 on August 22nd. We make stop 109-3/4. Stop was caught and we sell short 2000 at 109-3/4.

September 13th low 107. September 14th high 109-3/4. We reduce stop to 110-3/4. Stop is caught, and we buy 2000 at 110-3/4 September 27th high 113½. Last low 109-3/4, September 25th. We raise stop to 108-3/4. Stop was caught, and we sell short 2000 at 108-3/4.

We figure from June 1st low 96¼ to August 28th high 116½, which makes 106-3/8 the 1/2 point. We cover shorts at 106½ and buy 2000 at 106½, stop 105-3/8. Stop is caught, and we sell short 2000 at 105-3/8.

October 9th low 104-5/8. Last low, October 8th, 108½. We make stop 109-1/8 , which is caught, and we buy 2000 at 109-1/8. October 19th high 114½. We raise stop to 111½. The stop is caught, and we sell 2000 short at 111½, sell 2000 more at 107½, sell 500 more at 102½, and on November 7th, high 104¼ we reduce stop on all trades to 105-1/8. November 29th low 94. High same day 96¼. We reduce stop to 97¼. Stop was caught, and we buy 2000 at 97¼. December 11th high 99-3/4. Last low 95¼ on December 6th. We raise stop to 94¼. Stop is caught, and we sell short 2000 at 94¼.

December 26th low 92½. December 30th high 95¼. We make stop at 96¼. Stop was caught, and we buy 2000 at 96¼. Last low December 31st, 93-3/4. We place stop at 92-3 /4. Stop was caught, and we sell short 2,000 at 92-3/4.

## 1919

January 9, 1919, high 94-3/8. We make stop 95-3/8. January 21st low 88-3/4. January 22nd high 90-5/8. January 25th high 94. January 27th low 90-3/4. We make stop 89-3/4. Stop was caught, and we sell 2000 short at 89-3/4. February 10th low 88¼. February 4 th high 91. We make stop 92. Stop was caught, and we buy 2000 at 92.

The statement below covers trades from January 10, 1918 to February 10, 1919:

| | | | | | DEBIT | CREDIT |
|---|---|---|---|---|---|---|
| | | | | January 10, 1918 | | $406,870 |
| Sold | 2000 | at | 92½ | closed at 89 | | 7,000 |
| Bought | 2000 | " | 89 | " " 98 | | 18,000 |
| Sold | 2000 | " | 98 | " " 91-5/8 | | 12,760 |
| Sold | 1000 | " | 93-3/4 | " " 91-5/8 | | 2,120 |
| Bought | 2000 | " | 91-5/8 | " " 88-3/4 | $5,760 | |
| Sold | 2000 | " | 88-3/4 | " " 92-5/8 | 7,760 | |
| Bought | 2000 | " | 92-5/8 | " "108-3/8 | | 31,500 |
| Bought | 1000 | " | 99 | " "108-3/8 | | 9,380 |
| Bought | 500 | " | 104 | " "108-3/8 | | 2,190 |
| Bought | 200 | " | 109 | " "108-3/8 | 124 | |
| Sold | 2000 | " | 108-3/8 | " " 97 | | 22,760 |
| Sold | 1000 | " | 105½ | " " 97 | | 8,500 |
| Bought | 2000 | " | 97 | " "106¼ | | 18,500 |
| Bought | 1000 | " | 104½ | " "106¼ | | 1,750 |
| Sold | 2000 | " | 106¼ | " "105-3/4 | | 1,000 |
| Bought | 2000 | " | 105-3/4 | " "109-3/4 | | 8,000 |
| Bought | 1000 | " | 110-3/4 | " "109-3/4 | 1,000 | |
| Sold | 2000 | " | 109-3/4 | " "110-3/4 | 2,000 | |
| Bought | 2000 | " | 110-3/4 | " "108-3/4 | 4,000 | |
| Sold | 2000 | " | 108-3/4 | " "106-1/2 | | 4,500 |
| Bought | 2000 | " | 106-1/2 | " "105-3/8 | 2,240 | |
| Sold | 2000 | " | 105-3/8 | " "109-1/8 | 7,500 | |
| Bought | 2000 | " | 109-1/8 | " "111-1/2 | | 4,740 |
| Sold | 2000 | " | 111-1/2 | " " 97¼ | | 28,500 |
| Sold | 1000 | " | 107-1/2 | " " 97¼ | | 10,250 |
| Sold | 500 | " | 102-1/2 | " " 97¼ | | 2,625 |
| Bought | 2000 | " | 97¼ | " " 94¼ | 6,000 | |
| Sold | 2000 | " | 94¼ | " " 96¼ | 4,000 | |
| Bought | 2000 | " | 96¼ | " " 92¾ | 7,000 | |
| Sold | 2000 | " | 92-3/4 | " " 91-5/8 | | 2,240 |
| Bought | 2000 | " | 91-5/8 | " 89-3/4 | 3,760 | |
| Sold | 2000 | " | 89-3/4 | " 92 | 4,500 | |
| | | | | | $55,644 | $603,185 |
| | | | | Commissions | 13,050 | 68,694 |
| | | | | Net Profit | | $534,491 |

Bought 2000 at 92 - February 10, 1919. February 27th high 95-3/4. Low on February 25th 93½. We raise stop to 92½. Stop was caught. We sell short 2000 at 92½. March 5th low 91-5/8, same low as March 1st. Last high March 3rd at 94-5/8. We make stop 95-5/8. The stop was caught. We buy 2000 at 95-5/8. March 11th low 95½. We make stop 94½. The stop was caught. We sell short 2000 at 94½. March 19th low 94¼, stop 98. Stop was caught and we buy 200 at 98.

The market makes a series of narrow moves, and on April 23rd makes high at 103. April 25th low 99¾. We make stop 98¾. Stop was caught, and we sell short 2000 at 98¾. May 1st low 96½. May 3rd high 99¾. We make stop 100¾. Stop was caught, and we buy 2000 at 100¾. Buy 1000 at 104.

June 6th high 111¾. June 11th low 106¾. We raise stop to 105¾. The stop was caught, and we sell short 2000 at 105¾. June 16th low 103¼. We figure last low May 1st 96½ to June 6th at 111¾, making 1/2 point 104-1/8. We cover shorts at 104¼ and buy 2000 at 104¼, stop 103-1/8, and buy 1000 more at 109¼.

July 7th high 115-1/8. July 11th low 111-5/8. We raise stop to 110-5/8. Stop was caught. We go short 2000 at 110-5/8. July 24th high 113-3/8. We make stop 114-3/8. We sell 1000 more at 105, because it is one point under 1/2 point from 96½ to 115½.

August 21st low 98½. August 25th high 101-5/8. We reduce stops to 102-5/8. Stops are caught, and we buy 2000 at 102-5/8 with stop 99½.

September 4th high 107½. September 5th low 103¼. We place stop 102¼. Stop was caught and we sell short 2000 at 103¼. September 20th low 100½. We make stop 103½. Stop was caught. We buy 2000 at 103½.

October 10th high 112½. October 23rd low 108. We make stop 107. Stop was caught. We sell short 2000 at 107 and place stop at 110. Stop was caught. We buy 2000 at 110. November 5th high 112½, same high at October 10th. We sell out at 112 and go short 2000 at 112 with stop at 113½. We sell 1000 more at 107. December 1st low 101. December 3rd high 103¼. We make stop 104¼. Stop was caught. We buy 2000 at 104¼, with stop at 100. December 12 th low 100½.

## 1920

January 5, 1920 high 109. January 8th low 105¾. We make stop 104¾. Stop was caught, and we sell short 2000 at 104¾. January 19th low 104½. January 20th high 106. We make stop 107. Stop was caught. We buy 2000 at 107 with stop 104. Stop was caught. We sell 2000 at 100. Sell 1000 more at 99. February 27th low 92½. We reduce stop to 95½. Stop was caught, and we buy 2000 at 95½.

March 20th low 102¼. We raise stop to 101¼. Stop was caught. We go short 2000 at 101¼. March 25th low 100½. We make stop 103¼. Stop was caught. We buy 2000 at 103¼. April 7th high 107½. April 12th low 104. Make stop 103. Stop caught. We sell 2000 at 103. Sell 1000 more at 99.

May 24th low 89½. Last high June 22nd at 92½. We make stop 93½. Stop caught. We buy 2000 at 93½. June 14th low 92¾. Raise stop to 91¾. Stop caught. We sell 2000 at 91¾. June 23rd low 91½. June 26th high 93. We make stop 94. Stop caught. We buy 2000 at 94. July 8th high 95½. We make stop 92½. Stop caught. We sell 2000 at 92½ and sell 1000 at 87½.

August 9th low 84. August 7th low 96½. We make stop 87. Stop caught. We buy 2000 at 87. September 8th high 91½. August 23rd low 88-1/8. We make stop 87¼. Stop caught. We sell 2000 at 87¼. The decline follows, and we sell 1000 more at 85¼.

December 21st low 76¼. December 24th high 97-7/8. We make stop 80-7/8. The stop caught. We buy 2000 at 80-7/8. February 16th high 85. February 21st low 82-3/4. We make stop 81¾. Stop caught. We sell 2000 at 81¾. March 12th low 77¾. We make stop 80¾. The stop was caught. We buy 2 000 at 80¾.

The statement below covers trades from February 10, 1919 to March 15, 1921:

| | | | | | | | DEBIT | CREDIT |
|---|---|---|---|---|---|---|---|---|
| | | | | February 10, 1919 | | | | $534,491 |
| Bought | 2000 | at | 92 | closed at | | 92½ | | 1,000 |
| Sold | 2000 | " | 92½ | " | " | 95-5/8 | $ 250 | |
| Bought | 2000 | " | 95-5/8 | " | " | 94-1/2 | 2,250 | |
| Sold | 2000 | " | 94-1/2 | " | " | 98 | 7,000 | |
| Bought | 2000 | " | 98 | " | " | 98¾ | | 1,500 |
| Sold | 2000 | " | 98¾ | " | " | 100¾ | 4,000 | |
| Bought | 2000 | " | 100¾ | " | " | 105¾ | | 10,000 |
| Bought | 1000 | " | 104 | " | " | 105¾ | | 1,750 |
| Sold | 2000 | " | 105¾ | " | " | 104¼ | | 3,000 |
| Bought | 2000 | " | 104-1/8 | " | " | 110-5/8 | | 13,000 |
| Bought | 1000 | " | 109 | " | " | 110-5/8 | | 1,625 |
| Sold | 2000 | " | 110-5/8 | " | " | 102-5/8 | | 16,000 |
| Sold | 1000 | " | 105 | " | " | 102-5/8 | | 2,375 |
| Bought | 2000 | " | 102-5/8 | " | " | 102-1/4 | 750 | |
| Sold | 2000 | " | 103¼ | " | " | 103-1/2 | 500 | |
| Bought | 2000 | " | 103½ | " | " | 107 | | 7,000 |
| Sold | 2000 | " | 107 | " | " | 110 | 7,000 | |
| Bought | 2000 | " | 110 | " | " | 112 | | 4,000 |
| Sold | 2000 | " | 112 | " | " | 104¼ | | 1,550 |
| Sold | 1000 | " | 107 | " | " | 104¼ | | 2,750 |
| Bought | 2000 | " | 104¼ | " | " | 104¾ | | 1,000 |
| Sold | 2000 | " | 104¾ | " | " | 107 | 4,500 | |
| Bought | 2000 | " | 107 | " | " | 104 | 6,000 | |
| Sold | 2000 | " | 104 | " | " | 95½ | | 17,000 |

(Continued on next page)

| | | | | | | | DEBIT | CREDIT |
|---|---|---|---|---|---|---|---|---|
| Sold | 1000 | at | 99 | closed | at | 95½ | | $3,500 |
| Bought | 2000 | " | 95½ | " | " | 101¼ | | 11,500 |
| Sold | 2000 | " | 101¼ | " | " | 103¼ | $4,000 | |
| Bought | 2000 | " | 103¼ | " | " | 103 | 500 | |
| Sold | 2000 | " | 103 | " | " | 95½ | | 15,000 |
| Sold | 1000 | " | 99 | " | " | 95½ | | 3,500 |
| Bought | 2000 | " | 95½ | " | " | 91½ | 7,500 | |
| Sold | 2000 | " | 91¾ | " | " | 94 | 4,500 | |
| Bought | 2000 | " | 94 | " | " | 92½ | 3,000 | |
| Sold | 2000 | " | 92½ | " | " | 87 | | 11,000 |
| Sold | 1000 | " | 87¼ | " | " | 87 | | 500 |
| Bought | 2000 | " | 87 | " | " | 87¼ | | 500 |
| Sold | 2000 | " | 87½ | " | " | 80-7/8 | | 12,750 |
| Sold | 1000 | " | 85¼ | " | " | 80-7/8 | | 5,625 |
| Bought | 2000 | " | 80-7/8 | " | " | 81-3/4 | | 1,750 |
| Sold | 2000 | " | 81-3/4 | | " | 80-3/4 | | 2,000 |
| | | | | | | | $51,750 | $685,666 |
| | | | | Commissions | | | 18,000 | 69,750 |
| | | | | Net Profit | | | | $615,916 |

---

March 15, 1921, bought 2000 at 80-3/4. March 22nd low 80¾. We make stop 79¾. April 14th stop caught. We sell short 2000 at 79-3/4, stop 82-3/4. Stop caught. We buy 2000 at 82-3/4. May 6th high 86-1/2. We make stop 83-1/2. Stop caught. We go short 2000 at 83-1/2. Decline continues. We sell 1000 at 78-1/2. June 23rd low 70-1/2. We reduce stop to 73-1/2. Stop was caught and we buy 2000 at 73-1/2. June 30th low 73-5/8. We make stop 72-5/8. Stop caught. We go short 2000 at 72-5/8. July 16th low 71-1/2. July 20th high 73-1/2 . We make stop 74-1/2. Stop caught. We buy 2000 at 74-1/2.

September 19th, 26th and 30th high 80½. We sell out at 80 and go short 2000 at 80, stop 81½. October 17th low 77¼. October 20th, high 78-5/8. We make stop 79-5/8. Stop is caught, and we buy 2000 at 79-5/8. December 15th low 83-3/4. We raise stop to 82-3/4. Stop is caught, and we go short 2000 at 82-3/4.

## 1922

January 6th low 82. January 9th high 83½. We make stop 84½. Stop caught. We buy 2000 at 84½ and buy 1000 at 89½. Buy 500 at 94½. Buy 300 at 99½.

April 20th high 100½. April 18th last low 97. We raise stop to 96. June 6th high 103½, low 102-5/8 on June 5th. We raise stop to 101-5/8. Stop caught. We sell short 2000 at 101-5/8.

The statement below covers trades from March 15, 1921 to June 1922:

| | | | | | DEBIT | CREDIT |
|---|---|---|---|---|---|---|
| | | | | March 15, 1921 | | \$615,916 |
| Bought | 2000 | at | $80\frac{3}{4}$ | closed at $79\frac{3}{4}$ | \$2,000 | |
| Sold | 2000 | " | $79\frac{3}{4}$ | " " $82\frac{3}{4}$ | 6,000 | |
| Bought | 2000 | " | $82\frac{3}{4}$ | " " $83\frac{1}{2}$ | | 1,500 |
| Sold | 2000 | " | $83\frac{1}{2}$ | " " $73\frac{1}{2}$ | | 20,000 |
| Bought | 2000 | " | $73\frac{1}{2}$ | " " 72-5/8 | 1,750 | |
| Sold | 2000 | " | 72-5/8 | " " 74 | 3,750 | |
| Bought | 2000 | " | 74-1/2 | " " 80 | | 11,000 |
| Sold | 2000 | " | 80 | " " 79-5/8 | | 750 |
| Bought | 2000 | " | 79-5/8 | " " 82-3/4 | | 6,250 |
| Sold | 2000 | " | 82-3/4 | " " 84-1/2 | 3,500 | |
| Bought | 2000 | " | 84-1/2 | " "101-5/8 | | 24,250 |
| Bought | 1000 | " | 89-1/2 | " "101-5/8 | | 12,125 |
| Bought | 500 | " | 94-1/2 | " "101-5/8 | | 3,562.50 |
| Bought | 300 | " | 99-1/2 | "101-5/8 | | 637.50 |
| | | | | | \$17,000 | \$695,991.00 |
| | | | | Commissions | 5,950 | 22,950.00 |
| | | | | Net Profit | | \$673,041.00 |

---

June, 1922 sold short 2000 at 101-5/8. June 12th and 16th low $96\frac{3}{4}$. We make stop $99\frac{3}{4}$. Stop caught. We buy 2000 at $99\frac{3}{4}$. Buy 1000 more at 104. September 11th high $106\frac{1}{2}$. September 14th low $104\frac{1}{2}$. We make stop $103\frac{1}{2}$. Stop caught. We go short 2000 at $103\frac{1}{2}$. September 27th and 29th low $100\frac{3}{4}$. September high $102\frac{1}{2}$. We make stop $103\frac{1}{2}$. Stop caught. We buy 2000 at $103\frac{1}{2}$. Buy 1000 at 107. October 16th high $111\frac{1}{2}$. We make stop $108\frac{1}{2}$. Stop caught. We go short 2000 at $108\frac{1}{2}$. November 1st low $103\frac{1}{4}$. Make stop $106\frac{1}{4}$. Stop caught. We buy 2000 at $106\frac{1}{4}$.

November 9th high $110\frac{3}{4}$. Make stop $107\frac{3}{4}$. Stop caught. We sell 2000 at $107\frac{3}{4}$. November 28th low $99\frac{3}{4}$. December 2nd high $103\frac{1}{2}$. We make stop $104\frac{1}{2}$ and buy 2000 at $104\frac{1}{2}$. December 26th low $106\frac{1}{4}$. Make stop $105\frac{1}{4}$. Stop caught. We go short 2000 at $105\frac{1}{4}$.

<u>1923</u>

January 31st low 104. Make stop 107. Stop caught. We buy 2000 at 107. March 21st high $109\frac{1}{2}$. March 17th low $107\frac{1}{2}$. We make stop $106\frac{1}{2}$. Stop caught. We go short 2000 at $106\frac{1}{2}$.

The statement below covers trades from June, 1922 to March, 1923:

| | | | | DEBIT | CREDIT |
|---|---|---|---|---|---|
| | | June, 1922 | | | $673,041 |
| Sold 2000 | at 101-5/8 | closed at | 99-3/4 | | 3,750 |
| Bought 2000 | " 99-3/4 | " " | 103½ | | 7,500 |
| Bought 1000 | " 104 | " " | 103½ | $500 | |
| Sold 2000 | " 103½ | " " | 103½ | -- | -- |
| Bought 2000 | " 103½ | " " | 108½ | | 10,000 |
| Bought 1000 | " 107 | " " | 108½ | | 1,500 |
| Sold 2000 | " 108½ | " " | 106¼ | | 4,500 |
| Bought 2000 | " 106¼ | " " | 107¾ | | 3,000 |
| Sold 2000 | " 107¾ | " " | 104½ | | 6,500 |
| Bought 2000 | " 104½ | " " | 105¼ | | 1,500 |
| Sold 2000 | " 105¼ | " " | 107 | 3,500 | |
| Bought 2000 | " 107 | " " | 106½ | 1,000 | |
| | | | | $5,000 | $711,291 |
| | | Commissions | | 5,500 | 10,500 |
| | | Total Profit | | | $700,791 |

---

Sold 2000 at 106½
Sell 1000 " 103
Sell 500 " 98
Sell 300 " 93

June 30th, July 5th, 11th and 17th made lows at 89½ to 89¼, and on July 14th high 91½. We make stop on all trades at 92½. Stop caught and we buy 2000 at 92½. July 23rd high 92¾. July 21st low 91½. We make stop 90½. Stop caught. We sell short 2000 at 90½. July 31st low 85-3/8. August 2nd high 88½. We make stop 89½. Stop caught. We buy 2000 at 89½. August 30th high 94. August 8th low 92. Make stop 91. Stop caught. We go short 2000 at 91. September 25th low 85-5/8, same low as July 31st. We cover shorts at 86½ and buy 2000 at 86½, with stop 84½. We buy 1000 at 90. November 9th low 94. We make stop 93. Stop caught. We sell 2000 at 93. November 17th low 91-7/8. We make stop 94-7/8 and buy 2000 at 94-7/8. Buy 1000 at 98 and 500 at 103.

## 1924

February 7th high 109. February 8th low 106½. We make stop 105½. Stop caught. We go short 2000 at 106½. Sell 1000 at 101½. March 29th low 97. We figure low of 85-3/8 to high 109 and find 1/2 point 97. We cover shorts at 97½ and buy 2000 at 97½, stop 96. Stop is caught and we go short 2000 at 96.

The statement below covers trades from March, 1923 to April, 1924:

| | | | | March, 1923 | | DEBIT | CREDIT |
|---|---|---|---|---|---|---|---|
| | | | | | | | $700,791 |
| Sold | 2000 | at | 106½ | closed at | 92½ | | 28,000 |
| Sold | 1000 | " | 103 | " " | 92½ | | 10,500 |
| Sold | 500 | " | 98 | " " | 92½ | | 2,750 |
| Sold | 300 | " | 93 | " " | 92½ | | 150 |
| Bought | 2000 | " | 92½ | " " | 91½ | $2,000 | |
| Sold | 2000 | " | 90½ | " " | 89½ | | 2,000 |
| Bought | 2000 | " | 89½ | " " | 91 | 3,000 | |
| Sold | 2000 | " | 91 | " " | 86½ | | 9,000 |
| Bought | 2000 | " | 86½ | " " | 93 | | 13,000 |
| Bought | 1000 | " | 90 | " " | 93 | | 3,000 |
| Sold | 2000 | " | 93 | " " | 94-7/8 | 3,750 | |
| Bought | 2000 | " | 94-7/8 | " " | 105-1/2 | | 21,250 |
| Bought | 1000 | " | 98 | " " | 105-1/2 | | 7,500 |
| Bought | 500 | " | 103 | " " | 105-1/2 | | 1,250 |
| Sold | 2000 | " | 106-1/2 | " " | 97-1/2 | | 18,000 |
| Sold | 1000 | " | 101-1/2 | " | 97-1/2 | | 4,000 |
| Bought | 2000 | " | 97-1/2 | | 96 | 3,000 | |
| | | | | | | $11,750 | $821,191 |
| | | | | Commissions | | 6,325 | 18,075 |
| | | | | Net Profit | | | $803,116 |

---

Sold 2000 at 96. April 10th, 15th and 22nd low 95½. We make stop 98½. Stop caught. We buy 2000 at 98½. April 26th high 101. We raise stop to 98. Stop caught. We go short 2000 at 98. June 6th low 94-1/8. We make stop 97-1/8. Stop caught. We buy 2000 at 97-1/8 buy 1000 at 102 and 500 at 107. August 20th high 111¾. We raise stop to 108¾. Stop caught. We go short 2000 at 108¾. September 8th low 105¼. We make stop 108¼. Stop caught. We buy 2000 at 108¼. September 25th low 108¼. We raise stop to 107¼. Stop caught. We go short 2000 at 107¼. October 14th low 104¾. October 18th high 107¼. We make stop 108⅛. Stop caught. We buy 2000 at 108-1/8. Buy 1000 at 112. November 26th high 119¼. December 2nd low 116. We raise stop to 115 and buy 500 at 117. Buy 300 at 122.

1925

January 23rd high 129½. January 28th low 125¾. We make stop 124¾. Stop caught and we go short 2000 at 124¾. February 19th low 122. We sell 1000 at 121 and 500 at 116. March 30th low 112¼. April 8th high 115¼. We make stop 116¼. Stop caught.

The statement below covers trades from April, 1924 to April, 1925:

| | | | | | | DEBIT | CREDIT |
|---|---|---|---|---|---|---|---|
| | | | | April, 1924 | | | $803,116 |
| Sold | 2000 | at | 96 | closed at | 98½ | $5,000 | |
| Bought | 2000 | " | 98½ | " " | 98 | 1,000 | |
| Sold | 2000 | " | 98 | " " | 98-1/8 | | 1,750 |
| Bought | 2000 | " | 98-1/8 | " " | 108¾ | | 23,250 |
| Bought | 1000 | " | 102 | " " | 108¾ | | 6,750 |
| Bought | 500 | " | 107 | " " | 108¾ | | 875 |
| Sold | 2000 | " | 108¾ | " " | 108¼ | | 1,000 |
| Bought | 2000 | " | 108¼ | " " | 108¼ | 2,000 | |
| Sold | 2000 | " | 107¼ | " " | 108¼ | 2,000 | |
| Bought | 2000 | " | 108-1/8 | " " | 124¾ | | 33,250 |
| Bought | 1000 | " | 112 | " " | 124¾ | | 12,750 |
| Bought | 500 | " | 117 | " " | 124¾ | | 3,875 |
| Bought | 300 | " | 122 | " " | 124¾ | | 825 |
| Sold | 2000 | " | 124¾ | " " | 116¼ | | 17,000 |
| Sold | 1000 | " | 121 | " | 116¼ | | 4,750 |
| Sold | 500 | " | 116 | " | 116¼ | 125 | |
| | | | | | | $10,125 | $909,191 |
| | | | | Commissions | | 5,700 | 15,825 |
| | | | | Net Profit | | | $893,366 |

---

We buy 2000 at 116¼. April 18th high 118¼. Raise stop to 115¼. Stop caught. We go short 2000 at 115¼. April 30th low 112¾. We make stop 115¾. Stop caught. We buy 2000 at 115¾. April 21st high 120¼. Raise stop to 117¼. Stop caught. We go short 2000 at 117¼. June 5th low 113½. June 8th high 114½. We make stop 115½. Stop caught. We buy 2000 at 115½. June 15th high 117¼. June 18th low 115¾. Make stop 114¾. Stop caught. We go short 2000 at 115¾. June 29th low 113¼. Make stop 116¼. Stop caught. We buy 2000 at 116¼ and 1000 at 121. August 26th high 125-7/8. We raise stop to 122-7/8. Stop caught. We go short 2000 at 112-7/8. September 3rd low 118¼. Make stop 121¼. Stop caught. We buy 2000 at 121¼. September 15th high 125-7/8. Make stop 122-5/8. Stop caught. We go short 2000 at 122-5/8. September 28th low 118½. We figure from low 112¼ March 30th to high 125-7/8 August 26th and find 1/2 point 119, so we cover shorts and

Buy 2000 at 119¼ with stop 118<br>
" 1000 " 124¼<br>
" 500 " 127<br>
" 300 " 132<br>
200 " 137

November 7th high 139-3/8. We raise stop to 136-3/8. Stop caught. We go short 2000 at 136-3/8. Sold 1000 more at 131-3/8. November 10th low 128. Make stop 131. Stop caught. We buy 2000 at 131. November 14th high $138\frac{1}{2}$. We make stop $135\frac{1}{2}$. Stop caught. We go short 2000 at 135-1/2. November 24th low 126-5/8. We make stop 129-5/8. Stop caught. We buy 2000 at 129-5/8. December 8th high $137\frac{1}{4}$. Make stop $134\frac{1}{4}$. Stop caught. We go short 2000 at $134\frac{1}{4}$. December 22nd low $131\frac{3}{4}$. Make stop $134\frac{3}{4}$. Stop caught. We buy 2000 at $134\frac{3}{4}$.

## 1926

January 4th high $138\frac{1}{2}$. We make stop $135\frac{1}{2}$ Stop caught. We go short 2000 at $135\frac{1}{2}$. Later sell 1000 at 131 and 500 at 127. March 2nd low 120. Make stop 123. Stop caught.

The statement below covers trades from April, 1925 to March 5, 1926:

| | | | | | | | DEBIT | CREDIT |
|---|---|---|---|---|---|---|---|---|
| Balance brought forward April, 1925 | | | | | | | | \$893,366 |
| Bought | 2000 | at | $116\frac{1}{4}$ | closed | at | $115\frac{1}{2}$ | \$2,000 | |
| Sold | 2000 | " | $115\frac{1}{4}$ | " | " | $115\frac{3}{4}$ | 1,000 | |
| Bought | 2000 | " | $115\frac{3}{4}$ | " | " | $117\frac{1}{4}$ | | 3,000 |
| Sold | 2000 | " | $117\frac{1}{4}$ | " | " | $115\frac{1}{2}$ | | 3,500 |
| Bought | 2000 | " | $115\frac{1}{2}$ | " | " | $114\frac{3}{4}$ | 1,500 | |
| Sold | 2000 | " | $115\frac{3}{4}$ | " | " | $116\frac{1}{4}$ | 1,000 | |
| Bought | 2000 | " | $116\frac{1}{4}$ | " | " | 122-7/8 | | 13,250 |
| Sold | 2000 | " | 122-7/8 | " | " | $121\frac{1}{4}$ | | 3,250 |
| Bought | 2000 | " | $121\frac{1}{4}$ | " | " | 122-5/8 | | 2,750 |
| Sold | 2000 | " | 122-5/8 | " | " | 119 | | 7,250 |
| Bought | 2000 | " | $119\frac{1}{4}$ | " | " | 136-3/8 | | 34,250 |
| Bought | 1000 | " | $124\frac{1}{4}$ | " | " | 136-3/8 | | 12,125 |
| Bought | 500 | " | 127 | " | " | 136-3/8 | | 4,687.50 |
| Bought | 300 | " | 132 | " | " | 136-3/8 | | 1,311.50 |
| Bought | 200 | " | 137 | " | " | 136-3/8 | 125 | |
| Sold | 2000 | " | 136-3/8 | " | " | 131 | | 10,750. |
| Bought | 2000 | " | 131 | " | " | $135\frac{1}{2}$ | | 9,000 |
| Sold | 2000 | " | $135\frac{1}{2}$ | " | " | 129-5/8 | | 11,750 |
| Bought | 2000 | " | 129-5/8 | " | " | $134\frac{1}{4}$ | | 9,250 |
| Sold | 1000 | " | $134\frac{1}{4}$ | " | " | $134\frac{3}{4}$ | 500 | |
| Bought | 2000 | " | $134\frac{3}{4}$ | " | " | $135\frac{1}{2}$ | | 1,500 |
| Sold | 2000 | " | $135\frac{1}{2}$ | " | " | 123 | | 25,000 |
| Sold | 1000 | " | 131 | | " | 123 | | 8,000 |
| Sold | 500 | " | 127 | | " | 123 | | 2,000 |
| | | | | | | | \$6,125 | \$1,055,990.00 |
| | | | | Commissions | | | 9,625 | 15,750.00 |
| | | | | Net Profit | | | | \$1,040,240.00 |

We bought 2000 at 123. March 16th high 128-1/8. We make stop 125-1/8. The stop was caught. We go short 2000 at 125-1/8. March 30th low 117-5/8. Make stop 120-5/8. Stop caught. We buy 2000 at 120-5/8. April 6th high 123½. Make stop 120½. Stop caught We go short 2000 at 120½. April 15th low 117. Make stop 120. Stop caught. We buy 2000 at 120. April 29th high 124-5/8. We make stop 121-5/8. Stop caught. We go short 2000 at 121-5/8. May 17th low 118-1/8. Make stop 121-1/8. Stop caught. We buy 2000 at 121-1/8. Later we buy 1000 at 126-1/8 and buy 500 at 131 and buy 300 at 136 and 200 at 141. July 11th high 144-7/8. Make stop on all trades 141-7/8. Stop caught, and we sell short 2000 at 141-7/8. July 24th low 137¼. July 23 high 140½. We make stop at 141½. Stop caught. We buy 2000 at 141½. Later we buy 1000 at 145½, and 500 at 150. August 9th high 155¼. We raise stop to 152¼. Stop caught, and we go short 2000 at 152¼. August 12th low 147½. We make stop 150½. Stop caught, and we buy 2000 at 150½ . Later we buy 1000 at 155. August 17th high 159½. We raise stop to 156½. Stop caught. We go short 2000 at 156½. August 20th low 148½. We make stop 151½. Stop caught We buy 200 at 151½.

August 24th high 153. We make stop 150. Stop caught. We go short 2000 at 150. August 25th low 147-5/8. We make stop 150-5/8. Stop caught. We buy 2000 at 150-5/8. September 8th high 152¾. We make stop 149¾. Stop caught. We go short 2000 at 149¾. September 20th low 142¼. We make stop 145¼. Stop caught and we buy 2000 at 145¼. Later we buy 1000 at 150.

October 2nd high 154¾. Raise stop to 151¾. Stop caught. We go short 2000 at 151¾. We sell 1000 at 147 and sell 500 at 142 and 300 at 140. October 20th low 133¾. We make stop 136¾. Stop caught. We buy 2000 at 136¾, and later buy 1000 at 141¾ and buy 500 at 146¾. November 16th high 153½. We make stop 150½. Stop caught. We go short 2000 at 150½.

November 19th low 143½. We make stop 146½. Stop caught. We buy 2000 at 146½ and later buy 1000 at 151½ and 500 at 156½. December 17th and 27th high 160½. We sell out at 160 and go short 2000 at 160, because 159½ was high on August 17th. We place a stop at 162½.

## 1927

January 4th and 7th low 154. January 5th high 156½. We make stop 157½. Stop caught. We buy 2000 at 157½. January 13th high 159¼. We raise stop to 156¼. Stop caught. We sell 2000 short at 156¼. January 27th low 153½. We make stop 156½. Stop caught. We buy 2000 at 156½. February 24th high 162½. We make stop 159½. Stop caught. We go short 2000 at 159½. March 5th and 8th low 156½. March 7th high 157¾. We make stop 158¾. Stop caught.

The statement below covers trades from March 5, 1926 to March 10, 1927

| | DEBIT | CREDIT |
|---|---|---|
| Balance brought forward March 5, 1926 | | $1,040,240 |
| | Carried | Forward |

Brought Forward...$1,040,240

| | | | | | | DEBIT | CREDIT |
|---|---|---|---|---|---|---|---|
| Bought | 2000 | at | 123 | closed at | 125-1/8 | | $ 4,250.00 |
| Sold | 2000 | " | 125-1/8 | " " | 120-5/8 | | 11,000.00 |
| Bought | 1000 | " | 120-5/8 | " " | 120-1/2 | $ 125 | |
| Sold | 2000 | " | 120½ | " " | 120 | | 1,000.00 |
| Bought | 2000 | " | 120 | " " | 121-5/8 | | 3,250.00 |
| Sold | 2000 | " | 121-5/8 | " " | 121-1/8 | | 1,000.00 |
| Bought | 2000 | " | 121-1/8 | " " | 141-7/8 | | 41,500.00 |
| Bought | 1000 | " | 126-1/8 | " " | 141-7/8 | | 15,750.00 |
| Bought | 500 | " | 131 | " " | 141-7/8 | | 5,437.60 |
| Bought | 300 | " | 136 | " " | 141-7/8 | | 1,762.50 |
| Bought | 200 | " | 141 | " " | 141-7/8 | | 175.00 |
| Sold | 2000 | " | 141-7/8 | " " | 141-1/2 | | 750.00 |
| Bought | 2000 | " | 141-1/2 | " " | 152-1/4 | | 21,500.00 |
| Bought | 1000 | " | 145-1/2 | " " | 152-1/4 | | 6,750.00 |
| Bought | 500 | " | 150 | " " | 152-1/4 | | 1,125.00 |
| Sold | 2000 | " | 152-1/4 | " " | 150-1/2 | | 3,500.00 |
| Bought | 2000 | " | 150-1/2 | " " | 150 | 1,000 | |
| Sold | 2000 | " | 150 | " " | 150-5/8 | 1,250 | |
| Bought | 2000 | " | 150-5/8 | " " | 149-3/4 | 1,750 | |
| Sold | 2000 | " | 149-3/4 | " " | 145-1/4 | | 9,000.00 |
| Bought | 2000 | " | 145-1/4 | " " | 151-3/4 | | 13,000.00 |
| Bought | 1000 | " | 150 | " " | 151-3/4 | | 1,750.00 |
| Sold | 2000 | " | 151-3/4 | " " | 136-3/4 | | 30,000.00 |
| Sold | 1000 | " | 147 | " " | 136-3/4 | | 10,250.00 |
| Sold | 500 | " | 142 | " " | 136-3/4 | | 2,625.00 |
| Sold | 300 | " | 140 | " " | 136-3/4 | | 975.00 |
| Bought | 2000 | " | 136-3/4 | " " | 150-1/2 | | 27,500.00 |
| Bought | 1000 | " | 141-3/4 | " " | 150-1/2 | | 8,750.00 |
| Bought | 500 | " | 146-3/4 | " " | 150-1/2 | | 3,875.00 |
| Sold | 2000 | " | 150-1/2 | " " | 146-1/2 | | 8,000.00 |
| Bought | 2000 | " | 146-1/2 | " " | 160 | | 27,000.00 |
| Bought | 1000 | " | 151-1/2 | " " | 160 | | 8,500.00 |
| Bought | 500 | " | 156-1/2 | " " | 160 | | 2,250.00 |
| Sold | 2000 | " | 160 | " " | 157-1/2 | | 5,000.00 |
| Bought | 2000 | " | 157-1/2 | " " | 156-1/4 | 2,500 | |
| Sold | 2000 | " | 156-1/4 | " " | 156-1/2 | 500 | |
| Bought | 2000 | " | 156-1/2 | " " | 159-1/2 | | 6,000.00 |
| Sold | 2000 | " | 159-1/2 | " | 158-3/4 | | 1,500.00 |
| | | | | | | $7,125 | $1,324,965.00 |
| | | | Commissions | | | 14,075 | 21,200.00 |
| | | | Net Profits | | | | $1,303,765.00 |

---

We buy 2000 at 158-3/4. Later we buy 1000 at 163 and 500 at 168. April 11th and 16th, high 172-3/4. We make stop 169-3/4. Stop caught. We go short 2000 at 169-3/4. May 2nd low 164-1/2. We make stop 167-1/2. Stop caught. We discontinue trading in the old stock.

May 9th, we buy 2000 of new stock at 121½. June 1st high 125¾. June 4th low 123. We make stop 122. The stop was caught. We go short 2000 at 122. June 30th low 118-7/8. June 25th last high 121½. We make stop 122½. The stop was caught and we buy 2000 at 122½. Later we buy 1000 at 127 and 500 at 132. August 2nd high 138-3/8. August 1st low 134-5/8. We raise stop to 133-5/8. Stop was caught, and we sell 2000 short at 133-5/8. August 12th low 129¾. We make stop 132¼. Stop was caught and we buy 2000 at 132¼ and later buy 1000 at 136, 500 at 141, 300 at 145, 200 at 150 and 100 at 155.

September 16th high 160½. We make stop on all trades 157½. The stop was caught, and we go short 2000 at 157½. Later sell 1000 at 152½ and 500 at 147½. September 29th low 145½. We make stop 148½. Stop caught. We buy 2000 at 148½. October 4th high 154-5/8. We make stop 151-5/8. Stop was caught and we go short 2000 at 151-5/8 and later sell 1000 at 146-5/8, sell 500 at 141-5/8, 300 at 136-5/8 and 200 at 131-5/8. October 29th low 128-5/8. We make stops on all trades 131-5/8. Stops caught.

We buy 2000 at 131-5/8 and later we buy 1000 at 136-5/8 and 500 at 141-5/8. November 29th high 147-5/8. Same day low 144-5/8. We make stop 143-5/8. Stop was caught, and we go short 2000 at 143-5/8. December 9th low 138. We make stop 141. Stop caught. We buy 2000 at 141 and later buy 1000 at 145 and 500 at 150. December 24th high 155. We make stop 152. Stop was caught, and we sell short 2000 at 152 and later sell 500 at 147 and 300 at 142. On March 2, 1928 low 137½, just 1/2 point under low of December 9th. We could have covered shorts at 138 and bought with stop at 137, which would not have been caught, but we reduce stop to 140½, because the last three tops were at 140¼. The stop was caught.

The following statement covers trades from March 10,1927 to March, 1928:

| | | | | | DEBIT | CREDIT |
|---|---|---|---|---|---|---|
| Balance brought forward March 10, 1927 | | | | | | $1,313,765 |
| Bought | 2000 | at 158¾ | closed at | 169¾ | | 22,000 |
| Bought | 1000 | " 163 | " " | 169¾ | | 6,750 |
| Bought | 500 | " 168 | " " | 169¾ | | 875 |
| Sold | 2000 | " 169¾ | " " | 167½ | | 4,500 |
| | | NEW STOCK | | | | |
| Bought | 2000 | at 121½ | closed at | 122 | | 1,000 |
| Sold | 2000 | " 122 | " " | 122½ | $1,000 | |
| Bought | 2000 | " 122½ | " " | 133-5/8 | | 22,250 |
| Bought | 1000 | " 127 | " " | 133-5/8 | | 6,625 |
| Bought | 500 | " 132 | " " | 133-5/8 | | 812.50 |
| Sold | 2000 | " 133-5/8 | " | 132¼ | | 2,750 |
| Bought | 2000 | " 132¼ | " | 157½ | | 50,500 |

| | | | | | | DEBIT | CREDIT |
|---|---|---|---|---|---|---|---|
| Bought | 1000 | at 136 | closed at | | 157½ | | $21,500 |
| Bought | 500 | " 131 | " | " | 157½ | | 13,250 |
| Bought | 300 | " 145 | " | " | 157½ | | 3,750 |
| Bought | 200 | " 150 | " | " | 157½ | | 1,500 |
| Bought | 100 | " 155 | " | " | 157½ | | 250 |
| Sold | 2000 | " 157½ | " | " | 148½ | | 18,000 |
| Sold | 1000 | " 152½ | " | " | 148½ | | 4,000 |
| Sold | 500 | " 147½ | " | " | 148½ | 500 | |
| Bought | 2000 | " 148½ | " | " | 151-5/8 | | 6,250 |
| Sold | 2000 | " 151-5/8 | " | " | 131-5/8 | | 40,000 |
| Sold | 1000 | " 146-5/8 | " | " | 131-5/8 | | 15,000 |
| Sold | 500 | " 141-5/8 | " | " | 131-5/8 | | 5,000 |
| Sold | 300 | " 136-5/8 | " | " | 131-5/8 | | 1,500 |
| Sold | 200 | " 131-5/8 | " | " | 131-5/8 | | -- |
| Bought | 2000 | " 131-5/8 | " | " | 143-5/8 | | 24,000 |
| Bought | 1000 | " 136-5/8 | " | " | 143-5/8 | | 7,000 |
| Bought | 500 | " 141-5/8 | " | " | 143-5/8 | | 1,000 |
| Sold | 2000 | " 143-5/8 | " | " | 141 | | 5,250 |
| Bought | 2000 | " 141 | " | " | 152 | | 22,000 |
| Bought | 1000 | " 145 | " | " | 152 | | 7,000 |
| Bought | 500 | " 150 | " | " | 152 | | 1,000 |
| Sold | 2000 | " 152 | " | " | 140½ | | 23,000 |
| Sold | 500 | " 147 | " | " | 140½ | | 3,250 |
| Sold | 300 | " 142 | | " | 140½ | | 450 |
| | | | | | | $1,500 | $1,645,777.50 |
| | | | Commissions | | | 10,100 | 11,600.00 |
| | | | Net Credit | | | | $1,634,177.50 |

## 1928

We buy 2000 at 140½ and later buy 1000 at 144½ and 500 at 149½. March 22nd and 26th high 152. We raise stop to 149. Stop caught, and we sell short 2000 at 149, April 2nd and 11th low 145, same low as March 14th and 20th. We reduce stop to 148, although could have covered against double bottom. Stop caught. We buy 2000 at 148. April 12th high 154. We raise stop to 151, Stop was caught, and we sell short 2000 at 151. April 24th low 143¾. April 27th high 147. We make stop 148. Stop caught. We buy 2000 at 148. May 11th high 150¾. We make stop at 147¾. The stop was caught, and we go short 2000 at 147¾, and later sell 1000 at 142¾ and 500 at 137¾. June 11th low 132-5/8. Last low June 21st at 136¼. We make stop 137¼. Stop was caught, and we buy 2000 at 137¼. July 9th high 142. We make stop 139. Stop caught, and we go short 2000 at 139. July 17th low 134. We make stop 137. The stop was caught.

We buy 2000 at 137 and later buy 1000 at 142, 500 at 147 and 300 at 152. September 17th high 160-3/8. We make stop 157-3/8. Stop was caught, and we sell short 2000 at 157-3/8. September 21st low 155. We make stop 158. The stop was caught, and we buy 2000 at 158. Later buy 1000 at 162. October 15th high 166. We make stop

163. Stop caught. We go short 2000 at 163. October 26th low 159-1/8. We make stop 162-1/8. Stop was caught, and we buy 2000 at 162-1/8 and later buy 1000 at 167. November 16th high 172½ and we make stop 169½. Stop was caught and we go short 2 000 at 169½. Later sell 1000 at 164½, 500 at 159½ and 300 at 154½. December 17th low 149¾ and December 8th low was 150¼. Also note August 23rd and 28th lows were 149½ and 150½. These bottoms give us an indication to cover shorts around 150 and buy; besides from the last low of 132-3/8 on June 25th to the high 172½ on November 16th made 1/2 point at 152½ and 3 point stop was never caught. After low of 149¾ on December 17th, we made stop 152¾. Stop was caught, and we buy 2000 at 152¾. Later buy 1000 at 157¾, 500 at 162¾, 300 at 167¾, 200 at 172¾ and 100 at 177¾.

## 1929

On January 22, 1929, high 190¼. We make stop 187¼. Stop caught. We go short 2000 at 187¼. January 24th low 183½. We make stop 187½. Stop caught. We buy 2000 at 187½. January 25th high 192 ¾. We make stop 189¾. Stop was caught, and we sell 2000 at 189¾. January 30th low 179½. We make stop 182½. Stop was caught. We buy 2000 at 182½. February 2nd high 188. Make stop 185. Stop caught. We go short 2000 at 185, and later sell 1000 at 180. February 8th low 171-1/8. Make stop 174-1/8. Stop caught. We buy 2000 at 174-1/8. February 13th high 180. We make stop 177. Stop caught. We sell 2000 at 177 and later sell 1000 at 172. February 16th low 168¼. We make stop 171¼. Stop was caught, and we buy 2000 at 171¼. Later we buy 1000 at 176¼, 500 at 181¼, 300 at 186¼ and 300 at 190¼. March 1st high 193¾. We make stop at 190¾. Stop caught.

We go short 2000 at 190¾ and sell 1000 at 185¾. March 6th low 180½. We make stop 183½. Stop was caught and we buy 2000 at 183½. March 8th high 187¼. We make stop 184¼. Stop was caught, and we go short 2000 at 184¼. March 11th low 180½, same low as March 6th. We make stop 183½. Stop was caught and we buy 2000 at 184¼. March 28th high 183¾. Make stop 180¾. Stop caught.

We go short 2000 at 180¾. April 1st low 176¼. We make stop 179¼. Stop caught. We buy 2,000 at 179¼ and later buy 1000 at 184¼. April 5th high 189. We make stop 186. Stop caught. We go short 2000 at 186. April 9th and 17th low 183¾. Make stop 186¾. Stop caught. We buy 2000 at 186¾. April 30th high 190½. We make stop 187½. Stop caught. We go short 2000 at 187½. Later sell 1000 at 182½, 500 at 177½, 300 at 172½ and 200 at 167½. May 31st low 162½. We make stop 165½ . Stop was caught, and we buy 2000 at 165½. Later buy 1000 at 170½, 500 at 175½, 300 at 180½, 200 at 185½, 100 at 190½.

In the early part of July, the stock crosses 194, the highest in history, and not having broken an overnight bottom since the low of 162½ shows strong up trend. As we have 30 points' profit in the first purchase at 165½, we start a new pyramid and buy 2000 more at 195½. Buy 1000 at 200½. July 11th low 197½. We raise stop on all purchases to 196½. The advance continues, and we buy 1000 more at 205½. July 20th and 24th high 209¾ and 210. July 22nd, 24th and 29th made lows at 204½. We raise stops on all trades to 203½. Stops were not caught. We buy 500 more at 210½, 300 at 215½, 200 at 220½, and 100 at 225½. August 9th, the last low was 213½. We raise stops on all trades to 212½. The advance continues with no change in trend on the Overnight Chart. August 14th high 245. August 15th low 235-5/8. We raise stop on all trades to 234-5/8. August 19th low 237-5/8. We raise all stops to 236-5/8.

The rule to follow when you have big profits on a double pyramid is, do no guessing; wait until the Overnight Chart closes your trades by catching a stop one point under a previous low or follow up with a stop 10 points under each day's high level. This rule is to be applied only in active fast markets. For example, from August 14th high to August 15th low there was decline of 9-3/8 points. Therefore, 10 points from the next extreme high level would indicate that the trend was getting ready to turn down.

August 24th high 260½. August 29th low 251½, just 9 points' decline, and would not catch a 10 point stop. We raise all stops to 250½. September 3rd high 2 61¾, and a stop 10 points down would be 251¾. We sell out all long stock at 251¾.

The following statement covers all trades from March, 1928 to Sept. 5, 1929:

| | | | | | | DEBIT | CREDIT |
|---|---|---|---|---|---|---|---|
| March, 1928 balance brought forward | | | | | | | $1,634,177.50 |
| Bought | 2000 | at 140½ | closed | at | 149 | | 17,000 |
| Bought | 1000 | " 144½ | " | " | 149 | | 4,500 |
| Bought | 500 | " 149½ | " | " | 149 | 250 | |
| Sold | 2000 | " 149 | " | " | 148 | | 2,000 |
| Bought | 2000 | " 148 | " | " | 141 | 14,000 | |
| Sold | 2000 | " 141 | " | " | 148 | 14,000 | |
| Bought | 2000 | " 148 | " | " | 147¾ | 500 | |
| Sold | 2000 | " 147¾ | " | " | 137¼ | | 21,000 |
| Sold | 1000 | " 142¾ | " | " | 137¼ | | 5,500 |
| Sold | 500 | " 137¾ | " | " | 137¼ | | 250 |
| Bought | 2000 | " 137¼ | " | " | 139 | | 3,500 |
| Sold | 2000 | " 139 | " | " | 137 | | 4,000 |
| Bought | 2000 | " 137 | " | " | 157-3/8 | | 40,750 |
| Bought | 1000 | " 142 | " | " | 157-3/8 | | 15,375 |
| Bought | 500 | " 147 | " | " | 157-3/8 | | 5,187.50 |
| Bought | 300 | " 152 | " | " | 157-3/8 | | 1,612.50 |
| Sold | 2000 | " 157-3/8 | " | " | 158 | 1,250 | |
| Bought | 2000 | " 158 | " | " | 163 | | 10,000. |
| Bought | 1000 | " 162 | " | " | 163 | | 1,000 |
| Sold | 2000 | " 163 | " | " | 162-1/8 | | 1,750 |
| Bought | 2000 | " 162-1/8 | " | " | 169½ | | 14,750 |
| Bought | 1000 | " 167 | " | " | 169½ | | 2,500 |
| Sold | 2000 | " 169½ | " | " | 152¾ | | 33,500 |

| Transaction | Closed | DEBIT | CREDIT |
|---|---|---|---|
| Sold 1000 at 164½ | closed at 152¾ | | 11,750 |
| Sold 500 " 159½ | " " 152¾ | | 3,375 |
| Sold 300 " 154½ | " " 152¾ | | 525 |
| Bought 2000" 152¾ | " " 187¼ | | 69,000 |
| Bought 1000 " 157¾ | " " 187¼ | | 29,500 |
| Bought 500 " 162¾ | " " 187¼ | | 12,250 |
| Bought 300 " 167¾ | " " 187¼ | | 5,850 |
| Bought 200 " 172¾ | " " 187¼ | | 2,900 |
| Bought 100 " 177¾ | " " 187¼ | | 950 |
| Sold 2000 " 187¼ | " " 187½ | 500 | |
| Bought 2000 " 187½ | " " 189¾ | | 4,500 |
| Sold 2000 " 189¾ | " " 182½ | | 24,500 |
| Bought 2000 " 182½ | " " 185 | | 5,000 |
| Sold 2000 " 185 | " " 174¼ | | 21,500 |
| Sold 1000 " 180 | " " 174¼ | | 5,750 |
| Bought 2000 " 174-1/8 | " " 177 | | 5,750 |
| Sold 2000 " 177 | " " 171¼ | | 11,500 |
| Sold 1000 " 172 | " " 171¼ | | 750 |
| Bought 2000 " 171¼ | " " 190¾ | | 39,000 |
| " 1000 " 176¼ | " " 190¾ | | 14,500 |
| " 500 " 181¼ | " " 190¾ | | 4,750 |
| " 300 " 186¼ | " " 190¾ | | 1,350 |
| " 300 " 191¼ | " " 190¾ | 150 | |
| Sold 2000 " 190¾ | " " 183½ | | 14,500 |
| " 1000 " 185¾ | " " 183½ | | 2,250 |
| Bought 2000 " 183½ | " " 184¼ | | 1,500 |
| Sold 2000 " 184¼ | " " 183½ | | 1,500 |
| Bought 2000" 183½ | " " 187¾ | | 8,500 |
| " 1000" 188½ | " " 187¾ | 750 | |
| Sold 2000" 187¾ | " " 174½ | | 26,500 |
| Sold 1000" 182¾ | " " 174½ | | 8,250 |
| Sold 500" 177¾ | " " 174½ | | 1,750 |
| " 300" 172¾ | " " 174½ | 525 | |
| Bought 2000" 174½ | " " 180¾ | | 12,500 |
| Sold 2000" 180¾ | " " 179½ | | 2,500 |
| Bought 2000" 179¼ | " " 186 | | 13,500 |
| " 2000" 184¼ | " " 186 | | 1,750 |
| Sold 2000 "186 | " " 186¾ | 1,500 | |
| Bought 2000" 186¾ | " " 187½ | | 1,500 |
| Sold 2000" 187½ | " " 165½ | | 4,400 |
| " 1000" 182½ | " " 165½ | | 17,000 |
| " 500" 177½ | " " 165½ | | 6,000 |
| " 300" 172½ | " " 165½ | | 2,100 |
| " 200" 167½ | " " 165½ | | 400 |
| Bought 2000" 165½ | " " 251¾ | | 172,500 |
| " 1000" 170½ | " " 251¾ | | 81,500 |
| " 500" 175½ | " " 251¾ | | 38,125 |
| " 300" 180½ | " " 251¾ | | 21,375 |
| " 200" 185½ | " " 251¾ | | 13,250 |
| " 100" 190½ | " " 251¾ | | 6,150 |
| " 2000" 195½ | " " 251¾ | | 113,500 |
| " 1000" 200½ | " " 251¾ | | 51,250 |
| 1000" 205½ | " 251¾ | | 46,250 |
| 500" 210½ | " 251¾ | | 20,625 |
| 300" 215½ | " 251¾ | | 10,875 |

| | | DEBITS | CREDITS |
|---|---|---|---|
| Bought 200 at 220½ | closed at 251¾ | | 6,250 |
| Bought 100 " 225½ | " " 251¾ | | 2,625 |
| | | $33,425 | $2,833,577.50 |
| | Commissions | 24,700 | 58,125.00 |
| | Net Credit | | $2,775,452.50 |

---

Now that we have a total capital of $2,775,452.50, we can be ultra conservative and increase trading unit to 5000 shares. We sell 5000 short at 251¾. September 5th low 245¾. We make stop 248¾. Stop was caught, and we buy 5000 at 248¾. August 7th high 252½. We make stop 249½. Stop was caught, and we sell short 5000 at 249½. Later we sell 3000 at 244½ and 2000 at 239½. September 10th low 238. September 11th high 243¼. We make stop on all trades 244¼. September 13th and 15th low 230½. We reduce stop to 233½. Stop caught. We buy 5000 at 233½, with stop 229½ and then buy 3000 at 238½ and 2000 at 243½. September 19th high 247½. We raise all stops to 244½. Stops caught. We go short 5000 at 244½ and 3000 at 239½. September 21st low 232. We make stops at 235. Stops caught.

We buy 5000 at 235 and 3000 at 240. September 24th high 241¾. We make stop at 238¾. Stops caught. We go short 5000 at 238¾ and later sell 3000 at 233¾, 2000 at 228¾, 1000 at 223¾, 500 at 218¾, 300 at 213¾ and 200 at 208¾. October 4th low 206½. We figure from the low of 149¾ in December, 1928 to the high of 261¾ and get 1/2 point at 205¾, but we are in a panic, so we follow down with stop 3 points above the low or at 209½. Stop is caught, and we buy 5000 at 209½ and later buy 3000 at 214½, 2000 at 219½, 1000 at 22 and 500 at 229½. October 10th high 234, same high as September 26th. We figure from 261¾ high to 206½ low and get 234-1/8, the 1/2 point. We sell out at 233 and go short 5000 with stop 235-1/8. Then sell 3000 at 230-1/8, 2000 at 225-1/8, 1000 at 220-1/8, 500 at 215-1/8, and 300 at 210-1/8. December 21st low 205, just under the 1/2 point. Also note July 22nd, 24th and 29th lows, 204½, showing a strong resistance point, where we should cover shorts, but we reduce stops to 208. Stop caught. We buy 5000 at 208 and later buy 3000 at 213 and 2000 at 218. October 22nd high 218½. We raise all stops to 215½. Stops caught.

We go short 5000 at 215½. Later sell 3000 at 210½ and 2000 at 204, when 1/2 point and bottoms are broken, and sell 1000 at 199, and 500 at 194. October 24th low 193½. As this is a panic day, we pull stops down 5 points from the low. This covers shorts at 198½, and we buy 5000 at 198½. October 25th high 207. We know the 1/2 point is 205¾, so we sell out at 205 and go short 5000 at 205 with stop at 208. Later we sell 3000 at 200, 2000 at 195, 1000 at 190, 500 at 185, 300 at 180, 200 at 175 and 100 at 170. October 29th, the great panic, Steel declines to 166½. We must cover or follow down with stop 5 points from the low, so stop at 171½ is caught, and we buy 5000 at 171½, 3000 at 176½ and 2000 at 181½. October 31st high 193½. We raise stop to 188½. Stop caught. We go short 5000 at 188½. Then sell 3000 at 183½, 2000 at 178½, 1000 at 173½, and 500 at 168½. November 7th low 161½. We reduce stop to 166½. Stop caught. We buy 5000 at 166½ and we buy 3000 at 171½. November 8th high 175½. We make all stops 170½. Stops caught. We go short 5000 at 170½. Then sell 3000 at 165½, 2000 at 160½, and 1000 at 155½.

Here we figure from low 38, February 1, 1915, to high 261¾. and find 1/2 point 149-7/8. We also know the move started from 149¾ on December 17, 1928. Therefore, 150 is the strongest support level. On November 13th U. S. Steel sells at 150, but we do not wait for the last 1/8th. We cover all shorts at 151 and buy 5000 with stop at 148¾. Later we buy 3000 at 156 and 2000 at 161. November 15th high 167½. We make stop 164½. Stop is caught, and we go short 5000 at 164½. December 18th low 159-5/8. We make stop 162-5/8. Stop caught. We buy 5000 at 162-5/8. Then buy 3000 at 167-5/8. November 21st high 171-7/8. We make stop 168-7/8. Stop caught. We go short 5000 at 168-7/8. Then sell 3000 at 163-7/8. December 2nd low 159¼, only 3/8 under low of November 18th. We make stop 162¼. Stop caught. We buy 5000 at 162¼ and later buy 3000 at 167¼. December 5th low 164½. We make all stops 163½. Later we buy 2000 at 172¼, 1000 at 177¼, 500 at 182¼ and 300 at 187¼. December 9th high 189. We make stop 186. Stop caught. We go short 5000 at 186. Then sell 3000 at 181, 2000 at 176, 1000 at 171, and 500 at 166. December 13th low 164¼, same low as December 5th. We make stop 167¼. Stops caught. We buy 5000 at 167¼. Then buy 3000 at 172¼. December 14th high 174¾. We make stop 171¾. Stops caught.

We sell 5000 at 171¾. Later sell 3000 at 166¾. December 17th low 166¼. We make stop 169¼. Stops caught. We buy 5000 at 169¼. December 18th high 173½. We make stop 170½. Stop caught. We sell short 5000 at 170½. Later sell 3000 at 165½. Sell 2000 at 160½. December 23rd low 156¾. We make stop 159¾. Stop caught. We buy 5000 at 159¾. Later we buy 3000 at 163¾. December 29th low 163-5/8. We make all stops 162-5/8. Later we buy 2000 at 169-3/4.

## 1930

January 2nd high 173-5/8. Low same day 166. We make all stops 165. The price of 166-1/8 is the 1/2 point from 70½, low of June 23rd, 1921, and the extreme high 261¾. Therefore, a strong support and buying level. January 13th low 168-5/8. We make all stops 167-5/8, because since January 2nd the Overnight Chart has made lower tops. January 18th low 167¼. Stops are caught at 167-5/8, and we go short 5000 at 167-5/8, with stop at 170-5/8. Stop caught, and we buy 5000 at 170-5/8. We buy 3000 at 175-5/8, 2000 at 180-5/8 and 1000 at 185-5/8. February 14th high 189, same as December 9th high. February 17th low 184½. We make all stops 183½. February 18th high 189½. We raise stop to 186½. Stops caught. We go short 5000 at 186½ with stop 190. Later we sell 3000 at 181½. February 25th low 177. We make all stops 180. Stops caught. We buy 5000 at 180. March 1st and 7th high 184. We make stop 181. Stop caught

The following statement covers trades from September, 1929 to March 1930:-

| | | | | | | | DEBIT | CREDIT |
|---|---|---|---|---|---|---|---|---|
| | | | | September, 1929 | | | | $2,775,452.50 |
| Sold | 5000 | at | 251-3/4 | closed | at | 248-3/4 | | 15,000 |
| Bought | 5000 | " | 248-3/4 | " | " | 249½ | | 3,750 |
| Sold | 5000 | " | 249½ | " | " | 233½ | | 80,000 |
| " | 3000 | " | 244½ | " | " | 233½ | | 33,000 |
| " | 2000 | " | 239½ | " | " | 233½ | | 12,000 |
| Bought | 5000 | " | 233½ | " | " | 244½ | | 55,000 |
| " | 3000 | " | 238½ | " | " | 244½ | | 18,000 |
| " | 2000 | " | 243½ | " | " | 244½ | | 2,000 |
| Sold | 5000 | " | 244½ | " | " | 235 | | 47,500 |
| " | 3000 | " | 239½ | " | " | 235 | | 13,500 |
| Bought | 5000 | " | 235 | " | " | 238-3/4 | | 18,750 |
| " | 3000 | " | 240 | " | " | 238-3/4 | $1,250 | |
| Sold | 5000 | " | 238-3/4 | " | " | 209½ | | 146,250 |
| " | 3000 | " | 233-3/4 | " | " | 209½ | | 72,750 |
| " | 2000 | " | 228-3/4 | " | " | 209½ | | 38,500 |
| " | 1000 | " | 223-3/4 | " | " | 209½ | | 14,250 |
| " | 500 | " | 218-3/4 | " | " | 209½ | | 4,625 |
| " | 300 | " | 213-3/4 | " | " | 209½ | | 1,275 |
| " | 200 | " | 208-3/4 | " | " | 209½ | 150 | |
| Bought | 5000 | " | 209½ | " | " | 233 | | 117,500 |
| " | 3000 | " | 214½ | " | " | 233 | | 55,500 |
| " | 2000 | " | 219½ | " | " | 233 | | 27,000 |
| " | 1000 | " | 224½ | " | " | 233 | | 8,500 |
| " | 500 | " | 229½ | " | " | 233 | | 1,750 |
| Sold | 5000 | " | 233 | " | " | 208 | | 125,000 |
| " | 3000 | " | 230-1/8 | " | " | 208 | | 66,375 |
| " | 2000 | " | 225-1/8 | " | " | 208 | | 34,250 |
| " | 1000 | " | 220-1/8 | " | " | 208 | | 12,125 |
| " | 500 | " | 215-1/8 | " | " | 208 | | 3,562.50 |
| " | 300 | " | 210-1/8 | " | " | 208 | | 637.50 |
| Bought | 5000 | " | 208 | " | " | 215½ | | 37,500 |
| " | 3000 | " | 213 | " | " | 215½ | | 7,500 |
| " | 2000 | " | 218 | " | " | 215½ | 5,000 | |
| Sold | 5000 | " | 215½ | " | " | 198½ | | 85,000 |
| " | 3000 | " | 210½ | " | " | 198½ | | 36,000 |
| " | 2000 | " | 204 | " | " | 198½ | | 11,000 |
| " | 1000 | " | 100 | " | " | 198½ | | 500 |
| " | 500 | " | 194 | " | " | 198½ | 2,250 | |
| Bought | 5000 | " | 198½ | " | " | 205 | | 32,500 |
| Sold | 5000 | " | 205 | " | " | 171½ | | 167,500 |
| " | 3000 | " | 200 | " | " | 171½ | | 85,500 |
| " | 2000 | " | 195 | " | " | 171½ | | 47,000 |
| " | 1000 | " | 190 | " | " | 171½ | | 18,500 |
| " | 500 | " | 185 | | " | 171½ | | 6,750 |
| | 300 | " | 180 | | " | 171½ | | 2,550 |
| | 200 | " | 175 | | " | 171½ | | 700 |
| | 100 | " | 170 | | " | 171½ | 150 | |

| | | | | | | | DEBIT | CREDIT |
|---|---|---|---|---|---|---|---|---|
| Bought | 5000 | at | 171½ | closed | at | 188½ | | $85,000 |
| " | 3000 | " | 176½ | " | " | 188½ | | 36,000 |
| " | 2000 | " | 181½ | " | " | 188½ | | 14,000 |
| Sold | 5000 | " | 188½ | " | " | 166½ | | 110,000 |
| " | 3000 | " | 183½ | " | " | 166½ | | 51,000 |
| " | 2000 | " | 178½ | " | " | 166½ | | 24,000 |
| " | 1000 | " | 173½ | " | " | 166½ | | 7,000 |
| " | 500 | " | 168½ | " | " | 166½ | | 1,000 |
| Bought | 5000 | " | 166½ | " | " | 170½ | | 20,000 |
| " | 3000 | " | 171½ | " | " | 170½ | $3,000 | |
| Sold | 5000 | " | 170½ | " | " | 151 | | 97,500 |
| " | 3000 | " | 165½ | " | " | 151 | | 43,500 |
| " | 2000 | " | 160½ | " | " | 151 | | 19,000 |
| " | 1000 | " | 155½ | " | " | 151 | | 4,500 |
| Bought | 5000 | " | 151 | " | " | 164½ | | 67,500 |
| " | 3000 | " | 156 | " | " | 164½ | | 25,500 |
| " | 2000 | " | 161 | " | " | 164½ | | 7,000 |
| Sold | 5000 | " | 164½ | " | " | 162-5/8 | | 9,375 |
| Bought | 5000 | " | 162-5/8 | " | " | 168-7/8 | | 31,250 |
| " | 3000 | " | 167-5/8 | " | " | 168-7/8 | | 3,750 |
| Sold | 5000 | " | 168-7/8 | " | " | 162¼ | | 33,125 |
| " | 3000 | " | 163-7/8 | " | " | 162¼ | | 4,875 |
| Bought | 5000 | " | 162¼ | " | " | 186 | | 118,750 |
| " | 3000 | " | 167¼ | " | " | 186 | | 56,250 |
| " | 2000 | " | 172¼ | " | " | 186 | | 27,500 |
| " | 1000 | " | 177¼ | " | " | 186 | | 8,750 |
| " | 500 | " | 182¼ | " | " | 186 | | 1,875 |
| " | 300 | " | 187¼ | " | " | 186 | 375 | |
| Sold | 5000 | " | 186 | " | " | 167¼ | | 93,750 |
| " | 3000 | " | 181 | " | " | 167¼ | | 41,250 |
| " | 2000 | " | 176 | " | " | 167¼ | | 17,500 |
| " | 1000 | " | 171 | " | " | 167¼ | | 3,750 |
| " | 500 | " | 166 | " | " | 167¼ | 625 | |
| Bought | 5000 | " | 167¼ | " | " | 171-3/4 | | 22,500 |
| " | 3000 | " | 172¼ | " | " | 171-3/4 | 1,500 | |
| Sold | 5000 | " | 171-3/4 | " | " | 169¼ | | 12,500 |
| " | 3000 | " | 166-3/4 | " | " | 169¼ | 7,500 | |
| Bought | 5000 | " | 169¼ | " | " | 170½ | | 6,250 |
| Sold | 5000 | " | 170½ | " | " | 159-3/4 | | 52,500 |
| " | 3000 | " | 165½ | " | " | 158-3/4 | | 17,250 |
| " | 2000 | " | 160½ | " | " | 159-3/4 | | 1,500 |
| Bought | 5000 | " | 159-3/4 | " | " | 167-5/8 | | 39,375 |
| " | 3000 | " | 164-3/4 | " | " | 167-5/8 | | 8,625 |
| " | 2000 | " | 169-3/4 | " | " | 167-5/8 | 4,250 | |
| Sold | 5000 | " | 167-5/8 | " | " | 170-5/8 | 15,000 | |
| Bought | 5000 | " | 170-5/8 | " | " | 186½ | | 79,375 |
| " | 3000 | " | 175-5/8 | " | " | 186½ | | 32,625 |
| " | 2000 | " | 180-5/8 | " | " | 186½ | | 11,750 |
| " | 1000 | " | 185-5/8 | " | " | 186½ | | 875 |
| Sold | 5000 | " | 186½ | | " | 180 | | 32,500 |
| " | 3000 | " | 181½ | | " | 180 | | 4,500 |
| Bought | 5000 | " | 180 | | " | 181 | | 5,000 |
| | | | | | | | $41,050 | $5,733,677. |
| | | | | Commissions | | | 71,175 | 112,225. |
| | | | | Net Profit | | | | $5,621,452. |

We go short )
5000 at 181)

We go short 5000 at 181. March 13th low $177\frac{3}{4}$. March 11th and 14th high $182\frac{1}{2}$. We make stop $183\frac{1}{2}$. Stop caught. We buy 5000 at $183\frac{1}{2}$. Later buy 3000 at $188\frac{1}{2}$ and 2000 at $193\frac{1}{2}$. April 1st, 7th 10th and 16th, highs $198\frac{3}{4}$ to 197, but extreme high $198\frac{3}{4}$. The last low on April 3rd was $192\frac{3}{4}$. We make stops at $191\frac{3}{4}$. Stops caught. We go short 5000 at $191\frac{3}{4}$. Later we sell 3000 at $186\frac{3}{4}$, 2000 at $181\frac{3}{4}$, 1000 at $176\frac{3}{4}$ and 500 at $171\frac{3}{4}$.

May 5th low $166\frac{1}{4}$. We cover shorts and buy 5000 at 167, because 166-1/8 is the 1/2 point from 1921 low to 1929 high and because low on January 2nd, 1930 was 166. We protect purchases with stop at 165. Later we buy 3000 at 172. May 6th high 175. We figure 174-3/8 the 1/2 point from 150 to $198\frac{3}{4}$. Therefore, we sell out longs at 174 and go short 5000 at 174 with stop at 176. Then sell 3000 at 169. May 8th low $165\frac{3}{4}$. We cover shorts at $166\frac{1}{2}$ and buy 5000 at $166\frac{1}{2}$, with stop at 165. Later we buy 3000 at $171\frac{1}{2}$. May 14th high 175-3/8. We again sell out longs at 174 and go short 5000 at 174 with stop at 176. Later we sell 3000 at 169. May 20th low $166\frac{1}{4}$. We again cover shorts and buy 5000 at $166\frac{1}{2}$, with stop at 165. Later buy 3000 at $171\frac{1}{2}$. May 28th high 175. We sell out longs at 174 and sell 5000 short at 174 with stop at 176. Later we sell 3000 at 169.

June 7th, U. S. Steel sells at 166. We cover shorts at $166\frac{1}{2}$ and buy 5000 at $166\frac{1}{2}$ with stop at 165. Stop was caught same day and we go short 5000 at 165. Steel declines to 164 on June 7th. We can now make stop 167 or wait until the Overnight makes a turn, then place a stop 1 point above the top from which the Overnight Chart turns down again or follow down with a stop loss order 3 points above the low of each day.

The following statement covers trades from March, 1930 to June 7th, 1930, inclusive:-

| | | | | | DEBIT | CREDIT |
|---|---|---|---|---|---|---|
| | | | | Balance Forward | | $5,621,452 |
| Sold | 5000 | at | 181 | closed at 183½ | $12,500 | |
| Bought | 5000 | " | 183½ | " " 191-3/4 | | 41,250 |
| " | 3000 | " | 188½ | " " 191-3/4 | | 9,750 |
| " | 2000 | " | 193½ | " " 191-3/4 | 3,500 | |
| Sold | 5000 | " | 191-3/4 | " " 167 | | 123,750 |
| " | 3000 | " | 186-3/4 | " " 167 | | 59,250 |
| " | 2000 | " | 181-3/4 | " " 167 | | 29,500 |
| " | 1000 | " | 176-3/4 | " " 167 | | 9,750 |
| " | 500 | " | 171-3/4 | " " 167 | | 2,375 |
| Bought | 5000 | " | 167 | " " 174 | | 35,000 |
| " | 3000 | " | 172 | " " 174 | | 6,000 |
| Sold | 5000 | " | 174 | " " 166½ | | 37,500 |
| " | 3000 | " | 169 | " " 166½ | | 7,500 |
| Bought | 5000 | " | 166½ | " " 174 | | 37,500 |
| " | 3000 | " | 171½ | " " 174 | | 7,500 |
| Sold | 5000 | " | 174 | " " 166½ | | 37,500 |
| " | 3000 | " | 169 | " " 166½ | | 7,500 |
| Bought | 5000 | " | 166½ | " " 174 | | 37,500 |
| " | 3000 | " | 171½ | " " 174 | | 7,500 |
| Sold | 5000 | " | 174 | " " 166½ | | 37,500 |
| " | 3000 | " | 169 | " 166½ | | 7,500 |
| Bought | 5000 | " | 166½ | " 165 | 7,500 | |
| | | | | | $23,500 | $6,163,077 |
| | | | | Commissions | 19,875 | 43,375 |
| | | | | Net Credit | | $6,119,702. |

Error March 10, 1927 to June 7, 1930
509,600 shares at $25 per 100 should
be $50 per 100 round turn........... $127,403
Tax at $4.00 per 100 shares not figured
on 869,700 shares..................... 34,788 — 162,191.

TOTAL NET PROFITS.................$5,957,511.

June 7th, 1930

with 5000 shares short at 165.

June 11 low 160½; June 13 high 166. We make stop on shorts at 167. June 16 we sell 3000 at 161. June 18 low 155. We make stop on all trades at 158. Stop caught. We buy 5000 at 158. June 20 high 162½. We make stop 159¼. Stop caught. We go short 5000 at 159¼. June 25 low 151-5/8. We reduce stop to 154-5/8. Stop caught. We buy 5000 at 154-5/8. We could have bought at 152 with stop at 149 because 150 is 1/2 point from 1914 to 1929.

June 27 low 153½. We make stop 153. June 30 Steel crossed 157½, the tops of June 24 and 26 and for the first time since June 28 makes a higher top on the Overnight Chart. For this reason we buy 3000 more at 157½ and make stop on all trades at 154.

On June 30, 1930 the account stands:

| | | | | Profit |
|---|---|---|---|---|
| Sold | 5000 at 165 | closed at | 158 | $35,000 |
| " | 3000 " 161 | " " | 158 | 9,000 |
| Bought | 5000 " 158 | " " | 159¼ | 6,250 |
| Sold | 5000 " 159¼ | " " | 154-5/8 | 23,125 |
| | | | | $73,375 |
| | Less Commissions & Taxes | | | 9,720 |
| | | Net Profit | | $63,655 |
| | | June 7 Capital | | 5,957,511 |
| | | | | $6,021,166 |

with 5000 bought at 154-5/8 and stop on all trades at 154 and 3000 bought at 157½.

July 1st high 161-3/8. We raise stop to 158-3/8 because last high on June 20 was 162½ and failing to cross this level indicated lower. The stop was caught and we went short 5000 at 158-3/8.

July 8th low 153¾. Note low June 27th was 153½, from which the Overnight turned up for the first time since May 28, when the stock sold at 175. We cover shorts and buy 5000 at 153½ with stop at 152½ because this was a double bottom same as June 27th.

July 9 high 158¼; July 10th low 155¾. We raise stop to 154¾.

On July 10, when Steel rallies to 158½, we buy 3000 more at 158½ and make stop on all trades 155½.

July 14 high 163¾. We raise stops to 160¾ or 3 points from the high. We can either follow up with stop 1 point under each day's lowest or wait until the Overnight Chart makes a turn, then place stop 1 point under the Overnight bottom.

July 19 high 168¾. We sell out longs and go short 5000 at 168, because 169 is 3/8 point from 198¾ to 151-5/8. We make stop 170. July 21 low 162-5/8. In view of the fact that the Overnight Chart still shows up, we note last low at 164¼ on July 16. We calculate the 1/2 point from July 10th bottom, 155¾, to high at 168¾ and get 162¼ as the 1/2 point, so we cover shorts and buy 5000 at 163 with stop at 161.

July 23 high 168½. We sell out longs at 168 and go short July 25 low 164¼. We cover shorts and buy with stop at 162 or one point under the low of July 21. July 28 high 170. We sell out longs and go short. July 31 low 163. We cover shorts and buy at 163½ with stop at 162, because 163 is Resistance Level.

August 5 high 170¼, a double top against July 28. We sell out longs at 170 and go short with stop at 171. Sell more at 165; then sell more at 160 because it has broken bottoms of July 21 and July 31.

The last Resistance Level on July 10 was 155¾. The stock declined to 155½ on August 13. We cover shorts and buy at 156 with stop at 154¾. Then buy more at 161 where the Overnight Chart turned trend up. Steel advanced to 166¾ on August 16. August 18 reacted to 162⅝ and resumed advance. We raise stop to 161¾. August 20 high 168½. August 21 low 165¾. Make stop 164¾. August 27 and September 2nd high 172¼. September 4 low 167¼, still above main 1/2 point, 166¼ We make stop 165. September 8 high 173½. Note three tops, May 6, 14, and 28 at 175. The 1/2 point is 174-3/8. September 8 we sell out longs and go short at 173 with stop at 176. If it had crossed the 3 tops made in May, we would buy for long account.

September 16 declines and breaks low of September 4 and we sell more at 167; then sell more at 164, because it has again broken the main 1/2 point, 166¼. September 27 sell more at 159. September 30 breaks 155, under bottoms of July 10 and August 13; then rallies and makes two tops on October 1 and October 3 at 160½. We make stop 161½. Then sell more at 155; then at 149 sell more, because it has broken the low of November 13, 1929, the big 1/2 point.

October 10 and 14 low 144½. We cover all shorts and buy with stop at 142. October 11 and 15 highs 151½ and 152½. We sell out and go short on 2nd top. October 18 we cover shorts and buy at 145 with stop at 143. Then buy more at 150. October 28 high 154, over last 2 tops. We make stop 151. Stop was caught and we go short. Later sell more at 146. Then when it breaks 4 bottoms, sell more at 143.

November 8, 10 and 12 made bottom. We cover shorts on stop at 143 and buy. Then buy more at 147. The next point to watch is 150, the 1/2 point, where 4 tops were made November 15, 20, 21 and 25. Would sell out there and go short with stop at 151. Sell more at 145; then sell more at 140. Cover all shorts and buy for long account at 135, because this is the 1/2 point between 8-3/8 and 261¾, being half of the life fluctuation and the strongest point since 150.

It made double top December 18 and 20. We sell out longs and go short at 140. On December 29th it declines to 135¾. We cover shorts and buy because 135 is the 1/2 point. We buy a second lot at 141 and when it reacts on January 2nd we raise stop to 137. On January 7 and 9 it makes double top and we raise stop to 142, where again sell out and go short. On January 16 and 19 it makes double bottom at 138½. This is also the 1/2 point between 134-3/8 and 145, therefore we cover shorts and buy at 139 and protect with stop at 137. On January 24 and 27 double tops and lower than January 9. We sell out longs at 143 and go short again. On February 5th we cover shorts and buy at 138 because it is the same bottom as was made on January 2 and 19th. We buy more at 143. On February 16 we sell out longs at 148 and go short because it is a double top and under the 1/2 point and also just under the tops made on November 15 to 25.

On February 17 it makes a double bottom just above the 1/2 point of the last move. We cover shorts and buy at 145. On February 26 the stock advances to 152¼, failing to get 3 points above the 1/2 point. We raise stop to 149. Stop is caught and we sell out longs and go short.

On March 4th the stock declines to 143½, the 1/2 point between 134-3/8 and 152¼. We cover shorts at 144 and go long with stop 142. If the stocks crosses 152 and especially if it makes 153 it will be in a very strong position, and indicate much higher.

# CHAPTER 3

## *REVIEW OF THE BEAR AND BULL MARKETS*

### *SHOWING FORMATIONS*

### *BUYING AND SELLING POINTS*

### *1903-1939 DOW-JONES INDUSTRIAL AVERAGE*

AUTHOR:
"Truth of the Stock Tape"
"Wall Street Stock Selector"
"New Stock Trend Detector"

W. D. GANN
Statistician and Economist
82 WALL STREET
NEW YORK, N. Y.

2101 N. W. 18th TERRACE
MIAMI, FLA.

MEMBER
New Orleans Cotton Exchange
Commodity Exchange, Inc. N.Y.
American Economic Ass'n
Royal Economy Society

# REVIEW OF BULL AND BEAR MARKETS

Showing Formations and Buying
and Selling Points 1903-1939
Dow-Jones 30 Industrial averages

---

## 2nd BEAR MARKET

The 2nd Bear Market started on June 23, 1901 and reached final low on November 9, 1903. After that there was a period of accumulation which lasted until July 3, 1904.

**1903** END OF 2ND BEAR MARKET

Jul. The averages broke 53 and 51 and there was no rally or sign of support at these old levels, indicating great weakness and lower prices. After these old bottoms were broken, the next point to watch for support and bottom was 42, the low of Mch. 25, 1898.

Oct. 15 Low 42-1/4. Support came at the old bottom. A 2 weeks' rally followed to 45-1/2; then a 2 weeks' decline to Nov. 9, when the averages reached 42-1/8, a DOUBLE BOTTOM, just above the old bottom at 42 in Mch. 1898. This was TIME TO BUY with close stop loss orders. A rally followed and prices crossed 45-1/2, over the tops of the past 3 weeks ... the first sign that the minor trend had turned up and the Bear Market ended.

You should now review the 2nd Bear Market from the top at 78-1/4 in June, 1901, to the bottom at 42-1/8 on Nov. 9, 1903.

From 78-1/4 high to 42-1/8 low, the total range was ... 36-1/8 points. The greatest rally in the Bear Market was ... 8 points, from 59-5/8 to 67-7/8. Therefore, when the averages advanced 9 points or one point more than the greatest rally in the Bear Market, it would be a definite signal for a Bull Market and a safe place to buy.

**1904** 3rd BULL MARKET

ACCUMULATION ON SIDE BEFORE IT STARTS

Jan. 27 High 50-1/2, up 8-3/8 points from the low at 42-1/8, not yet 9 points to confirm Bull Market ready to go ahead.

Feb. 6 In this week prices broke under the lows of the two previous weeks, indicating a reaction. The averages failing to reach old bottoms at 51-1/2 to 53, indicated that the selling was not yet over.

SECONDARY REACTION ... SAFE TO BUY

Mch. 12 Low 46-1/2, a decline of 4 points from the top and a loss of one-half the gain from 42-1/8 to 50-1/2. This reaction lasted 6 weeks from the top and held for 3 weeks in 1-1/2 point range; then crossed tops of 3 previous weeks, indicating higher prices.

Apr. 7 High 49-7/8. Failed to reach last top at 50-1/2, a sign that it was not yet ready to go up. A slow decline followed, lasting 6 weeks.

May 18 Low 47-1/2, off only 2-3/8 points in 6 weeks, indicating very little selling; also volume of sales very small. This was dullness at bottom. A slow advance started and it required 7 weeks for prices to cross the top at 50-1/2.

SAFEST PLACE TO BUY

Jul. 16 Prices crossed 51 and advanced to 62-1/2, up over 10 points from the bottom and a greater advance than the rally of 8 points in the previous Bear Market. From Nov. 9, 1903 to July 9, 1904, prices held in a range of 8 points and most of the time in a 4-point range ... a period of 8 months of accumulation on the side, getting ready for a Bull Market. Study this formation of sideways accumulation 4 points above the low levels so that you will know what it means when you see it again. After July, 1904, prices advanced to 63, the old bottom; reacted one point in one week; then the advance was resumed. The old tops at 68 were crossed in November. There was no reaction and prices moved right on up, indicating a strong Bull Market. The next point to watch would be around the old tops at 78 to 78-3/4.

1905

Mch. 15 The averages made 78-1/4.

22 Reacted to 76-1/2.

Then went thru old tops, advancing to 80 before end of March.

The next old top was 84-1/2 made Sep. 4, 1895.

Apr. 14 High 83-3/4, just under old bottom at 84-1/2. Prices held 3 weeks in 2-1/2 point range at top; then broke under 3 weeks' bottoms, indicating minor trend down, and stocks should have been sold out.

May 22 Failing to make bottom at 78, the old top, indicated lower. On May 22 the averages reached 71-3/8. The last old top in July and August was 72-3/4.

Jun. 3 In this week crossed top of previous week, indicating higher. After low of 71-3/8 the next 4 weeks each bottom was higher.

Jun. 17 and 24 ... In these weeks the high was 75-1/4 and the following week crossed tops, indicating higher.

Nov. The averages advanced to 84-1/8, the old tops. Then reacted to 81. The advance was resumed and prices crossed old tops at 84-1/2. The next old high was 94-1/2 made in March and April, 1892.

Dec. The averages advanced to 96; reacted to 94 and held for three weeks, making bottoms at 94 and failing to break 94, an indication of strong uptrend and higher prices. There was no change in trend at this level and no weekly bottoms broken. Refer to rule, "When Stocks Advance into New High Ground."

1906

Jan. 19 High 103. END OF BULL MARKET.

This was 8-1/2 points above old top. When prices of averages or stocks reach 100 to 106 there is nearly always heavy selling, but when prices get above 100, you must wait for a signal that top has been made by prices breaking the low of the previous week or weeks.

Jan. 27 In this week there was a narrow range of one point and slightly lower than 103.

Feb. 3 In this week prices broke under the lows of 2 previous weeks. Breaking back (under 100) to 98-1/2 indicated that minor trend had turned down. There was a rally of one week to 100-1/2 or 2 points up.
Then the following week prices broke 98, a more definite indication of lower prices and a time to sell short.

Review of Bull Market - Nov. 1903 to Jan. 1906:
The greatest reaction was from April, 1905 to May, 1905--
83-3/4 to 71-3/8 or 12-3/8 points.
The smallest reaction was 4 points.
Therefore, you must watch for a decline of more than 12-3/8 points to indicate a definite change in the main trend.

## 3rd BEAR MARKET

DISTRIBUTION ON SIDE BELOW TOP LEVELS.

Mch. 10 The averages declined to 92-7/8, down 10 points and broke under 4 weeks' bottoms at 94, indicating lower. SELLING SIGNAL.
A rally of one week followed to 96-3/4.
A reaction followed in the next week to 93.
A rally the following week to 96-3/4, making a double top. In the weeks ending Feb. 17 and 24 there were two tops at 97-1/4. Therefore, these tops at 96-3/4 gave sign of good selling.
A decline followed, breaking bottoms at 93.

May [illegible] Low 86-1/2, down 16-1/2 points from 103. Breaking more than 12-3/8 points, the greatest reaction in the previous Bull Market, indicated main trend down and a Bear Market would follow. There was an old top at 86-3/4 on April 7, 1893, and a top at 83-3/4, in April, 1905, indicating that a rally could occur from this level. Refer to rule ...
After first sharp decline there is a secondary rally which is safe to sell on. The market advanced 5 weeks.

Jun. 4 High 95-1/4, lower than the last tops at 96-3/4, indicating weakness. Held last week in one-point range and following week broke lows of three previous weeks, indicating minor trend down again. SELLING SIGNAL.

Jul. 13 Low 85-1/4, still above old top at 83-3/4 and one point under low of May 3, 1906, a sign of support for a rally.

Jul. 7 and 14-- During those weeks the highs were 87-7/8 and 87-3/4.

21 Crossed 88, over 2 weeks' tops ... Minor trend up ... BUYING SIGNAL.
The next week a rapid advance followed.

Oct. 9 High 96-3/4, the THIRD TOP at same level. The week's range was less than one point ... Signal to SELL OUT AND SELL SHORT.
SAFE SELLING LEVEL ... In the following week prices broke broke under 3 weeks' lows ... a safe place to sell short.

Nov. 17 Low 92-3/8.

Dec. 15 A rally followed. High 95-3/4.

A reaction of two weeks to 93 followed.
Then a rally for two weeks.

**1907**

Jan. 7 High 96-3/8, the 4th time at this level but lower than first two ...
SAFE POINT TO GO SHORT with close stops.

12 In this week the range was 3/4 point, a narrow week same as Oct., 1906.

19 In this week prices broke under 3 weeks' lows and then broke minor bottom at 93.

Feb. 2 Declined to 90-1/8.
Rallied two weeks to 93-1/4, the old bottoms. The top of this last rally was in a range of 5/8 point. Dull and narrow at top of small rally was a sign of weakness.

Mch. 9 During this week prices broke low of 86-3/8 and 85-1/4, a very bearish indication. A rapid decline followed.

14 SILENT PANIC... Some stocks, like Union Pacific and Reading, which were active leaders at that time, broke 20 points in one day.
Our rule says, cover shorts and buy on panic days.

14 Low 76-1/4, just under old tops at 78.
A rally followed to 82.
SECONDARY REACTION ...SAFEST TO BUY.

25 Stocks had a secondary reaction after the panicky decline and made a slightly lower bottom at 75-3/8, less than one point under Mch. 14 low, a double bottom and place to buy with stop, as main trend was down. But with averages down 28 points from the top at 103 and down 21 points from Jan. 1907, a rally was due.

May 3 High 85, up less than 10 points. Note rally from July, 1906 to Jan. 1907 was 11 points, making 10 to 11 points up a point to watch for a change in trend. There were 3 weeks' tops at 84-3/4 to 85; then prices broke under 3 weeks' lows, an indication that the trend had turned down and SHORT SALES should be made. The market worked lower and rallies were small, not more than 3 points.

Aug. Prices broke 75, the low of March, 1907, and in the same month broke 71, under the low of May, 1905, making the position very weak.
Refer to our rule: In the LAST STAGE OF A BEAR MARKET rallies get less as market gets weaker. After May, 1905, low was broken, at what point should we expect resistance, support or bottom? Review:
Oct. 1898, low 51-1/2; Jun. 1900, low 53-1/2; Sep. 1900, low 53; Jul. 1904, last low after main trend turned up was 52-1/4 and last bottom in May, 1904, was 47-3/8, so the first important points would be 53-1/2 to 51-1/8.

Nov. 15 PANIC BOTTOM ... Low 53 ... time to buy.
Last week of fast decline was 4 points on averages.
Next week after low there was a 2-point range.
In the following week there was a fast advance, crossing top of previous week at 55. Minor trend turned up ... A SAFE POINT TO BUY.
This was a SHARP SINGLE BOTTOM and indicated that BEAR MARKET HAD ENDED.

Review of 3rd Bear Market: Four Sections or movements down.

Greatest rally in the Bear Market ... 11 points. Therefore, there must be an advance of 12 points or more to show main trend up.

## 4TH BULL MARKET

Dec. 7 In this week the high was 61-3/4.
Three weeks' rally ... up 8-3/4 points ... not enough to confirm main trend up as the averages must advance 12 points.
17 Low 56-7/8, a 5-point reaction in 2 weeks. You would buy as this was a SECONDARY REACTION WITH HIGHER BOTTOM.
28 In this week the market was narrow, within range of previous week.

**1908**

Jan. 4 In this week the averages crossed 60, above 3 weeks' tops .... a SAFER POINT TO BUY as trend was up.
Later crossed 62, over last rally ... DEFINITE SIGNAL FOR HIGHER.
18 Advanced to 65-7/8 in this week. Low was 64-1/4, making the range 1-5/8 points, a narrow week at the top. In the following week broke bottom of previous week, indicating further reaction.
Feb. 8 Low 58-7/8, down 7 points from 65-7/8 top and 2 points higher than low of December, 1907, the first higher bottom.
15 SECOND HIGHER BOTTOM ... SAFER TO BUY. In this week the range was 3/4 point and the following week the range was 1-1/2 points; crossed top of previous week ... safer to buy because 2nd higher bottom from sharp panic bottom.
Mch. 7 Crossed 62, top of Dec. 1907, and tops of 3 weeks in Jan. & Feb. 1908.
May 21 In this week crossed 65-7/8, old top of Jan. 1908, a DEFINITE SIGNAL FOR HIGHER prices and a bull market to follow ... a safe point to buy or to buy more if you had already bought at lower levels.
Fast moves come after secondary tops are crossed.
The next point to watch for a reaction was around the old bottoms of March, 1907, at 75 to 76. The market advanced right thru these levels with no reaction, showing strong uptrend.
The next point to watch was the top at 85 in May, 1907.
Aug. 10 High 85-3/8. The market was advancing very fast and in the same week that top was reached at 85-3/8, it reacted to 80-5/8; then rallied to 84-1/2, holding 2 weeks at a lower top, indicating good selling under old tops.
Sep. 19 In this week broke under 4 weeks' bottoms, indicating MINOR TREND DOWN and lower prices.
Sep. 22 Low 77-1/8, down 8-1/4 points from the top. Last reaction Jan. 1908 to Feb. low was 7 points, making this a BUYING POINT, just above old bottom of March, 1907. This was only 3 weeks from secondary tops at 84-1/2.
Oct. 3 During this week crossed top of previous week ...SAFER TO BUY. The advance continued and crossed old tops at 85-1/2, which indicated higher.
Nov. 13 High 88-3/8. THREE SECTIONS OR MOVES UP IN BULL MARKET.
Dull at top. Range 1-3/8 points for the week.
The next week broke low of previous week, indicating TOP FOR REACTION.
Held 4 weeks between 86-1/8 and 87-1/2.
Then following week broke under 4 weeks' bottoms, indicating lower.

Dec. 26 In this week the low was 83-3/8, just under old tops at 85.
A rally followed to 87. Made tops 2 weeks at 87, under old top.
Then reacted to 84-1/8.

**1909**

Feb. 20 In this week made top at 86-3/4, the 2nd LOWER TOP.
Declined and broke lows of 7 weeks past.

Feb. 23 Last low 80, down 8-3/8 points from the top of 88-3/8 in Nov. 1908 ... same number of points as reaction from August to Sept. 1908, making this a BUYING POINT. This was the 4th reaction in the Bull Market, but made higher bottom than low of Sep. 22, 1908, indicating main trend still up. A rally followed to 83-1/4; reacted to 81-1/2; then crossed 83-1/2, a SAFER BUYING POINT.

May Crossed top of 88-3/8 made in August, 1908, and did not react at all -- A sure sign of much higher prices. Next point to watch was old tops in 1906 and 1907 at 96-3/4 to 97-1/2.

Jul. Went thru all these tops with no reaction.

Aug. 14 In this week the high was 99-1/8; reacted 3 weeks to 96. Holding above old tops showed strength.

Oct. 2 High 100-1/2, under 1906 top at 103. FINAL TOP.

23 Low of reaction 95-7/8, same as last low in Sep. and at old tops.

Nov. 4 High 100-1/2, a DOUBLE TOP.
In the following week reacted to 98-1/8.

19 Then rallied to 100-1/2 on Nov. 19, THE 3rd AND LAST TOP. END OF BULL MARKET.

REVIEW: The advance from the low of 53 on Nov. 15, 1907 to the high of 100-1/2 on Nov. 19, 1909, was ... 47-1/2 points. During that time the greatest reaction was ... 8-1/2 points. The last reaction was ... 4-3/4 points. Therefore, when the average broke back over 5 points, it would be the first indication of a change in trend and when they broke back over 9 points, it would be a signal that the main trend had turned down.

## 4th BEAR MARKET

Dec. 2 Declined to 96-5/8, just above old bottoms and the 3rd time at those levels. A rally followed.

11 High 99, a 4th TOP LOWER ... a SIGNAL TO SELL.
Held for 3 weeks in less than one point range.
Then broke 4 weeks' bottoms.

**1910**

Jan. 15 In this week broke 96. This was 4th time at this level and went lower never rallying more than 4 points and rallies lasting only 10 days to 2 weeks ... a sign of great weakness in a Bear Market.

Jul. 26 Low 73-5/8. There was a sharp decline in the last week, but closed well up from the bottom and failed to go 5 points under 77, the last low of Sep. 1906 and less than 2 points under the low of 75-3/8 made in Mch. 1907. This was a PANIC BOTTOM and rule will be given in next lesson for proving why this was a SAFE POINT TO BUY.

END OF 1st SECTION OF BEAR MARKET

Aug. 6 In this week the range was 76 to 78 and in the following week the averages crossed 78, top of 2 previous weeks, indicating change in trend and a SAFER POINT TO BUY.
Next apply Space Rule. The greatest rally or secondary move up was 4-3/4 points and there was a 2nd rally in June, 1910 of 4-1/4 points. Therefore, to change trend the averages must advance more than 5 points from 73-5/8 or to above 79.

Aug. 13 During this week they crossed 79 and on Aug. 17 advanced to 81-1/2, under old bottoms and to tops of 3 previous weeks' levels.

Sept. 6 A SECONDARY REACTION followed to a low of 78-3/8, only 3-1/8 points' decline, became dull and narrow and made bottoms for 4 weeks near same level ... a sign of support and a SAFE BUYING POINT.

Oct. 1 Crossed tops of 5 previous weeks and later crossed 82, above old tops, indicating strong uptrend.

" 18 High 86. There were 2 old tops in June at 86-3/8 and 86-1/4.

" 29 In this week broke the low of the previous week.
Rallied one week to 85-3/4.
Then broke lows of 3 previous weeks.
Held for 2 weeks in a narrow range.

Dec. 6 Low of sharp decline to 79-5/8, just above secondary bottoms at 78-3/8 to 78-5/8, a higher bottom and support and buying level. This was 6-3/8 points' decline. Rallied to 28; reacted to 80-1/2, making higher bottom; then crossed 83, indicating higher.

**1911**

Feb. 4 High 86, same level as top of Oct. 18, 1910 - A DOUBLE TOP and SELLING LEVEL. Held 3 weeks in narrow range.

Mch. 4 Declined to 81-7/8.
A 2-weeks' rally followed to 84.

Apr. 22 Then declined to 81-1/4, making two bottoms near same level. Holding more than one point above low of Dec. 1910 indicated support and not yet ready to decline.

Jun. 19 High 87, making 5/8 to 1 point above old tops.
Market became very dull and narrow, holding for 6 weeks between 86-5/8 and 85-5/8, in one point range. This was a point to watch and wait for a definite change in trend as there were 3 tops at same level.

Aug. 5 In this week the SELLING SIGNAL came when the averages declined to 85, breaking under 9 weeks' bottoms ... a sign that the distribution on the side had been completed and that the downtrend would be resumed.
Note DISTRIBUTION ON SIDE after 1st Section of Bear Market. The averages held in a range of 6 to 7 points between 80 and 87 from Dec. 1910 to July 1911.
A sharp, severe decline followed, with volume of sales increasing.

Sep. 25 Low of Bear Market 73. This was a PANICKY DECLINE and the averages made a DOUBLE BOTTOM against low of 73-1/2 on July 26, 1910. BUYING POINT.
A quick rally followed.

5th BULL MARKET

Crossed 2 weeks' tops, a second indication that the trend was up

Oct. 14 High 78, under old bottoms of 1910, a selling level for a reaction. There had been only two weeks' rally so they were not yet ready to go further before a reaction.

27 Low 74-7/8 after two weeks' SECONDARY REACTION, a higher bottom and SAFER PLACE TO BUY.

Nov. 11 In this week the averages crossed 78-1/2, tops of 4 previous weeks, indicating main trend up and safe to buy at this level. Reactions were very small and prices worked higher.

**1912**

Mch. 22 Prices crossed 87, the old tops. This was the 4TH TIME AT SAME LEVEL (Refer to Rule) and there was no reaction from old tops, an indication of a strong uptrend. The advance continued with only small reaction.

Sep. 30 High 94-1/8, under old bottoms at 96 made in 1909 and failing to reach these old bottoms was a sign of weakness. END OF BULL MARKET.
The averages made 3 weeks' tops at 94, holding in one-point range.

Oct.19 During this week broke under the laws of 3 previous weeks, indicating MINOR TREND DOWN.

REVIEW: From 73 low in Sep. 1911 to 94-1/8 high in Sep. 1912 the averages had advanced 23-1/8 points. The greatest reaction had been 3-3/4 points. Therefore, they must react over 4 points to indicate a greater decline.

## 5th BEAR MARKET

Woodrow Wilson, a Democrat, was elected President.

Nov. 16 The averages declined to 89-1/2, down 4-5/8 points, a second indication of lower prices and a better SHORT SALE on any rally.
A weak rally followed, lasting two weeks. High 91-1/4.

Dec. 7 In this week broke 89 and a faster decline followed.

" 11 Low 85-1/4, just under 4 old tops and a point for a rally.
A slow advance followed lasting 3 weeks.

**1913**

Jan. 19 High 88-1/2, up only 3-1/4 points -- A weak SECONDARY RALLY.
The following week the averages broke 85, indicating a Bear Market and lower prices followed with weak rallies.

Jun. 11 Low 72-1/8, the THIRD BOTTOM at the same level and only one point under the low of October, 1911, a BUYING POINT with close stops.
The greatest rally from 94 to 72-1/8 (a decline of 21-7/8 points) was 3-1/4 points. Therefore a rally from 72-1/8 of 4 points or more would indicate that the trend was turning up.

21 Rallied to 75-3/4.
Held for three weeks on the side in a range from 75-3/4 to 74-5/8, a narrow but no lower bottom.

Jul. 9 In this week crossed 76, above 5 weeks' tops and up more than 4 points -- a second indication of change in trend.

Sep. 12 High 83-1/2. Note two weeks' tops at 83-3/4 and 83-1/2 in February, 1913, which was the last rally before a big decline started. Prices held two weeks on the side in a narrow range; then broke under 3 weeks' lows-- MINOR TREND DOWN.

**1913**

Dec. 16 Low 75-1/4, back to last low of July, 1913, and at 5 old weekly tops, support level for a rally.
The averages made bottoms for six weeks between 76 and 75-1/4 showing support and a PLACE TO BUY.

" 27 Crossed 78, tops of 7 previous weeks A SAFER POINT TO BUY

**1914**

Feb. 3 High 83-1/8, the SECOND TOP at this level.
Prices hold 3 weeks in 5/8-point range; then broke under 3 weeks' low indicating lower.

Mch. 6 Low 81-1/8, a very narrow, dull market.

" 20 High 83-1/2, THIRD TOP at same level.
Was dull and narrow for 3 weeks in range of 1-1/2 points.
Then broke under lows of 7 weeks, a definite indication of lower prices.

Apr. 25 Low 77, just above old tops of Nov. and Dec. 1913.
A slow rally followed.

Jun. 10 High 81-7/8, just under old bottoms.

" 25 Low 79-1/4, slow and narrow.

Jul. 8 High 81-3/4, last high and 4TH TOP at lower level -- a sure SELLING SIGNAL and a time to go short.

28 Broke bottom at 78, a definite signal for lower prices.
The market was declining on heavy volume of sales and WAR NEWS was causing heavy selling from Europe.

30 The averages broke 75, the low of Dec. 1913 and the same day broke triple bottoms at 73-1/2, 73, and 72-1/8, making the 4th time at this level and closing under 72 was a definite sign for much lower prices.

" 31 STOCK EXCHANGE CLOSED ON ACCOUNT OF WAR.

Dec. 12 Exchange opened and the averages started at 64-3/8.
In 1907 the low was 53 and in 1898 and 1900 the lows were made at 53 so these old bottoms should be the next support and buying points.

Dec. 24 Low 53-1/8 ... END OF BEAR MARKET.

REVIEW: From the last high at 94-1/8 on Sep. 30, 1912, to the low of 53-1/8 on Dec. 24, 1914 ... a decline of 41 points ... the greatest rally was from 72-1/8 to 83-3/8 or 11-1/4 points. Therefore, when the averages advance above 64-1/2, they will indicate strong uptrend.

**1915**

## 6th BULL MARKET

Jan. 23 High 58-1/2, only 5-3/8 point rally, not enough to show big move up was ready. Then SECONDARY REACTION AFTER PANIC ... SAFER TO BUY.

Feb. 24 Low 54-1/4, a higher bottom by more than one point and a good buying level.

Mch. 27 This week the averages crossed 58-1/2, top of first rally ... a second signal that main trend was up and a Bull Market under way: SAFEST BUYING POINT.

Apr. 10 The averages crossed 64-1/2 ... the THIRD DEFINITE INDICATION of main trend up and higher prices. This was a POINT TO BUY more stocks.

" 30 The market advanced fast and made high at 71-3/4, under 4 old bottoms at 71-1/2 to 73-1/2 ... SELLING LEVEL.

May Prices held one week between 70 and 71-3/4, above tops of two previous weeks. Then broke fast on U-Boat scare.

" 14 Low 60-3/8, but only two weeks' decline and failed to reach top at 58-1/2 ... a sign of good support. This was a natural reaction in a Bull Market ... 11-point decline and SAFE TO BUY. Then the advance was resumed. There were two weeks' tops at 65-1/2. When these were crossed prices moved up faster.

Jun. 22 High 71-7/8, same top as April and under old bottoms. It was only natural that some selling and resistance would be met.
A two weeks' reaction followed to 67-7/8, down only 4 points.

Jul. 24 During this week the averages crossed 72 on big volume and very active. This was the place to buy more stocks.
The advance continued with reactions of only 3 to 5 points.

Sep. 20 The averages crossed old tops at 81-3/4 to 83-1/2 and did not react, proving STRONG UPTREND. The next old tops were 91 to 94.

Oct. 2 High 92.

" 6 Prices reacted to 88-1/4, a small reaction; then went thru 94, the top of Sep. 1912. The next tops were at 100-1/2, the high of 1909.

Dec. 27 High 99-1/8, just under 1909 tops ... a SELLING LEVEL as prices were up 47 points with only one 11-point reaction.
The advance slowed down and in 4 weeks there was a gain of only one point ... indicating good selling.

**1916**

Jan. 8 Prices broke under lows of 3 previous weeks ... a sign that the MINOR TREND had turned DOWN.

31 Low 90-5/8, not yet down over 11 points, to overbalance the greatest reaction.

Feb. 11 Rallied to 96-1/8, a lower top and selling level.

Mch. 2 Low 90-1/8, same as Jan. 31 low. The averages would have to break this level to indicate lower. A rally followed.

" 16 High 96, slightly lower than Feb. 11 top ... A SELLING LEVEL.

Apr. 22 Low 85, just above old tops ... a BUYING LEVEL as this was a sharp panic, decline lasting only 3 weeks from last top at 94-1/2 in early April.
A quick rally followed.

Jun. 12 High 93-5/8, under old bottoms and at April top ... A SELLING LEVEL.

Jul. 1 This week made low at 87-5/8. A rally of one week followed.

" 13 Low 86-1/2, a higher bottom than April and above old tops, A BUYING POINT. A rally to 89-3/4 followed. Then reacted to 88.
Held for 3 weeks with bottom at 88, showing good support.
Then crossed tops at 90-1/2, indicating higher.

Sep. 21 Averages crossed tops at 96 and went thru 1915 top at 99-1/8; 1909 top at 100-1/2; also thru 103, the high of 1906 ... STRONG SIGNALS FOR HIGHER PRICES.

Oct. 5 High 104-1/8...new high by 1-1/8 points and a signal for higher prices.

" 14 Reacted to 99, the old top of Dec. 1915, a BUYING LEVEL as this was only a 5-point reaction and the greatest reactions from 1914 lows were 11 and 15 points. This was a 9-points' reaction and in two weeks prices crossed the top of 104, showing strong uptrend.
You now must follow rules to determine how far averages can go into new high ground. The rules say 7, 10, 15, 20, or 24 points but the safest

rule says, wait until minor trend turns by breaking under previous **weekly bottom.**

Nov. 21 High 110-1/8. This was 7-1/8 points higher than old top of 1906 and 10 **points above** 1909 top.
The averages made two weeks' tops at 110-1/8. **FINAL TOP.**

Dec. 2 Then broke under two weeks' lows, turning minor trend down and ending **Bull Market.**

REVIEW: The ending of this 6th Bull Market was the culmination of the greatest advance in the Industrials up to that time ... up 57 points in 23 months...with the greatest reaction 14 points and the last reaction 7 points. Therefore, a decline of 7 points or more would be the first signal for lower prices, and breaking 88, the last reaction point, would be a definite signal for a Bear Market to start.

## 6th BEAR MARKET

During December a wide-open break occurred on heavy scale, the averages breaking 99 and indicating SAFE SHORT SALES.

Dec. 21 Low 90-1/8, down 20 points in 4 weeks' time and at old tops . . BUYING LEVEL. A rally was due and a sharp advance followed.

**1917**

SECONDARY RALLY AFTER TREND TURNED DOWN:

Jan. 3 High 99-1/8, under old bottoms and at old tops ... a SELLING LEVEL on 9-point rally, the first secondary rally ... safe short sales. DISTRIBUTION ON SIDE after trend turned down ... Prices held for 3 weeks in a narrow range from 97-7/8 to 95.

Feb. 2 Prices broke fast on U-BOAT SCARE and fear that the United States would enter the World War. Low 87, down 23 points from 110 top and 12 points from the last top. Note 85, the low of April, 1916, and 86-1/2, the low of July, 1916, where last advance started, making 87 to 85 a support or BUYING LEVEL, especially as this was a panicky decline, with prices breaking 10 to 25 points in two days. Remember our rule, always buy in panics for a quick rally. The rally followed with reactions of only 4 to 5 points.

Mch. 20 High 98-1/4, just under old bottoms and tops .... A SELLING LEVEL.

May 9 Low 89-1/8, same level as Dec. 1916 ... a point for a rally.

Jun. 9 High 99, the THIRD TOP at the SAME LEVEL and a SAFE POINT TO GO SHORT as market became dull on this rally. Held 3 weeks in a narrow range. Then broke under 3 weeks' bottoms and went lower.

Jul. 19 Low 90-1/2, old bottom. A small rally followed.

Aug. 6 Last rally. High 93-7/8. Held narrow for 4 weeks.
Then broke under 5 weeks' lows.

Sep. 12 BROKE OLD BOTTOMS at 87 and 85, indicating a very weak market and much lower prices. Rallies were small, only 3 to 5 points. A panicky decline followed.

Nov. 8 Low 68-5/8. Note last bottom at 67-7/8 in July, 1915. A rally followed.

" 23 High 74-1/4, a 5-5/8 point rally in two weeks.
Then a sharp decline of 4 weeks, ending in a weak, panicky market.

19 Low 66, just 2-1/2 points under November low and 1-7/8 points under last low of July, 1915, making 66 a BUYING LEVEL. 6th BEAR MARKET ENDED

REVIEW: The greatest rally in the 6th Bear Market from the high of 110-1/8 in November, 1916 to the low of 66 in December, 1917 was 12 points. The last rally was 5-5/8 points. Therefore, the first indication of higher prices would be a rally of 6 points or more and the signal for a change in the main trend would be a rally of over 12 points.

## 7th BULL MARKET

Dec. 29 The advance started, crossing the top of the previous week and giving the FIRST MINOR INDICATION of a change in trend. The advance was rapid, reaching 72-1/2 the first week. There were old bottoms and old tops around 72 but the following week the advance went right thru these old resistance levels, showing great strength.

**1918**

Jan. 2 The averages advanced to 76-5/8, up 10 points from the low. At this level they were UNDER THE OLD BOTTOMS of Dec. 1913 and up to the top of the last rally before the final decline started. Then a reaction of two weeks occurred.

15 Declined to 73-3/8. This was a secondary reaction and prices held well above the old tops at 72, showing great strength. The fact that after a 3 weeks' sharp rally of more than 10 points, the market only reacted 2 weeks and only lost 3 points, showed good support and strength, making this a SAFE POINT TO BUY on a SECONDARY REACTION.
The advance was resumed and the averages crossed 78, up 12 points from the low level and exceeding the greatest rally in the bear market, a definite indication that the main trend had turned up. Also, crossing the previous high, indicated the MAIN TREND UP.

Feb. 19 The averages advanced to 82. This was up to old tops and old bottoms, as you can see on the chart, and was a natural point for a reaction. During the week that prices reached top, the range was 82 and 80-1/2, ... 1-1/2 point range. The following week, prices broke back under the low of the previous week, indicating the first change in the minor trend and a signal for a reaction.

Apr. 11 The averages declined to 75-1/2, a reaction of 6-1/2 points, about the average reaction in bull markets. Note that there were 3 weeks' tops at 76. Therefore, this was a logical support and BUYING POINT. The market held around these bottoms for 4 weeks, showing good support.

May 15 Advanced above the tops of 3 previous weeks; crossed the old top at 82 and advanced to 84. This was again under old bottoms and a point where a MINOR REACTION could take place.

Jun. 1 The averages reacted to 78, down 6 points. Then held in a narrow trading range for several weeks.

Sep. 3 Advanced to 83-7/8, just under the old top. A modern reaction followed.

" 11 The averages were down to 80-1/2, holding well above the last low level of June 1. The fact that this reaction was not as great as the previous reaction which was 7 points, this one being only 6 .. was still an indication that the main trend was up and that stocks were still SAFE TO BUY.

Oct. 18 The advance was resumed and the top at 84 crossed. High was 89. Note old bottoms around 87 to 90. The next week the market held in a narrow trading range. The second week it broke the bottom of two previous weeks and reacted to 84, off 5 points, the FIRST INDICATION that the minor trend was changing to the down side. Then followed a secondary rally.

Nov. 9 The averages reached 88, one point under the previous high. Failing to reach the old top, after the minor trend had turned down, was a SELLING SIGNAL on the SECONDARY RALLY.

25 The averages broke under the bottom of the first reaction at 84, indicating a further decline, and reached 79-7/8. Then followed a 2 weeks' rally to 84-1/2, a THIRD LOWER TOP, just under the first old bottom, a SELLING LEVEL.

**1919**

Feb. 8 The market gradually worked lower but narrowed down into a trading range of about 2 points and the averages reached a low of 79-1/8. Note OLD TOPS AROUND THIS LEVEL and the last weekly bottom from which the advance started, was around 77-1/2. Therefore, this bottom was higher than the previous bottom and only 3/8 point under the low of November, 1918, ... an indication of support. The market held for 4 weeks between 81-3/4 and 79-1/8.

22 The averages crossed the tops of 4 weeks at 82 .., a signal for higher prices and a SAFE POINT TO BUY.

Mch. Reached old top of 89 and only reacted a little over 2 points, showing great strength.

Apr. Crossed the last old top at 89 and advanced right on up with only minor reactions.

Jul. 14 The averages reached high of 112-1/4. This was 2 points into new high ground, crossing the old top of Nov. 1916, and a SIGNAL FOR HIGHER PRICES later.

19 The range this week was 110-1/4 to 112-1/4, a very narrow range at the top after a big advance. The following week the averages broke back under 110 and broke the bottoms of two previous weeks, A SIGNAL that the minor trend was turning down FOR A REACTION. The fact that the market had advanced from 79-1/8 to 112-1/4 without ever having a 5-point reaction was an indication that a temporary reaction was in order.

Aug. 20 A sharp, quick decline followed, lasting a little over 4 weeks, making bottom at 98-1/2. This was down to old tops and a natural support level just under 100. The fact that the reaction only ran 4 weeks, then the advance was resumed, was an indication that it was still a bull market and that prices were going higher. A SAFE PLACE TO BUY on this reaction would have been after the high of the last week's decline, 100-3/4, was crossed.

Oct. Prices advanced right on up with nothing more than 3 to 4 point reactions, crossing the old high at 112 in October.

Nov. 3 Advanced to 119-5/8, FINAL HIGH. This was 9-1/2 points above the old high of 1916 and 7 points above the high of July 14, 1919. Remember, our rule says that prices can advance 7 to 10 points into new territory and then react.

COMPARISON: In 1916, after the old high of 103 was crossed, the averages advanced to 110 or 7 points into new high ground. In 1919, the averages went 9-1/2 points into new high territory before the Bull Market ended and the trend turned down. During this last run in 1919 the volume was very heavy in the last 60 days. Everybody was bullish and buying stocks and talking about the greatest boom in history and higher prices than had ever been seen, but the end came and top was reached. A sharp decline followed, wiping out people who had overtraded on margin and had bought on hope instead of facing facts and following the trend.

REVIEW: In the 7th Bull Market, which started at 66 low in December, 1917, and culminated at 119-5/8 on November 3, 1919, the greatest reaction was from 89 to 79-1/8, or 9-7/8 points, and the last reaction before the end of the bull campaign was from 112-1/4 to 98-1/2, a decline of 11-3/4 points. Therefore, the signals to watch for a definite indication that a bear market was starting, would be a decline of more than 12 points or the breaking of the last low at 98-1/2 or the breaking of the low of the first sharp decline after final top.

## 7th BEAR MARKET

Nov. The lows of the last 3 weeks were 114-7/8 to 115-1/2.

Dec. 13 A sharp, severe decline followed, with prices breaking under these last 3 weeks' bottoms, showing a definite change in the MINOR TREND to the DOWN side.

22 Low 103-1/2, down 16 points from the high and exceeding the greatest reaction in a bull market, which was 11-3/4 points. This was a definite signal that the trend had turned down and that prices would go lower but the market had not yet had the secondary rally, which always occurs after the first sharp decline. The averages held for five weeks, making bottoms around 104 to 103-1/2. This was above the old top levels at 103 and a natural point for support. The fact that bottoms were made for five weeks at this level showed that there was good support and this was a point to COVER SHORTS AND BUY and wait for a secondary rally to sell on again.

1920

Jan. 3 The SECONDARY RALLY occurred, reaching high of 109-7/8, a rally of a little over 6 points and up under the old top level of 1916, SELLING LEVEL. There was heavy selling on this rally and prices failed to hold. The second week, the range was 108-3/4 to 106-1/2 and the following week prices broke the lows of the previous week and also broke under five weeks' bottoms around 103-1/2 ... a definite indication that the main trend had turned down because the bottom of the secondary reaction had been broken. The decline continued, the averages reaching 102; then rallied to 104-1/2, just under the old bottom, holding dull and narrow for one week.

Feb. 7 Heavy selling broke out and a sharp, severe decline followed, the averages breaking 98-1/2, the last bottom made in August 1919, another confirmation that the MAIN TREND was DOWN and that a bear market was under way. The decline was swift and severe with very small rallies; in fact, it was a panicky decline.

Feb. 25 Low 90. This was a support and BUYING LEVEL against old top of October, 1918 and February, 1920. There were two weeks' bottoms around this level, one at 90-1/2 during the week ending February 14 and the last bottom at 90, showing that there was support around this level and a point to buy.

Mch. 6 The averages crossed the top of the previous week, the THIRD SIGNAL that the minor trend was turning up. The greatest rally on the way down was 6 points. Therefore, when the averages advanced more than 6 points, they indicated a further rally.

" 13 The averages crossed 98 and failed to halt at the old bottoms around 99.

Apr. 8 Advanced to 105-5/8, just 2 points under the series of old bottoms where the main trend turned down, making this a SAFE SELLING LEVEL on an advance of 15 points after the market had declined 30 points. After 2 weeks at the top in a narrow trading range; the market started to break.

24 Broke back under the bottoms of the past five weeks, indicating that the MAIN TREND had again turned DOWN. A sharp decline followed with very small rallies.

May 19 Low 87-3/8, just 2-5/8 points under the low of February and down to a series of old tops and bottoms from which a moderate rally could occur. The market held for two weeks, making two bottoms just under 88; then the rally followed.

Jul. 8 High 94-1/2, a rally of 7 points, which is a fair-sized rally in a weak, bear market. During the last week, the range was 94-1/2 to 93 ... 1-1/2 point range. SELLING LEVEL. The following week the averages broke back under the low of this week and broke the lows of the 3 previous weeks, indicating that the main trend would continue down. All support levels were broken.

Aug. 10 The averages reached 83-1/4. A rally followed to 89-7/8 ... another rally of less than 7 points, practically the same as the last rally and a point at which to again SELL SHORT. The decline continued with only rallies of 2 to 3 points in the averages.

Nov. 19 Low 73-1/8.

Dec. 4 Top of rally 77-5/8 ... 4-1/2 point rally. Remember, the rule is that the lower prices get in a bear market, the smaller the rallies are because the market is getting weaker all the time, and is a safer short sale.

21 Low 66-3/4. BUYING LEVEL. This was down near the old low of 1917, which was 66, and the point to watch for support and a rally. Remember, the rule is, buy against old bottom and protect with a stop loss order. The last three weeks of the decline ran from 77-1/2 to 66-3/4. The last week of the decline was 69-5/8 to 66-3/4.

The following week the averages crossed the top of the previous week and advanced to 71-7/8, indicating a change in the minor trend, but a rally of 7 points or more, which would exceed the past two rallies, would indicate a further advance. This was confirmed by the averages advancing above 75.

1921

Jan. 3 The averages advanced to 76-1/2, just under old bottoms and a point from which there should be a reaction.

Jan. 11 The averages reacted to 72-3/8. Holding one point above the low of Nov. 1920, was an indication of support and a point at which to BUY FOR A RALLY, protected with stop loss order under the old bottom. The advance was resumed and the previous minor tops were crossed.

Feb. 16 Reached 77-1/4, under the old bottom, where a minor reaction was indicated.

Mch. 11 Low 72-1/4. This was down to OLD BOTTOM LEVELS AND OLD TOP, a natural support point. A slow advance followed.

May 5 High 80 market very dull and narrow on this advance. Note that 80 was under a series of old bottoms which occurred between September, 1918 and February, 1919, making this a natural SELLING LEVEL, where you should go short, especially as the market became dull and narrow. The averages were up 13-1/4 points, which was an average rally in a bear market.

14 The averages broke back under the lows of the previous weeks' bottoms, showing that the MINOR TREND was again turning DOWN. From this level the decline continued with very small rallies.

Jun. 20 Low 64-7/8. This was one point under the low of Dec. 1917; and 2 points under the low of Dec. 1920, a point to watch for support and resistance. A rally followed. This was a slow, feeble advance.

Aug. 2 High 70, a 5-point rally in 5 weeks, not enough to indicate a change in the main trend. The following week, prices broke under the lows of the past 5 weeks.

24 Low 64, 2 points under the low of Dec. 1917 and back to the lows of the weekly bottoms where the advance started in May, 1915, but the fact that the averages failed to break 3 points under the lows of 1917, where the bear market ended at that time, was an indication of support and a BUYING POINT, as the volume of sales ran very low, indicating that liquidation had run its course. But the safest and best indication for buying would be to wait until the market showed that it could rally by crossing the tops of previous weeks.

REVIEW: From the top at 119-6/8 on November 3, 1919, to the low of 64 on August 24, 1921, the greatest rally in the 7th Bear Market was 15 points and the last rally to May, 1921, was 13 points. Therefore, the first indication of a greater advance and a change in the main trend would be when the averages advance more than 13 to 15 points.

## 8th BULL MARKET

Sep. 3 The averages crossed 66, the highs of the two previous weeks, making this a SAFER PLACE TO BUY.

10 Crossed 70, the top of the last rally, a further confirmation of higher prices, making the market a safer purchase on reactions. The averages reached 71-7/8. This was an old bottom and old top level and resistance point for a reaction, but the reaction was very small.

Oct. 17 Low 69-1/2. The averages held for 6 weeks between 71-5/8 and 69-1/2, indicating that there was good buying just above or around the old top at 70, and when the averages made bottom a SECOND TIME, 4 weeks later, at 69-1/2, it was a SAFE POINT TO BUY.

**1921** 8th BULL MARKET (Continued)

Oct. 29 The safest and best point was when the main trend turned up by crossing 72. This was confirmation of MAIN TREND UP and showed that accumulation had been completed; that liquidation was over.

Dec. 15 The averages crossed 80, the last top of May 1921, another definite indication of a Bull Market and higher prices. The advance continued and reactions were very small.

**1922**

Sep. 11 The averages made 102, the high of April, 1920. From this level there was 2 weeks' reaction to 96-1/4. Holding above 3 weeks' bottoms where last advance started, indicated good support and a BUYING LEVEL for higher prices.

Oct. 14 High 103-1/2. Note the last high in April, 1920, was 105-1/2. Therefore, the averages were reaching a level from which a reaction could take place, especially as they had advanced from 64 to 103-1/2 without any important reaction. The market held in a narrow range for two weeks, then the third week broke the low of the two previous weeks, indicating temporary top and a reaction to follow. The decline continued and after the averages held for one week with a moderate raally, the lows at 96 were broken.

Nov. 27 Low 92, down 11-1/2 points from the top, a natural reaction in a Bull Market. There was a series of old tops and bottoms around 92, a support and BUYING POINT, especially as the reaction had run 7 weeks from the top, which is about the average reaction in a bull market when the decline exceeds 4 weeks. However, the SAFEST POINT TO BUY would have been when the averages crossed 96, three weeks' tops, which they did in the week ending Dec. 9, 1922. The advance continued with very small reaction.

**1923**

Mch. 20 High 105-3/8, at the old top of April, 1920. SELLING LEVEL. The market gave a definite indication that there was heavy selling at this level because for 3 consecutive weeks the high was around the same level and for 2 weeks the low was around 103-7/8.

24 Broke under 2 weeks' bottoms ... a signal for a bigger reaction and a point to sell out long stocks and GO SHORT.

REVIEW: From the low of 64 on August 24, 1921, to the high of 105-3/8 on March, 1923, the greatest reaction in the 8th Bull Market had been 11-1/2 points. Therefore, a decline of 12 points or more from the high would indicate main trend down but breaking the last series of four weeks' bottoms around 97 would be the first definite indication that the main trend had turned down and that the Bull Market had ended for the present.

## 8th BEAR MARKET

May 21 Low 93, holding one point above the low of Dec. 1922, from which the last run in the Bull Market occurred.

May 29 Rallied to 97-5/8, under the old bottom. A SELLING LEVEL. The decline continued and broke 92, the low of Dec. 1922, another definite confirmation that this was a bear market and going lower. The trend continued down.

Jul. 12 Low 87-5/8, old top and bottom levels, from which a rally could occur.

" 20 High 91-3/4, just under the two previous bottoms and a SELLING LEVEL. Market held for two weeks, then declined.

31 Reached 87, holding slightly under the bottom of July 12, which INDICATED A RALLY, especially as the market became very dull and narrow. When it crossed the top of the previous week at 88-1/2, it indicated a moderate further rally.

Aug. 29 High 93-3/4, which was under the old bottom level and just above the last rally. The market held for two weeks in a range of 1-1/2 points. SELLING LEVEL.

Sep. 15. Declined rapidly, breaking back under the four weeks' bottoms and indicating that the minor trend had again turned down.

Oct. 27 Low 85-3/4, just one point under the low of July 30 and down to a line of old bottoms and tops in previous campaigns. The market was very dull and narrow here but the volume was exceedingly small, indicating that temporarily, at least, liquidation had run its course and the market was making bottom and should be bought for a rally, especially as this was really a DOUBLE BOTTOM.

REVIEW: The greatest rally in the 8th Bear Market from the top at 105-3/8 on March 20, 1923 to the low at 85-3/4 on Oct. 27, 1923 was 6-1/2 points, from 87 to 93. Therefore, when the averages could advance more than 6-1/2 points, it would be an indication that the main trend was up and time for a Bull Market to start.

## 9th AND GREATEST BULL MARKET

This was really a continuation of the Bull Market that began in August, 1921, as the reaction from the top in 1923 was 20 points, which would only be considered a natural reaction and a resting point or accumulation period for the big Bull Market to follow.

Nov. 3 The SAFEST PLACE TO BUY would have been around 88-1/2 during the week ending Nov. 3 after the market had crossed the highs of 3 previous weeks. The advance continued and later crossed the tops at 93 to 93-1/2, indicating that the main trend was up. When prices got above 94, it would have been a still safer place to buy or pyramid, if you had already bought at lower levels.

1924

Feb. 6 High 101-3/8. This was under a series of 4 weeks' bottoms, where the market broke away from after the trend turned down from 105-1/2 ... a natural point or SELLING LEVEL for a reaction. The range at the top for the week ending Feb. 9, was very narrow, only about a point. A sharp decline followed, breaking the bottoms of the three previous weeks, indicating that the minor trend had again turned down. In the latter part of February the averages declined to 95-3/8.

March There was a SECONDARY RALLY to 98-3/4. This was a very feeble rally, requiring 3 weeks to go up a little over 2 points ... A SAFE RALLY TO SELL ON. But a safer time to sell was when the averages broke 96, under 3 weeks' bottoms. The trend continued down with very small rallies.

May 20 Low, 88-3/8. This was 2-1/2 points above the low of Nov. 1923 and 1-1/2 points above the low of July, 1923, making this a TRIPLE BOTTOM and a SAFE PLACE TO BUY, especially as the volume of sales was very small and the market holding for several weeks in a narrow trading range, indicating that liquidation had run its course and that there was not enough selling to break the previous low levels. But a safe rule to follow would be to wait until the market had definitely proved its strong position by crossing the tops of previous weeks. The market held for three weeks between 88-3/8 and 90-1/2. Then crossed 3 weeks' tops.

Jul. 14 During this week crossed other tops at 92-3/8, indicating a definite change in the trend to the upside and a SAFE POINT TO BUY as accumulation had taken place between 90 and 86.

Aug. 20 High 105-1/2, the same top as March, 1923, and same top as April 1920. The THIRD TIME at this level made it a natural SELLING LEVEL for at least a temporary reaction. During the second week the averages broke under the previous week and declined to 102-7/8.

Sep. 6 This week a rally followed.

" 24 High 104-5/8. Failing to reach the old top by 1 point and only a two weeks' rally indicated weakness. SELLING LEVEL - lower top.

Oct. 14 Low 99-1/8, final and last low before the big advance. SELLING LEVEL. This was down to old bottom and top level and a natural resistance point and a 6-point reaction in about 7 weeks, the average time for a reaction in a bull market after it exceeds 3 weeks and the average number of points for stocks at these levels.

Nov. 3 The safe point at which to buy would be to wait until after the market confirmed that it had made bottom, which it did promptly, by crossing the tops of the two previous weeks, during the week ending Nov. 3, indicating higher prices. The advance was rapid. The averages crossed the triple top at 105, making the FOURTH TIME AT THIS LEVEL ... a definite indication of a BULL MARKET and higher prices. The next point to watch was the high in history ... the old top of November 1919. The averages went right on thru the old top of 119-5/8 without a reaction, indicating a very strong market.

1925

Jan. 22 High 123-5/8, a new high point, and there had been no reaction of as much as 5 points since the averages started up from just above 88 in May 1924.

Feb. 16 The averages reacted to 118, just under the old top, and the advance was resumed.

Mch. 6 High 125-5/8.

" 30 Low 115, a reaction of 10 points and 4-5/8 points under the old top of 119-5/8. Our rule says that a reaction under an old top should never be greater than 5 points if the main trend is to continue up. This reaction was only 24 days, a little over three weeks, which is a natural reaction in a Bull Market, and this would have been the point at which TO BUY stocks, or you could have waited until the tops of the previous weeks were crossed, or until the averages advanced above the old top of 120 again, and then bought. They promptly advanced and crossed the high of 125-5/8 reached on March 6, and continued right on up with only small reactions.

Nov. 6 High 159. Market was very active and moved rapidly at this level.
" 10 The averages reacted to 151.
" 13 High 157-3/4. Lower top ... SELL.
" 24 Low 148-1/4, less than a 3 weeks' reaction and 11 points on averages, a natural reaction in a Bull Market. BUYING LEVEL.

1926

Feb. 11 High 162-3/8, another new high. Here the market held for several weeks, moving up and down. The fact that the averages could not go 5 points above the top of November 6, indicated that some distribution was taking place and the market making top for a reaction. SELLING LEVEL. You should have sold, especially as soon as the weekly bottom of previous week was broken. The market declined fast.
Mch. 30 Just one year from where the advance started at 115, the averages reached low of the reaction at 135-1/4, down 27 points from the top and the greatest reaction. The decline lasted only a little over 6 weeks, which is a natural reaction in a big Bull Market.
Apr. 6 The market rallied to 142-3/8.
" 16 A reaction to 136-1/4, higher bottom, BUYING LEVEL.
" 24 A rally to 144-7/8.
May 19 A reaction to 137-1/8, making the THIRD HIGHER BOTTOM between March 30 and May 19, indicating good support at these levels. This third higher bottom was a SAFE PLACE TO BUY. However, a safer place to buy would be to wait until after the top of April 24 was crossed, showing a definite change to the upside. The market advanced rapidly, crossing all tops of previous weeks.
Aug. 9 High 166-1/8.
" 11 Low 161-5/8.
" 14 High 166-5/8, a DOUBLE TOP against the previous top. SELLING LEVEL.
" 25 Low of reaction, 160-1/2.
Sep. 7 High 166, a THIRD TOP slightly lower ... a SELLING INDICATION, especially as the market had made no gains since August 9. A definite change in the minor trend was made when it broke the low of August 26. The market declined fast.
Oct. 19 Low 145-5/8, down a little over 20 points but not as much reaction as from February 11 to March 30, and holding the previous weekly bottom ... another six weeks' reaction ... an average reaction in a Bull Market. BUYING LEVEL. You should watch for the resumption of the main trend.
Dec. 18 High 161. This was up to the old top levels and bottom levels where a reaction could take place. SELLING LEVEL.

1927

Jan. 25 Low 152-3/4, a DOUBLE BOTTOM, the same low as Nov. 19th and a PLACE TO BUY with stop loss order, especially as weekly tops had been crossed on the upside.
Feb. 28 High 161-7/8.
Mch. 7 Low 158-5/8.

**1927** — 9th BULL MARKET (Continued)

Mch. 17 High 161-3/4, three times at the same level. SELLING LEVEL.

" 28 Low 158-1/2, a DOUBLE BOTTOM. BUYING LEVEL. Two times at the same level and no weekly bottoms broken. The main trend was still up. A SAFE PLACE TO BUY would be when the averages cross 162, getting above three tops. The market started moving up fast at the end of March.

Apr. 22 Reached a high of 167-3/8, getting above all previous tops, a signal for higher prices.

" 28 Low 163-1/2, down to old top levels and a natural BUYING POINT. The advance was resumed on big volume and a very active market.

May 31 High 172-7/8.

June 3 A reaction to 169-5/8.

" 6 High 171-1/8, a slightly LOWER TOP.

" 14 Low 167-0/8.

" 16 High 170-1/4, making the THIRD SLIGHTLY LOWER TOP, an indication for a reaction. SELLING LEVEL.

27 Low 165-3/4, down 7 points from the high of May 31st, a 4 weeks' reaction ... just under the top of April 22nd and still above the low of April 30th ... A BUYING INDICATION.

Jul. 9 A safer rule to follow would be to wait until the trend turned up, which it did this week, crossing the top of 3 previous weeks. Then advanced right on thru, crossing all tops.

Aug. 2 High 185-1/2, low 182-5/8 the same week; closed at the low and at practically the same level as the previous week. SELLING LEVEL ... Advancing to a new high and closing on the bottom was an indication of a further reaction. To play safe, you should have sold out long stocks and waited.

12 Low 177-1/8, an 8-point reaction, only a natural reaction. One week's reaction, not declining to old tops. The following week, the averages crossed the tops of the previous week. BUYING LEVEL. Advanced to the level of August 2 and closed strong, at the top, the highest closing in history up to that time and an indication of higher prices. The following week stocks advanced to new high levels.

Sep. 7 High 197-3/4. Remember the rule: Watch selling at all even levels, that is, 100, 200, 300, etc. SELLING LEVEL.

" 12 Reacted to 194.

Oct. 3 Made extreme high at 199-7/8, just under 200 ... SAFER SELLING LEVEL. Looking back, you will find 3 bottoms, in fact, 4 weekly bottoms around 194; therefore, this would be a level to watch. If you had not sold out around 200, where a change in trend was indicated, then you would sell when the market broke back under 3 weeks' bottoms, after an advance from 165 to 200, as this would be an indication for a reaction.

18 After opening at high levels, the market broke 194 this week and declined to 190, indicating LOWER PRICES. A rapid decline followed.

29 Low 179-1/2, a decline of 20 points from the top, not as great as the decline from Feb. 11 to Mch. 30, 1926, which was 27 points. This was another 3 weeks' reaction. A natural reaction in a Bull Market and a BUYING LEVEL, but it would be safer to wait until the averages crossed the top of the previous weeks. There was a narrow week on the side: High 185-1/4, low 181. The following week the bottom was higher, 181-1/2, and the averages crossed the top at 185-1/2. The advance continued.

1927

Nov. 30 High 198-7/8, just under old tops and still under 200...SELLING LEVEL.

Dec. 8 Low 193-1/8, a 5-point reaction. Did not break 1 point under the bottom of the previous week. BUYING LEVEL.

1928

Jan. 3 High 203-3/8. Crossing 200 was a SIGNAL FOR MUCH HIGHER PRICES.

" 16 Low 194-1/8, a 9-point reaction, only a natural reaction of 15 days and holding above the low of Dec. 8 ... BUYING LEVEL.

" 24 Advanced to 201.

Feb. 3 Low 196-3/8, the SECOND HIGHER BOTTOM and a level at which to BUY and protect with a stop loss order.

" 9 High 199-3/8.

" 20 Last low 191-3/8, breaking 2 points under the low of Dec. 8. With the market at these high levels, this was not enough to indicate lower prices. It should break at least 3 points under the previous lows to show a definite change in trend. The market remained for 3 weeks in a narrow trading range. In the second week the extreme low was 191-3/8 and the high 194-1/4, closing at the top, an indication of higher prices. You would buy and protect with stop loss orders under the old bottoms. The advance was resumed and prices went thru the 200 level and crossed the old top of Jan. 3 at 203-3/8, a DEFINITE INDICATION OF HIGHER PICES.

May 14 High 220-7/8. Opened at the top this week and closed near the bottom, closing under the low of previous week ... the FIRST SIGNAL OF TOP for reaction.

" 22 Declined to 211-3/4.

" 25 Advanced to 217-3/4, a LOWER TOP.

" 28 Declined to 214, holding above the bottom of the first reaction.

Jun. 2 High 220-3/4, a DOUBLE TOP. SELLING LEVEL. Closed at the high on Saturday but opened down about 2 points on Monday morning, an indication that there was good selling at the top. This was the third top around this level and three consecutive weeks' selling had been met, therefore a reaction was indicated, but a definite change in the minor trend came when the averages broke 214, the low of the previous week.

12 Low 202-5/8, down from the old top of Jan. 3, still holding above the 200 level. BUYING LEVEL. This nearly always happens after prices cross high levels at figures like 200; and they stay above the level until the Bull Campaign is completed.

23 This was a narrow week: High 204-1/4, low 202, slightly lower than June 12. After a 3 weeks' sharp decline, this narrow range at the bottom indicated that selling was over and TIME TO BUY stocks again, as a natural reaction of about 4 points had run from the top, which is all you could expect in a real Bull Market. The SAFE PLACE TO BUY would be when the averages crossed 205 the following week, getting above the top of the previous week. Advance was resumed.

Jul. 5 High 214-1/2.

" 16 Low 205-1/8, a two weeks' reaction and a higher bottom, still holding well above the 200 level. BUYING LEVEL. The advance was then resumed and prices crossed 215, the previous top.

Aug. Later crossed 221 into new high ground, where you could AGAIN BUY stocks with confidence.

**1928**

Sep. 27 Low 236-7/8, a 5-point reaction, a very small reaction with prices at this level and an indication that prices were going higher.

Oct. 5 High 243.

" 8 Low 236-3/4, a higher bottom. Then, in the latter part of October, prices crossed the top of Sep. 7 and a rapid advance followed with reactions very small, only 3 to 5 points on the averages. SIGNAL FOR HIGHER PRICES.

Nov. 28 High 293-5/8, just under the 300 level and a point to watch for reaction before the even figure was crossed. SELLING LEVEL. A sharp quick decline followed.

Dec. 8 Low 255-1/8, down 38-1/4 points, the greatest decline since the Bull Market started, but this decline lasted only 10 days. The following week, the high was 272 and the low 264, making higher bottoms ... A DEFINITE INDICATION TO BUY. The following week, prices crossed the top of the previous week at 272 and advanced rapidly.

**1929**

Jan. 2 High 307.

" 8 Low 297, a 10-point reaction.

" 11 Low 301-5/8.

15 Low 297-5/8, holding above the bottom of Jan. 8, an indication of strength and in view of the fact that the averages did not get below the top for the week ending Dec. 29th, showed that there was still good buying and indicated higher prices. BUYING LEVEL. The advance followed.

Feb. 5 High 324-1/2. SELLING LEVEL. On Monday morning the market opened unchanged from Saturday's close; advanced from 319-1/2 to 322; then broke fast and later broke the low of the previous week at 312.

16 Low 295, down 27 points from 322, double bottom against Jan. 15 . BUYING LEVEL.

Mch. 1 High 324, making a DOUBLE TOP . SELLING LEVEL. Quick rally followed.

" 6 Low 305-1/8.

" 16 High 320, making a third lower top ... SELLING LEVEL for reaction. The decline followed. Broke 3 weeks' bottoms around 303 to 306.

30 Low 281-1/2, a decline of 43 points from the high of 324-1/2 made on Feb. 5. Strictly on a space movement, this would be a BUYING LEVEL because the greatest previous decline since the averages started up in August, 1921 was 44 points in 10 days, from Nov. 28, 1928, high of 299 to Dec. 1928, low of 255. One of my rules is that reactions or advances can run to around 40 points when prices are at an extreme level. You could have bought on this extreme decline because it was a sharp, panicky break, or you could have waited until the trend turned up by crossing the previous week's top. The market held for two weeks in a range from 294 to 308; then crossed the 308 top, showing that the trend had turned up again and making it a SAFER PURCHASE.

May 11 High 331, or 6-1/2 points above the top of Feb. 5 and March 1. The rally failed to hold and the following week the high was 324-1/2, the same level as the previous old top ... SELLING LEVEL. Breaking back under the low of the previous week, indicated a further reaction.

May 27 Low 290, down 41 points from 331 high, a smaller reaction than the two previous reactions, which were 43 and 44 points. You will note that there were several old bottoms around 292, making this a logical support point and as it was a decline of only 16 days, less than 3 weeks, it was a natural support or BUYING POINT in a Bull Market. However, you could have waited until the top of the low week was crossed at 306, then bought on a reaction around that price. It reacted to around 302. Then, the advance was resumed and the market moved up fast, crossing the old top at 331 and advancing to a new high level.

Jul. 8 High 350-1/4. The low for the two previous weeks was 332 and 331.
" 11 Low 343.
" 12 High 349-3/4, a slightly LOWER TOP . . SELLING LEVEL.
" 16 Low 340.
" 23 High 349-1/2. Three weeks' tops at this point . SELLING LEVEL. A reaction followed.
29 Low 336-3/8; made low for two weeks at this level, making four weeks' bottoms in a range of less than 3 points, indicating good support and BUYING LEVEL. The advance was resumed.
Aug. 3 New high 358-3/8.
" 7 Low 338-1/2, a 10-point reaction.
" 8 High 352, a lower top.
" 9 Low 336-1/8, a 12-point reaction and not enough to show any change in the main trend. There were 2 weeks' bottoms around this level ... BUYING POINT. Then the advance was resumed.
Sep. 3 High of history 386-1/8, making 50 points' advance on the last run in 25 days and 90 points from the low of Mch. 30, 1929. From May 27 low of 290, there was an advance of 96 points. SELLING LEVEL.
7 The range this week was 386-1/8 high and 367-3/8 low, making a higher top and then breaking back to a lower bottom than the previous week. This is what we call a SIGNAL TOP or final top, making a new high and the same week breaking the low of the previous week and closing lower.

REVIEW: From the extreme low of 64 on August 24, 1921, to the extreme high of 386-1/8 on September 3, 1929, the greatest reaction in the Bull Market was 44 points; the last reaction before final top was 41 points; the last small reaction 10 points. Therefore, breaking back more than 10 points was the FIRST SIGNAl that the trend had changed; breaking back under the 4 weeks' bottoms around 336-1/2, was the SECOND DEFINITE SIGNAL that the main trend had changed, and when this level was reached, the averages had broken back over 44 points, giving the THIRD DEFINITE SIGNAL that the main trend had turned down and that a real BEAR MARKET was starting.

## 9th BEAR MARKET

Oct. 4 The averages reached 320-1/2, down 66 points from the top in one month. A sharp, quick SECONDARY RALLY followed, lasting one week.
" 10 High 358-3/4 ... SELLING LEVEL.
" 19 This week declined to 321, the same bottom as Oct. 4. High was 333 the next week; then the bottom at 320-1/2 was broken and a wide-open decline followed.
29 Averages at 212-3/8 and over 16,000,000 shares traded in...the largest day's sales in the history of the New York Stock Exchange. PANIC ... BUYING LEVEL for rally. A quick advance followed.

Oct. 31 High 273-1/2. There was heavy selling on this rally. SELLING LEVEL after 60-point rally. Decline continued.

Nov. 6 Low 232-1/8.

" 7 Moderate rally to 239-1/8.

" 13 Then followed a sharp decline, reaching final low Nov. 13, 1929, at 195-3/8. The averages were down 190 points in 70 days. Look back on your chart and you will find a period of tops and bottoms between 194 and 200, which was the reason for support and bottom at this level. On this decline the volume of trading was smaller, indicating that liquidation had run its course and that stocks were meeting support. BUYING LEVEL IN PANIC.

In fast markets of this kind, by keeping up a daily high and low chart and watching the first time tops of previous days are crossed, you get the first indication to buy. But I would consider that when the averages rallied above 212 again, the bottom of Oct. 29, it would be an indication that the rally would go further and would consider this a SAFE BUYING LEVEL. Movements were very rapid at this time, up and down.

" 21 High 250.

" 26 Low 235-1/2. SECONDARY REACTION ... BUY.

Dec. 4 High 264-5/8. SIGNAL FOR HIGHER PRICES.

" 5 Low 251-1/2. Then the advance was resumed.

" 7 High 263-1/2, failing to reach the last top at 273 and a 4 weeks' rally, market was high enough for a reaction, which followed quickly. Lower top ... SELLING LEVEL.

" 21 Low 227-1/4.

" 26 Low 226-3/8. This was the secondary reaction after the first advance from a panic bottom, stocks reacting more than 50% from the first run-up. This would be the PLACE TO BUY with close stop loss orders.

**1930**

Jan. 4 A safer place to buy would be after the high of the previous week was crossed, which occurred this week when the averages crossed 246 ... SIGNAL FOR HIGHER. After that there were 4 bottoms around 242 to 244 and 3 weekly tops around 252 to 253-1/2. The fact that the market held for 4 weeks without breaking the bottom, was another indication of good support and A PLACE TO BUY. But, again, it was still safer to buy when it crossed the 4 weeks' tops at 254. The advance continued and crossed the top at 267-1/2.

Feb. 13 High 275, under old bottom and top ... SELLING LEVEL. Note high of last rally on Oct. 31, 1929, was 273-1/2. The averages made top 4 weeks around 274 to 276, indicating a reaction.

Mch. 1 After 2 weeks' reaction, the averages declined to 260 during this week. Holding above the old top level was an indication of support. BUYING LEVEL. Advance was resumed and averages rallied above the top of 276; reacted to 268-3/4 and made bottom for 3 weeks and failing to break them indicated higher. Advance continued.

Apr. 17 High 297-1/4 ... SELLING LEVEL ... top of SECONDARY RALLY. Why did the averages stop at this level? Look back over your chart and you will find a series of bottoms from 292 to 298. The averages were up over 100 points from the extreme low and at a point to watch for a change in trend, to sell out longs and go short. There were 3 weeks' highs around this level, one 296-1/4, one 297-1/4 and one at 295. The averages advanced for 7 weeks without breaking below the previous weeks' bottoms, therefore, the first signal for a change in the minor trend would be breaking bottoms of the previous weeks.

Apr. 26 During this week the averages broke the lows of 3 previous weeks, indicating MINOR TREND had turned DOWN and it was SAFE TO SELL out longs and go short. The greatest reaction was 40-5/8 points. The last reaction before the last advance of 37 points was 15 points. Therefore, the first break of 15 points would be a second signal or indication that the trend had turned down.

May 3 This week broke under 282, more than 15 points down, and declined the same week below the last bottom at 260.

10 Declined to 249-1/2 this week. Note 4 weeks' old tops around 252 to 253, indicating SUPPORT around this level FOR A SECONDARY RALLY. Remember, according to the rules, after the first sharp decline running 3 weeks or more, there is always a secondary rally. This first decline had run three weeks and had declined 47 points, therefore, the rally was sharp and quick.

17 Averages advanced to 277 this week. There was one week's reaction to 261, followed by one week's rally to 276-3/4, DOUBLE TOP ... SELLING LEVEL. Also note series of old tops around 274-75, making this a selling level and a place to go short. But the safe place to sell would be around 269, when the averages broke back under the low of the previous week, after making 3 weeks' tops. The next definite indication of weakness and lower prices, was when the averages broke the weekly bottom at 261.

Jun. 14 This week the averages broke the 4 weeks' bottoms around 244-43.

" 24 Low 207. This was at the end of four weeks' sharp decline. While the main trend was definitely down, a RALLY WAS DUE.

Jul. 5 The averages crossed the high for the previous week, advancing to 229 ... SIGNAL FOR RALLY. Then followed one week's reaction.

12 Declining to 215 this week, making a higher bottom than the previous week and holding above the low of Oct. 29, 1929, an indication of temporary support ... BUYING LEVEL.

31 The advance was resumed and the averages crossed the 2 weeks' tops at 229, advancing to 243 on July 31 ... SELLING LEVEL. There were 4 weeks' top around 241 to 243, indicating that the market was meeting resistance. The reason for this, if you will look back, was 4 weeks' bottoms around 243 to 245 in February, 1930, showing that this would be a resistance point. Then there was a quick reaction lasting 2 weeks.

Aug. 16 Averages declined to 214-1/2 this week, making a DOUBLE BOTTOM against low in July. This was the third higher bottom ... BUYING LEVEL, protected with close loss orders, especially as the reaction only lasted 2 weeks. Then followed another advance.

Sep. 10 High 247-1/4. This was the last and final high. SELLING LEVEL. Note that this was under the bottom of 250 made in Feb. 1930 and the prices failed to reach the low at 250 made on the decline in May. The chart will show you plainly that with 4 weeks' tops around 241 to 243 and then 2 weeks' tops on the next rally, at 244-1/2 to 247-1/4, the market was meeting with good selling around this level.

**1930**

Sep. 20 But the FIRST DEFINITE INDICATION that the MINOR TREND had turned DOWN and the market was again a safe short sale, came during this week when the averages broke back under the lows of the 3 previous weeks. Volume of sales increased and the decline was fast.

Oct. 4 This week the averages broke the last bottom at 207.

" 11 This week broke the low of Nov. 13, 1929, at 195-3/8, SIGNAL FOR BIG DECLINE.

Nov. 15 Low 168-3/8. Note the series of old tops in July and August, 1926, around 166, making this a logical POINT FOR RALLY after such a sharp, severe decline in 9 weeks' time. BUYING LEVEL.

29 A 10-day rally followed. Averages made tops two weeks at 191-1/4 ... SELLING LEVEL under old bottoms. Failed to reach old bottom at 195-3/8, made in Nov. 1929, an indication of weakness. If you look back over your chart, you will find 3 weekly bottoms around 191 and 192 made in March, 1928, and also in the week ending Nov. 1930, you will see that the top on the last rally was 199. Therefore, the averages failing to reach this high, indicated lower.

Dec. 3 The first signal came this week when the averages broke back under 3 weeks. The decline was swift and wound up in a panicky decline.

17 Extreme low 154-1/2. Referring to Feb. 1927, you will find 2 bottoms at 154-1/4 and the last low at that time at 152-3/4. There was a series of tops and bottoms in this zone, making this a logical POINT FOR SUPPORT and a rally. A quick rally followed to 170; then a reaction to 158-1/2, with bottoms for 2 weeks at this point, making it a SAFER BUYING POINT.

**1931**

Jan. 9 High 175-1/2 ... SELLING LEVEL. This was a 3 weeks' rally but failed to hold. Then followed a secondary reaction lasting 2 weeks.

19 Low 160-1/2. This was the SAFE POINT TO BUY, protected with stop loss orders under the 2 bottoms at 158-1/2. A rally followed. There were 3 weekly tops around 172 to 172-3/4. When these tops were crossed, it was a still SAFER POINT TO BUY.

Feb. 14 These tops were crossed during this week and the top at 175-1/2 was crossed ... BUYING LEVEL. The market advanced sharply.

24 Reached high at 196-7/8, against the old bottom of Nov. 13, 1929, and the last high on Nov. 1, 1930, making this a logical SELLING LEVEL, the old bottom becoming top. From the low of 154-1/2 on Dec. 17, 1930, to this high of 196-7/8, the greatest reaction was 15 points, therefore breaking back more than 15 points from the top would be a definite signal for lower prices. The first indication that the MINOR TREND had turned DOWN again was the breaking of a weekly bottom at 187-1/4 made in the week ending Feb. 28.

Mch. 7 This week the averages declined below 180.

" 13 Declined to 175-7/8, the old top of Jan. 9, 1931, a logical POINT FOR RALLY. The rally followed, lasting only one week, advancing to 189-1/4 during the week ending March 21 ... SELLING LEVEL. The main trend turned down and the following week the averages broke under the bottom at 175, indicating definitely that the main trend was again down. The next point to watch was the old bottom at 154-1/2 made in Dec. 1930. The averages did not hesitate or rally at this point because selling was heavy. They went right on thru this low.

Apr. 29 Declined to 141-3/4.

May 9 The averages rallied to 156-1/8, just above the old bottom at 154-1/2 ... SELLING LEVEL. It was one-week rally and the trend continued down.

Jun. 2 Made 120, low of a panicky decline. This was down to the old top of 1919, which was a logical POINT TO BUY for a rally, especially after such a sharp, severe decline. A sharp quick rally followed to 139-1/2; then a reaction to around 128, making 2 weeks' bottoms around this level, showing good support and a point to BUY ON A SECONDARY REACTION.

27 This week the averages crossed 2 weeks' tops at 140 and advanced quickly to 157-7/8, just above the last top at 156-1/8 and against the old bottom of 154-1/2 made in Dec. 1930, a logical SELLING LEVEL, and really only a 3 weeks' rally. The next 2 weeks the tops were lower.

Jul. 11 This week the averages broke under the low of the previous week, showing that the trend had turned down again. Stocks were again a SHORT SALE.

Aug. 6 The averages declined to 132-1/2, made 3 weeks' bottoms around this level. RALLY DUE.

15 Rallied to 146-1/2, making the third lower bottom. Then held in a range from 148 to 136 the next two weeks.

Sep. 5 A sharp decline started this week and the averages broke back under 132, where there were 4 weeks' bottoms, INDICATING MUCH LOWER PRICES. The decline became worse and the volume of selling was heavy. The averages went right on thru the old bottom at 120 without rallying, an indication of much lower prices.

Oct. 5 Low 85-1/2. You will note that the last low from which this Bull Market started on October 27, 1923, was 85-3/4. Therefore, 85-1/2 or anywhere from 88-3/8 to 85 was a logical BUYING POINT for a rally, especially at the time of a panicky decline. A sharp, quick rally followed with only small reaction.

" 24 Averages advanced to 110-1/2.

" 29 Then there was a SECONDARY REACTION to 98-1/4, just under 100, a SUPPORT LEVEL, as there were old tops and bottoms around these levels. The advance was resumed and the averages crossed four weeks' tops around 108 to 110.

Nov. 9 High 119-1/2, under the low of June 2, 1931 and at the old top of Nov. 1919 ... the logical place to SELL OUT LONGS AND GO SHORT and not to buy until this old bottom and top level could be crossed. The greatest reaction from 85-1/2 low in October to this high was 11 points, therefore breaking back 11 points from the high would be an indication of lower prices and breaking the previous weekly bottom would indicate trend down again.

21 The market broke back quickly more than 12 points and during this week broke the bottoms of 4 previous weeks, indicating definitely the main trend down.

Dec. 12 This week the averages broke the low at 85-1/2, another indication that the main trend was down and the Bear Market would continue and the rallies were very small.

**1932**

Jan. ow 70. The last low on Oct. 17, 1921 was 70 and the other old bottoms

66 and 64. The two weeks previous, the market had rallied from 72. Therefore, this bottom was only 2 points under the previous bottom, indicating that SUPPORT was coming at this time ... BUYING LEVEL. A sharp rally followed.

Jan. 14 High 89-1/2. This was just above the old bottom at 85-1/2. The market met SELLING around this LEVEL.

Feb. 10 Declined to 71, holding 1 point above the previous bottom and making 3 bottoms around this level ... a POINT TO BUY with stop loss order. A rally followed.

Mch. 8 High 89-1/2, a DOUBLE TOP against Jan. 14, making the third time that the market had advanced to around those levels and failed to go thru. The market became very dull and narrow, showing there was not much buying power at the top of the rally, indicating stocks were still a SHORT SALE.

19 The FIRST DEFINITE INDICATION came during this week when the averages broke back under the previous week's bottom and broke 3 bottoms around 81 to 83-1/2, continuing right on down.

Apr. 7 This week they broke 70, where there were three bottoms, indicating the market was in a very WEAK POSITION and that the main trend was still down. Remember our rule: The lower stocks get, the smaller the rallies until the final clean-out comes and final bottom is reached. The decline continued and the old bottoms at 66 to 64, made back in 1921 and 1917, were all broken. There was no indication of support, showing that the final stage of the panic was on and that stocks would not rally until liquidation had run its course. After breaking 64, the next point to watch was 53, the low of 1914, a support level for several other years in the past.

May 4 The averages declined to 52-1/2, getting support at the old bottom, a quick rally followed.
High 60, only a 3-day rally which failed to hold. The decline continued and the averages broke the old bottoms at 52 and 51-1/2. The next point to watch for bottom was the old lows of Mar. 25, 1898 at 42 and the next lower bottom of Apr. 19, 1897 at 38-1/2. The last low Nov. 9, 1903 was 42-1/8. Therefore, there were old triple bottoms around the 42 level, a logical place to watch for bottom, anywhere between 42 and 38-1/2. Our rule says that where there is a series of old bottoms, there should be support.

Jun. 2 Low 43-1/2.

" 4 A quick rally to 51-1/2. The first rally of as much as 8 points since the averages started down from 89-1/2. This rally failed to hold.

9 The averages went back to 44-1/2.

16 They rallied to 51. Failing to reach the previous top showed that liquidation was still going on and stocks were for sale on rallies. The decline continued and the averages broke the low at 43-1/2.

8 Low 40-1/2, receiving support 1-1/2 points under the old support level at 42, thus ENDING THE GREAT BEAR MARKET.

In 34 months the Dow-Jones 30 Industrial averages were down 345-1/2 points, wiping out a gain of more than 30 years. This proves what happens when people lose confidence and everybody gets loaded up and continues to buy on the way down, and finally all have to sell. Prices swung to extreme low levels, the same as they did on the advance, going to extreme and unwarranted high levels. But that is when the man who has knowledge and time makes money, by knowing when to take advantage of extremes, when the public buys on hope and sells on fear.

The FIRST SIGNAL that the market was NEARING BOTTOM came in the week of June 11 when the averages held in a narrow trading range of less than one point and the following week rallied 11 points, making the first high above a previous week since the trend turned down on Mch. 9th at 89-1/2. Then, from 51-1/2, the last high, the averages declined for 3 weeks. Certainly stocks were low enough at these old panic levels for a blind man to know that they were low enough to buy, but having declined so long, people had lost all hope and fear controlled them. Therefore, you could have waited for a definite indication that the trend had turned up and still bought stocks very near the low levels.

REVIEW: Figuring the last decline or last stage of the Bear Market from 119-1/2 high on Nov. 9, 1931, to 40-1/2 low on July 8, 1932, the greatest rally was 19 points, from 70 to 89-1/2, and the next rally around 8 points. Therefore, when the averages advanced more than 8 points, it was the first signal that they were going higher. Advancing more than 19 points indicated a still further advance.

## 10th BULL MARKET

Jul. There were 2 weeks' tops at 44-3/4 and 44 1/2.

" 16 This week the averages crossed 45, advancing above the 2 weeks' tops, an indication that the minor trend had turned up and that stocks were now SAFE TO BUY.

30 The averages crossed 53 in this week, getting above 9 weeks' tops, and crossed the tops of previous rallies, being up more than 10 points. This was an indication that the main trend had turned up and with the averages at 52, they were a SAFE PURCHASE for a further advance. The advance was rapid as, naturally, it would be after such a sharp decline and heavy liquidation, cleaning out everybody.

Sep. 8 The averages advanced to 81-1/2, having made higher bottoms and higher tops every week after the low of July 8, advancing for nine weeks. The averages were up under old bottoms and were up 41 points or an advance of 100% from low levels and would have to cross 89 to give a definite indication of a real Bull Market and higher prices. There had been no secondary reaction, which always comes after the first sharp advance. Therefore, your FIRST SIGNAL TO SELL out would be the first week that the averages broke the low of the previous week's bottoms, especially after an advance of nine consecutive weeks.

17 This signal came during this week when the averages broke under the previous bottoms, declining sharply to 64-1/2, down 17 points in 10 days. As they held just above tops of previous weeks and above the old bottom at 64 in 1921, it was a POINT FOR A RALLY. The averages rallied to 76 and made top the next week at 75-1/2. Failing to get above the bottom at 77 reached in the top week was an indication of GOOD SELLING

**1933** 10th BULL MARKET (Continued)

Oct. 31 A secondary reaction to 86-1/2. This was the SAFEST PLACE TO BUY on the SECONDARY REACTION, protected with stop-loss order under the old bottom. The advance was resumed and the market worked higher with very small reactions.

Dec. 11 High 104-1/2, making a THIRD LOWER TOP ... SELLING LEVEL ... and indicating that the market was still meeting resistance. A two weeks' reaction followed.

20 Low 93-1/2. Note series of tops in Oct. 1933, around this level. The market made four weeks' bottom at 93-1/2 to 96-1/2, indicating good support at this level, especially after rallying to 101-3/4 and coming back to 96 ... a SAFE POINT TO BUY, protected with stop-loss orders. The advance was resumed and the market moved on up.

**1934**

Feb. 5 High 111-1/2, getting 1 point above the old high of July 17, 1933 ... SELLING LEVEL. The volume of trading was very heavy and the market too weak to cross the top at 112-1/2 and a quick, sharp decline followed.

10 Low 103, a decline of 8-1/2 points from the top and a definite signal that the market was meeting with heavy selling. The greatest reaction from 82-1/2 low to 111-1/2 was 11 points. The first quick decline of 8-1/2 points was not enough to give a DEFINITE SIGNAL that the market was GOING LOWER. A rally followed.

15 High 109-1/2, failing by 2 points to reach the old top, an indication of GOOD SELLING.

Mch. 3 The next definite signal that the market was going lower came during this week when the averages broke back under the lows of 3 previous weeks. The decline continued.

27 Low 97, down 14-1/2 points, indicating a reversal on space movement, but there were 3 bottoms around 96 ... BUYING LEVEL ... and holding above these bottoms indicated a rally. A rally followed.

Apr. 11 High 107 ... SELLING LEVEL. The market made tops 2 weeks at this level and the bottoms for three weeks were around 102-1/2, indicating again that there was good selling.

May 5 This week averages broke under the 3 weeks' bottoms, indicating that the main trend had again turned down. The decline continued.

14 Low 89. There was a rally to 96 ... SELLING LEVEL ... and a reaction to 90, making 5 weeks' bottoms around these levels ... BUYING LEVEL.

Jun. 19 High 101, failing to reach the bottoms of the previous advance around 100, an OLD SELLING LEVEL. This was only a 3 weeks' rally and there was good selling. A reaction followed to 94-1/2, breaking the bottoms of previous weeks and breaking back under top levels.

Jul. 14 There was another feeble rally during this week to 99-1/2, a lower top Heavy selling and a sharp, severe decline followed.

26 Low 84-1/2. There was a 3-million share day at the bottom, the largest for months, which indicated there was heavy liquidation and that the market was making final bottom. Holding at exactly the SAME LEVEL as July, 1933, and holding above the low of Oct. 21, 1933, indicated good support and, again, the fact that the averages never came back to the old top at 81-1/2, made Sept. 8, 1932, indicated that after this top was crossed, it had become a bottom and a BUYING LEVEL. A rally followed quickly.

**1934**

Aug. 25 High 96 ... SELLING LEVEL. Then came a secondary reaction.

Sep. 17 Low 85-3/4, making a higher bottom. In fact, there were two weeks bottoms at this same level. This was a SAFE BUYING POINT. After a TRIPLE BOTTOM around the same level and then a higher bottom, it was an indication of good support and stocks should have been bought.

Oct. 17 High 96, back to the same level at Aug. 24 ... SELLING LEVEL. There were four weekly tops around this level.

Nov. 10 This week a reaction to 92, the last low level. Going back over the charts you can see a series of bottoms and tops around this level. This would make it a logical reaction and a SUPPORT POINT on 1 to 2 weeks' reactions. A rally followed promptly.

Dec. 24 This week the averages crossed 96, where there were 6 weekly tops, an INDICATION of HIGHER PRICES. Dec. 5th, high 104-1/2; Dec. 20th, low of reaction 99, back to the old support level.

**1935**

Jan. 7 High 107. This was back to the same top reached in Mch. 1934 . . SELLING LEVEL.

" 15 Low 99, back to the bottom of Dec. 20 ... BUYING LEVEL.

" 21 High 103.

Feb. 6 High 99-1/2, the THIRD TIME and SLIGHTLY HIGHER.

" 18 High 108-1/2, 1 point above the old high of March, 1934, and just under the old top ... SELLING LEVEL. Selling developed at this old top level and a decline started.

Mch. 18 Low 95-1/2, back to the same level where it had crossed a series of old tops ... a logical support and BUYING LEVEL. Selling on this decline was light and it was only one month's reaction after the market had given up-signals by crossing a series of tops around 104 to 106, but the safe place to buy was after the market had given a definite up-signal again by crossing the tops of previous weeks.

Apr. 6 This week the averages advanced and crossed the tops of the 3 previous weeks, indicating the MAIN TREND was again turning UP.

27 The averages advanced and crossed 108 this week and also crossed the old top at 111-1/2 and advanced to 112-1/2. There was a reaction the following week to 107-3/4, just back to the old top. This was a SAFE BUYING POINT after the averages had gone thru to a new high and INDICATED HIGHER PRICES.

May 24 High 117-1/2. The market made 3 weekly tops at this level, just under the old bottom of 119-5/8 and the old top of Nov. 9, 1931 ... SELLING LEVEL. It was natural that the market should meet selling around these old levels. A moderate reaction followed.

Jun. 1 Low 108-1/2, right back on the old top and a SAFE PLACE TO BUY, failing to get back to the low levels reached in the early part of May. This was really one week's reaction and the advance was promptly resumed.

15 This week crossed the 3 weeks tops at 117-1/2 and went on thru the old bottoms and old tops at 120, only hesitating around 121-1/2 and reacting about 4 points. The market continued to work higher with very small reactions.

Aug. 14 High 129-1/2.

" 20 Low 125, this reaction holding well above the old top and bottom levels.

**1935**

Sep. 18 High 135-1/2. At this level there were some old bottoms and tops of the previous campaign and it was natural for a reaction of moderate proportions. SELLING LEVEL.

Oct. 3 Low 127, a two weeks' reaction. The market made 3 weekly bottoms around 128 to 127, holding 2 points above the last low of 125...BUYING LEVEL. The advance was resumed and the averages crossed the top at 135-1/2, indicating still higher prices.

Nov. 20 High 149-1/2. There were two old tops around 147 to 148 in the previous campaign, making this a resistance level for at least a reaction ... SELLING LEVEL.

Dec. 19 Low 138-1/4 ... BUYING LEVEL; then followed a rally.

**1936**

Jan. 10 High 148-1/2, making a slightly lower top ... SELLING LEVEL.

" 21 Low 142-1/2, making a higher bottom than the previous bottom ... BUYING LEVEL. From the time that the low was reached July 26, 1934 at 84-1/2, the greatest reaction had been 12 points. There had been reactions of 10 points right along. The reaction of 11-1/4 points from Nov. 20, 1935, to Dec. 19, 1935, was a normal reaction and until the market broke back under some previous bottom or more than 12 points, all indications were that it was still a Bull Market and the main trend up.

Feb. The averages crossed the high of 149-1/2 and continued on up.

Mch. 6 High 159-1/2. Note the old top in June and July, 1931 at 157-1/2, making this a point from which the market should react ... SELLING LEVEL. There was also a bottom at 154-1/2.

13 Low 149, another 10-1/2 point reaction, the same reaction which had been occurring right along, and lasting only one week ... BUYING LEVEL. The advance continued and the averages moved to a new high for the present move.

Apr. 6 High 163, the low for the week was 159-1/2, making this a narrow week at the top ... SELLING LEVEL. The previous week's high being 161-3/4, showed very little range. In the following week the averages broke the low of the previous week, indicating a change in the minor trend. A sharp decline followed.

30 Low 141-1/2, down 21-1/2 points and the greatest reaction which had occurred since the low at 84-1/2. This decline was a little over 3 weeks, a normal reaction in a Bull Market ... BUYING LEVEL. The last low Dec. 19, 1935, was 138-1/4, from which the averages advanced to a new high, therefore this was an important level that should be broken if a Bear Market was going to start and the averages should continue down more than three weeks if the main trend was going to turn down. The market did not continue down but immediately started to advance.

May 23 This week there were two tops around 152-1/2 and a third higher bottom.

" 30 The averages advanced to 153-1/2 during this week. Then reacted to 148-1/2, holding above the old top level, indicating strength. This was a GOOD REACTION TO BUY ON. Continued up.

Jun. 27 High 161.

Jul. 11 This week reacted to 154, the old bottom of June 1931. Failing to decline into the second or third week, indicated strength.

18 The averages advanced to new highs ... SIGNAL FOR HIGHER.

Aug. 10 High 170-1/2 ... SELLING LEVEL.
" 21 Low 161, a 9-point reaction in eleven days ...BUYING LEVEL.
Sep. 8 Advanced to a new high 171 ... SELLING LEVEL; then followed a reaction.
" 23 Low 165, holding above the last top levels of the previous weeks ... BUYING LEVEL. Reaction was only 9 points, which was an INDICATION OF strength and HIGHER prices. The market continued higher.
Oct. 19 High 179.
" 26 Low 173, again only one week's reaction and the averages advanced to new high levels.
Nov. 18 High was 187 ... SELLING LEVEL.
Dec. 21 Low 175, a 12-point reaction. BUYING LEVEL. The advanced was resumed.

1937

Jan. 22 High 187, DOUBLE TOP ... SELLING LEVEL.
" 27 Low 182-1/2, a 5-point reaction ... BUYING LEVEL.
Feb. 11 High 191, a new high ... SIGNAL FOR HIGHER.
" 24 Low 185, a 6-point reaction ... HIGHER SUPPORT LEVEL.
Mch. 8 High 195-1/2, END OF BULL MARKET. Why should this be top? Going back to Nov. 13, 1929, you find the low at 195-1/2. Going back to the last high, Feb. 24, 1931, you find the high 197-1/4 and especially in view of the fact that from 1931 the main trend turned down again and continued on down, made this a logical SELLING POINT AGAINST OLD BOTTOMS AND OLD TOPS. But to be sure that this level would not be crossed, you must wait until the bottom of the previous week has been broken and the space movement exceeded.

REVIEW: From July 26, 1934, low 84-1/2 to Mch. 8, 1937, high 195-1/2, the greatest reaction was 21-1/2 points, from 163 to 141-1/2 in April, 1936. Therefore, when the averages broke back more than 21-1/2 points, it would be an indication the Bear Market was starting and main trend had turned down. The last reaction was 12 points when the averages declined to 175 in Dec. 1936. Therefore, breaking back over 12 points would be the first indication that the main trend had turned. There were 3 weeks' bottoms around 185 to 186 in Feb. 1937, and breaking these bottoms would indicate the first change in the main trend.

## 10th BEAR MARKET

The first decline was sharp and severe.

Mch. 27 This week the averages declined to 183-1/2, breaking under the bottoms of the previous 4 weeks and under the lows of the last reaction of Mch. 6 ... a decline of 12 points. Decline continued. SAFER SHORT SALE when they broke 185.
Apr. 9 Low 175. Note the last bottom in December, 1936 was 175, making this the logical support point ... BUYING LEVEL for rally. There were 2 weeks' bottoms at 176.
22 The market rallied to 185, under the old bottom and a SELLING LEVEL. A sharp decline followed, breaking 176, the old bottom and support level.
28 Low 169.

May 7 High 176-1/2, rallied back under the old bottoms, a natural SELLING POINT.

18 Low 166. Note old bottoms around 165 and old tops around 170, making this a point from which the market could rally ... BUYING LEVEL.

24 High 176, back to the old bottom and top levels and a SELLING POINT which the averages failed to go thru. Broke back under previous bottoms and declined sharply.

Jun. 17 Low 163. Note there was an old bottom at 164-3/4 and a top on April 6, 1936, at 163, making this a support and BUYING LEVEL. There was also last low at 161 on August 21, 1930, making this a RALLY POINT. Up to this time there had been no real secondary rally after the trend turned down and you should watch for definite indications of a change in the minor trend to buy for a rally. The averages rallied to 172 and reacted to 166. This was the REACTION TO BUY ON, protected with a stop under old bottoms. The advance was resumed and the averages crossed the tops of previous weeks and crossed 176, which was an INDICATION OF HIGHER PRICES. The market advanced slowly this time on very much lower volume than when the top was made in March 1937.

Aug. 14 High 190-1/2, a LOWER TOP than the main top ... SELLING LEVEL. There were two weeks' bottoms at 185-1/2 to 190-1/2; every bottom had been higher on the weekly chart since the advance started.

21 Therefore, during this week, when the averages broke back under 2 weeks bottoms, the trend had again turned down and you should SELL SHORT. From 163 to 190-1/2, the greatest reaction was 5 points. Therefore, when they broke back more than 5 points, overbalancing the space movements, it was a DEFINITE SIGNAL FOR LOWER PRICES. The decline was rapid and when the averages declined to a series of tops and bottoms at 176, there was no hesitation or any sign of support. The decline continued on down and the old bottom at 163 was reached. There was no rally or no support indicated. Then, finally, broke the low at 160 and continued on down.

Sep. 24 Low 147. This was down into old top levels where there were several weekly bottoms ... BUYING LEVEL.

30 High 156-1/2, a 9-1/2 point rally. This was up under old bottoms and old top levels of previous campaigns, making this a SELLING LEVEL.

Oct. 19 A panicky decline followed, reaching low at 115-1/2. The volume of sales at this time was the heaviest for many months. Note resistance level at 117 in June, 1936, and the old top and bottom levels at 119-1/2 in 1931, making this a support point for a rally, especially on a panicky decline ... and BUYING LEVEL. There was a sharp advance.

29 High 141-1/2. This was under a series of old bottoms and under the old bottom of April 30, 1936, making it a SELLING LEVEL for a reaction. A sharp quick reaction followed.

Nov. 23 Low 112-1/2, just 3 points under the previous bottom and down to the old 1933 and 1934 tops, a POINT FOR A RALLY.

Dec. 8 High 131 ... SELLING LEVEL.

" 13 Low 121-1/2, a SECONDARY REACTION and there were two bottoms around this level ... BUYING POINT.

21 High 131 ... SELLING LEVEL ... same top as Dec. 8.

29 Low 118, slightly HIGHER BOTTOM and sign of some support BUYING LEVEL.

Jan. 15 High 134-1/2 ... SELLING LEVEL ... went over two previous tops but made top here for two weeks and could not advance. The following week broke back under the low of the previous week, indicating a reaction.

Feb. 4 Low 117-1/2, a DOUBLE BOTTOM, same low as Dec. 29, a PLACE TO BUY with a close stop loss order, as the market was holding above the Oct. 19 bottom also.

23 High 133, a LOWER TOP than January 15, an indication of good selling around this level, where there were old bottoms and tops ... SELLING LEVEL.

Mch. 12 This week the averages broke back under 2 weeks bottoms at 127-1/2, turning the MINOR TREND DOWN again. A sharp decline followed. The double bottoms at 118 were broken, indicating extreme weakness, and no rally occurred from these bottoms. The last low at 112-1/2 was broken and there was no rally or support around the old tops at 110 and 108, indicating that the market was in a very weak position. There was heavy selling and everyone was bearish and had lost hope. Rallies were small, only 4 to 5 points. Remember our rule. In the last stages of a Bear Market, the lower prices get, the smaller the rallies are.

31 Low 97-1/2, END OF PANICKY DECLINE and END OF BEAR MARKET. Why should the averages stop at this point and receive support? Look back on your chart and you will see that on March 18, 1935, the low was 95-1/2, a point from which the real Bull Market got under way; in Nov. 1935, there was a series of tops around 96, making 97-1/2 to 95-1/2 a strong support level and a POINT TO BUY at the end of a panicky decline. But you should follow rules and watch for definite indication that the trend was turning up.

REVIEW: From the high of 195-1/2 on Mch. 8, 1937, to the low of 97-1/2 on Mch. 31, 1938, the greatest advances in the Bear Market was 27-1/2 points, from 163 to 190-1/2, and 22 points, from 112-1/2 to 134-1/2. The last rally was 15 points, from 117-1/2 to 133. The last small rally was 6 points, from low of 121-1/2 on Mch. 12 to high of 127-1/2 on Mch. 16, 1938. Therefore, the first indication of a change in the minor trend would be an advance of more than 6 points. Advancing more than 15 points would indicate uptrend again.

## 11th MINOR BULL MARKET

Apr. 2 The market started to rally, first indication of higher prices.

" 9 The averages crossed 108-1/2, the top of the previous week, a SECOND SIGNAL FOR HIGHER PRICES.

18 High 121-1/2, up 23-1/2 points, more than the rally from 112-1/2 to 134-1/2 in the previous Bear Market. This was the THIRD SIGNAL that prices were going higher, but note the series of bottoms around 121, making this a SELLING LEVEL for a reaction, and at 119 to 120, going back in the past, was a series of bottoms and tops, making it always an important point, an indication that a SECONDARY REACTION was DUE, which always follows the first sharp rally after final bottoms are made.

May 27 The market worked down slowly. Low 106-1/2, 9 points above the low of March 31. At this level stocks were very dull and narrow, showing that there was no selling pressure and that this SECONDARY REACTION was a PLACE TO BUY. This was a 3 weeks' reaction from top at 120. You should now watch for the first indication that the minor trend was turning up again. The averages had made a top at 114 and 112-1/2.

June 11 The averages crossed 112-1/2 this week, advancing to 116. Then the following week reacted to 112-1/2 on very small volume, a SURE INDICATION TO BUY.

25 The averages crossed 116, the last top, during this week and went right on thru 120-121, the old tops. There was heavy buying and a rapid run-away market. There was no reaction from the old tops at 133 to 134-1/2. Each weekly bottom was higher.

July 25 High 146-1/4. This was under old bottoms. Note 2 weekly bottoms in Oct. 1937. The market made 3 weeks' tops around 146 ... SELLING LEVEL.

" 28 Reacted to 139.

Aug. 6 Rallied to 146-1/2, making a second or double top . . SELLING LEVEL. Then followed a sharp, quick decline.

" 12 Low 136-1/2.

" 24 High 145, a THIRD LOWER TOP, where you should SELL OUT AND GO SHORT as the decline to 135-1/2 had broken under the bottoms of 3 previous weeks. The averages reacted to 136-1/2; rallied to 143-1/2, making a FOURTH LOWER TOP, a sure and SAFE INDICATION TO SELL for lower prices.

Sep. 14 Low 130-1/4--down against old top levels but had broken previous weekly bottoms, an indication of lower prices.

21 High 140-1/2, a FIFTH LOWER TOP ... SELLING LEVEL. A sharp, quick decline followed on war news, when Hitler was getting ready to take Czecho-Slovakia and the rumors were that there would be war if Hitler did not have his way, which he did.

" 26 Low 127-1/2.

" 27 A 5-point rally to 132-1/2.

" 28 Low 127-7/8, a slightly higher bottom than Sep. 26, ... BUYING LEVEL. Stocks showed great resistance and everything indicated that the market was making bottom. The Allies compromised with Hitler and war was averted. You will note at 128 there was a series of old tops and bottoms in past history and a natural support level. More reasons will be given later why this was a SURE BUYING POINT. Then you should watch for the first indication that the trend was turning up. The last rally was 5 points and the greatest rally on the decline 10 points. Therefore, when the averages advanced 6 points, they indicated higher and when they advanced 10 points indicated a still further advance. This they did promptly. You could have bought stocks after the averages were up 5 and 10 points and made plenty of money. The advance continued and the averages moved right on thru the old top at 146, indicated that it was a strong uptrend. You could have bought more stocks after the averages crossed 146 and still made big profits. Reactions were small and there were no weekly bottoms broken.

Nov. 10 High 158-3/4 ... SELLING LEVEL. Note top of last rally in September, 1937, at 157-1/2, an indication that stocks would meet selling around this level. But you must follow your rule to determine when the trend is changing.

REVIEW: From the low of 97-1/2 on Mch. 31, 1938, to the high of 158-3/4 on Nov. 10, 1938, there was one reaction of 15 points on the way up and the greatest reaction was 19 points. The smallest reaction was October 14 to 18, 153-1/2 to 148-1/2, 5 points, and the last reaction from 155-1/2 to 150-1/2 was 5 points. Therefore, when the market broke back 5 points or more, it would indicate lower prices and breaking 150-1/2 would be a signal for lower and breaking back under 148-1/2 would be under a series of weekly bottoms and turn the main trend down.

## 11th MINOR BEAR MARKET

The decline followed promptly.

Nov. 28 The averages reached 145. This was a natural support point for a rally and BUYING LEVEL because it was down against a series of old tops around 146 to 145. The market had not yet had the secondary rally, which is always indicated after the first sharp break. Therefore, you could have bought around 145 for a rally.

1939

Jan. 4 High 155-1/2 ... LOWER TOP. The market held for several days, in fact, made 2 weekly tops at 155-1/2, just 3 points under the high of Nov. 1938, indicating that it was meeting heavy selling on this secondary rally. This was a point for you to SELL OUT LONG STOCKS AND GO SHORT.

Jan. 14 The FIRST SIGNAL that the minor trend had turned down again and that stocks indicated LOWER PRICES came during this week, when the averages broke back under the bottoms of 3 previous weeks and continued on down.

26 Low 136-1/8. Note 3 weekly bottoms around this level in July, 1938, and tops around this level in Oct. and Dec. 1937, making this a point from which a rally could take place. A quick rally followed and the market worked higher.

Mch. 10 High 152-1/2, a THIRD LOWER TOP and at the breakaway point of the previous moves ... SELLING LEVEL. The low for the week was 148-1/2. In the following week when the averages broke back under 148-1/2, it was the first confirmation that the minor trend was turning down again. You should have sold out stocks and gone short. The market moved down fast, breaking all support levels.

31 In this week broke the low at 136, indicating a very weak position, and continued on down. There was no support of any importance or any rally from the old bottoms at 128, made in September 1938, showing that the market was weak and the main trend still down.

Apr. 11 Low 120-1/8 ... BUYING LEVEL. This was a natural support level against old tops and bottoms. Note the last rally before the last decline to 120 during the week ending May 14, making this a logical and natural support point.

REVIEW: From the high at 158-3/4 on Nov. 10, 1938, to the low of 120-1/8 on Apr. 11, 1939, the greatest rally was 16 points and the smallest rally 10-1/2 points. Therefore, when the market advanced 11 points from 120-1/8, it would be an indication that the minor trend was turning up and advancing more than 16 points would turn main trend up again. From the last high point at 152-1/2, made on Mch. 10, 1939, to the low at 120-1/8, the greatest rally was 5 points, therefore an advance greater than 5 points would be the first indication that bottom had been made and the minor trend, at least, was going to turn up.

## 12th MINOR BULL MARKET

A quick rally followed.

Apr. 13 The averages reached 129-1/4, up 9 points. 128 was the old bottom in Sep. 1938 ... SELLING LEVEL. Therefore, it was only natural that from around this level a secondary reaction would take place.

14 Low 124-1/2, a higher bottom ... BUYING LEVEL. Then followed a rally.

15 High 130-1/2, crossing the previous top by 1-1/4 points ... SELLING LEVEL.

19 A secondary reaction to 124-3/4 making a slightly higher bottom . BUYING LEVEL.

22 High 130, same level as Apr. 15 ... SELLING LEVEL.

26 Low 126-1/2, a THIRD HIGHER BOTTOM ... BUYING LEVEL.

" 28 High 131-1/2 ... SELLING LEVEL.

May 1 Low 127-1/2, a FOURTH HIGHER BOTTOM ... BUYING LEVEL.

" 10 High 134-1/2, under old bottoms ... SELLING LEVEL. A reaction followed.

" 17 Low 128-1/2, a FIFTH HIGHER BOTTOM and a support level around the old 128 top and bottom ...BUYING LEVEL. After this last low level the market advanced and tops were crossed. The advance continued.

June 9 Reached high at 140-3/4, again up to old bottom and top levels where resistance was met ... SELLING LEVEL. This advance from the extreme low of 120-1/8 in April had carried the averages up over 20 points, an indication of higher prices after a secondary reaction.

16 Low 134, back to an old top ... BUYING LEVEL.

21 High 138-1/2, a LOWER TOP, an indication of good selling ... SELLING LEVEL. A decline started. The support level at 134 was broken.

30 Low 128-7/8, holding above the series of support levels made in April and May, 1939. This was a BUYING POINT on the SECONDARY REACTION. A slow advance started and the averages crossed highs of previous weeks.

Jul. 13 Crossed 138, the top of June 21, SIGNAL FOR HIGHER PRICES.

" 17 Crossed 140-3/4 the high of June 9.

" 25 High 145-3/4, at old top levels of July and August, 1938, and at top of last rally of March 21, 1939, a point for at least a reaction ... SELLING LEVEL.

Aug. 1 Low 142-1/2.

" 3 High 145-3/4, same high as July 25, making a DOUBLE TOP . . SELLING LEVEL.

If you will go over the charts carefully and study all important movements and resistance levels, you will learn how to apply the rules successfully in future market campaigns. The more you study, the greater your success will be.

August 4, 1939

# CHAPTER 4

## *SEASONAL CHANGES IN STOCKS*

W. D. GANN
82-88 WALL STREET
NEW YORK

Scientific Advice
and Analytical Reports
on Stocks and Commodities
or of "Truth of the Stock Tape"
"Wall Street Stock Selector"
" Tunnel Thru the Air"

Member
American Economic Ass'n
Royal Economic Society
Cable Address
"Ganwade New York"

## SEASONAL CHANGES ON STOCKS

The average of stocks and many of the individual stocks make important bottoms and tops according to the Seasonal Changes, which are as follows:

The Winter Quarter begins December 22nd, and 15 days from this date is January 5th and 6th, which are always important dates to watch at the beginning of each year, as stocks often make extreme high or extreme low around these dates and a change in trend takes place. When stocks make low in December just before or just after the 22nd, a January rise usually follows. Dividends are payable on the first of January, and people buy for the dividends, which brings about a rally which often culminates around the 3rd to 7th. However, in some years, the January advance lasts until around the 20th to 21st.

February 5th is 45 days from December 22nd, and minor changes often take place around this date and, sometimes, very important tops and bottoms are reached.

March 21st is 90 days from December 22nd. This is the date when the Sun crosses the Equator and Spring begins. The Spring rally in the Stock Market often starts around this date or culminates, if stocks have been advancing previous to this date.

May 6th is 46 days from March 21st or 135 days from December 22nd and equals the 135° angle. Watch for important change in trend around this date.

June 22nd is 93 days from March 21st, which equals 90°, and, of course, it is opposite December 22nd and is important for seasonal change, as Summer begins at this date.

July 7th is 15 days from June 22nd and 6 months or 180 days from January 7th. July being a dividend month, advances or declines often culminate around this date and an important change in trend takes place. It is the next important date to watch after June 22nd.

August 8th is 47 days from June 22nd but the Sun has only moved 45°, which equals the 45° angle. This is a very important date for change in trend, and you should watch stocks that make tops and bottoms around this date.

September 23rd is 93 days from June 22nd, but the Earth or Sun has only travelled 90°. The Sun crosses the Equator at this time and is 180 ° or opposite the point where it crosses the Equator on March 21st. Fall begins at this date, and stocks make important changes in trend.

November 8th is 46 days from September 23rd and equals 45°. You will find by checking over the records that many important tops and bottoms and changes in trend occur around this date.

December 22nd is 91 days from September 23rd and 6 months or 180 days from June 22nd. This is where Winter begins, and it is important to watch for important changes in trends.

## MONTHLY CHANGES

Stocks make important changes in trend every 30, 60, 120, 150, 210, 240, 300, 330 and 360 days or degrees from any important top or bottom. These seasonal changes or monthly changes based on the beginning of any seasonal changes are important to watch for tops and bottoms.

January 21st is 30 days or 30° from December 22nd, and the Sun changes signs at this date.

February 19th is 60 days or 60° from December 22nd, and the Sun or Earth makes another change in sign.

April 20th is 120 days or 120° from December 22nd.

May 22nd is 150 days or 150° from December 22nd and 60° from March 21st.

July 23rd is 210° from December 22nd and 120° from March 21st.

August 23rd is 240° from December 22nd.

October 23rd is 300° from December 22nd.

November 22nd is 330° from December 22nd.

All of the above dates are important to watch for changes in the major and minor trends.

Next to the 30 day change in trend, the most important are those that occur every 7th, 10th, 14th, 20th and 21st day. You will find some variation in these due to the fact that the Sun changes sign every 30 days and that the Moon returns to its own place every 28 days and that there is a New Moon around 29 days from the previous New Moon. Sometimes the change will occur on the 28th day from a previous top or bottom, and, at other times, on the 33rd or 34th day, due to the changes in the Moon and the time between these changes and the time that the Earth or Sun changes signs.

The dates when companies are incorporated and the dates when stocks are first traded in on the New York Stock Exchange or other Exchanges causes them to make tops and bottoms at slightly different dates than these dates for seasonal changes.

For example: UNITED STATES STEEL was incorporated February 25, 1901 and trading began on the New York Stock Exchange on March 28, 1901. This is why Steel makes so many important changes in trend in the month of February and March. Steel's seasonal changes in trend, based on the date of incorporation, are as follows:-

February 25th to April 12th equals $45^{\circ}$.

April 27th equals 60 days or $60^{\circ}$ from February 25th.

May 28th equals $90^{\circ}$ from Feb.25th.

June 12th equals $135^{\circ}$ from Feb.25th. June 28th equals $120^{\circ}$ from Feb. 25th.

July 30th equals $150^{\circ}$ from Feb. 25th.

August 30th equals $180^{\circ}$ from Feb. 25th.

October 30th equals $240^{\circ}$ from Feb. 25th.

October 14th equals $225^{\circ}$ from February 25th.
November 29th equals $270^{\circ}$ from Feb. 25th.

December 28th equals $300^{\circ}$ from Feb. 25th.

January 11th equals $315^{\circ}$ from Feb. 25th.
January 27th equals $330^{\circ}$ from Feb. 25th.

February 25th equals $360^{\circ}$ or 365 days from Feb. 25th.

By checking over the dates when United States Steel has made minor and major tops and bottoms, you can see how often they have come out very closely to these dates for seasonal changes in trend.

## UNITED STATES STEEL QUARTERLY CHART

This chart is made up according to the quarterly seasonal changes and begins and ends each quarter according to the seasonal changes and not according to United States Steel's individual seasonal changes. The date at the bottom of each quarter is the date when the extreme low is made and the date at the top is the date when the extreme high was made during the Quarter.

The major and minor swings given below are taken from the overnight chart on U S Steel from 1901 to date and show most all of the minor swings each month. A study of these tops and bottoms will convince you of the value of these seasonal changes and will show you how tops and bottoms come out 30, 60, 90 days apart, and also will show you that the 7, 10, 14, 15, 20 and 21 day periods work with remarkable regularity.

1901

March 28th - Trading began in U S Steel and an advance started.

April 30th - Reached top of rally, extreme high of quarter, and made second top on May 6th.

May 9th - The day of the Northern Pacific panic. Steel reached extreme low for the quarter.

June 3 rd and 5th - Last top at 52 -3/8. June 24th - Extreme high for quarter. Never crossed last top. Trend turned down.

July 15th - Extreme low for quarter. July 22nd - Low of reaction.
July 27th - Top of rally.

August 6th - Low of reaction.

September 3rd - Top of rally. Slightly lower than July 27th.
September 13th - Low of reaction. Sept. 26th - Second low of reaction. Narrow market followed from rally to Sept.28th.

October 28th and November 1st to 5th - Lows of reactions.

November 19th - Top of sharp rally; extreme high for quarter.
November 21st and 27th - Low of reaction.

December 7th - Top of sharp rally.
December 12th - Low of reaction; extreme low of quarter.
December 24th - Last low of reaction and low for quarter. Rally followed.

1902

January 6th - High for year and high for quarter.
January 21st to 26th - Low of reaction.

February 26th - Top of rally.

March 12th and 21st - Lows of reactions in narrow market.

April 4th - Low of reaction since January high.
April 25th - High of rally and high for quarter.

June 19th - Extreme low of reaction and low for quarter.
June 24th - Second low of reaction.

July 2nd - Extreme low for quarter.

August 7th - Low of reaction.

September 5th - Top of rally; extreme high for quarter.

September 24th and 29th - Low of reaction.

October 20th - High of rally and high for quarter.

November 7th - Sharp decline started.

December 12th and 15th - Extreme low of year and of quarter. bear year, high in January - low in December.

1903

January 5th and 7th, - Top of rally. Slow market. High for quarter.

February 5th and 9th - Top of rally; 3/4 of point above Jan.7th top.

March 9th - Extreme low of quarter. March 21st - Top of small rally. Trend turned down. March 22nd - High of quarter. Just starting.

April 24th - Low of reaction.

May 5th - Top of small rally. Decline started.

June 19th - Low of reaction and low of quarter. Small rally to July 1st.

July 1st - High of quarter.

August 6th - Low of reaction. Aug. 18th top of rally.

September 8th - Fast decline started. Sept. 21st low of quarter. Sept. 29th - Low for small rally.

October 13th - Low for rally. Oct. 28th - Top of rally and high of quarter.

November 10th - Low of year.

December 11th and 22nd - Extreme low of quarter. Same lows as Nov. 10th. A bear year, high in January - low in December.
December 30th - High of quarter.

1904

January 6th - Low of reaction and extreme low of quarter.
January 22nd - Top of small rally.

March 18th - High of small rally. Very dull and narrow.
March 28th - High of quarter.

May 14th - Low 8-3/8 -- of it's history.

June 24th - 9-1/2 last low of reaction and low of quarter. Trend turned up.

August 3rd and 8th - Top of rally in slow, dull market.
August 22nd - Last low of reaction.

September 17th - Top of rally and high for quarter. Sept.23rd Last low of reaction 15 before big advance turned trend up.
September 24th - Low of quarter. Just started.

November 1st - Started upward, more active.
November 30th - Extreme high of year and high for quarter.

December 8th - Low of sharp reaction. Dec. 13th - Low of second reaction.
The year of final low bear market ended.

1905

January 7th - Low of reaction. Jan.25th - Same low again. Low of quarter.

March 13th - High of rally. Extreme high of quarter.
March 23rd - Low of reaction.

April 6th and 18th - Top of Spring rally and extreme high of quarter

May 22nd - Extreme low of reaction and low of quarter.

June 2nd and 6th - About same low as May 22nd.

June 19th - Trend turned up.
June 23rd - Low of quarter.

August 3rd - Low of small reaction.
August 29th - Same high as April 18th.

September 7th and 11th - Low of reaction.
September 18th - High of quarter.

October 3rd and 23rd - Top of rally.

November 10th and 13th - Low of reaction and of quarter.

December 12th - High of rally and of quarter.
December 18th - Low of reaction.
December 26th - Extreme high of year.

1906

January 5th - Low of small reaction.
January 25th - High of rally and of quarter.
January 30th - Same low as January 5th.

February 2nd - High of rally.
February 7th and 9th - Top of small rally, from which big decline followed and broke low of January 5th and 30th.

March 21st - Extreme low of reaction. Low of quarter.

April 16th - Extreme high of rally and of quarter.
April 21st and 25th - Lower top.

May 2nd - Low of sharp decline and low of quarter.

June 5th - Top of rally, only small rally from 22nd to 23rd; then went lower.

July 3rd and 13th - Extreme low of year and quarter. Trend turned up.

August 4th and 9th - Lows of small reactions.

September 6th - Top of rally and high of quarter.
September 28th - Extreme low of reaction and of quarter.

October 12th - Extreme high of year and of quarter.

November 12th - Low of reaction.

December 12th and 15th - High of rally.
December 19th and 24th - Low of reaction.

1907

January 7th - Extreme high of year and of quarter.
January 31st - Low of sharp decline.

February 8th and 15th - High of rally.

March 14th - Low of silent panic and low for quarter.
March 26th - Extreme low of quarter. Low made 1½ points lower than March 14th.

April 10th - Top of rally and high of quarter.

May 3rd - Top of small rally. Decline started.
May 27th - Extreme low of reaction.

June 17th and 22nd - Make lows 3/4 of point above May 27th low.

July 8th - Top of rally and high of quarter.

August 12th and 17th - Lows of reactions.

September 7th - Top of rally. Sept. 16th - Low of quarter.
September 21st - Top of small rally. Trend continued down.
September 23rd - High of quarter just starting.

October 23rd - Low 21-7/8, extreme low of year and of quarter.

November 6th and 12th - Top of rally.
November 19th and 26th - Lows of reactions.

December 6th - Top of rally.
December 16th and 26th - Lows of reactions and low of quarter. A bear year closed, only four points above the low of the year.

1908

January 2nd - Extreme low of year. Jan. 20th - Top of rally.

February 10th - Low of reaction. Advance started.

March 16th - High of quarter. March 24th - Top of rally.

April 4th - Low of reaction and of quarter.
April 28th - Top for small reaction.

May 3rd - Low of reaction. May 18th - High of rally and of quarter.
May 27th - Low of reaction.

June 2nd - Top of small rally.
June 24th - Low of reaction and of quarter. Slightly above May 27th low.

August 10th - Top of rally and high of quarter.
August 15th - Low of reaction.

September 8th - Same high as August 10th. Sept. 22nd - Low of sharp reaction. Sept. 24th - Low of quarter just started.

November 14th - Extreme high of year, 58-7/8 and high of quarter.

December 21st - Low of reaction. Sharp rally to Dec. 29th.

1909

January 6th - Low of reaction. Rallied to 8th.
January 14th - Low of reaction.
January 22nd - High of month and of quarter from which big decline followed.

February 23rd - Extreme low of year from which big bull market followed and low of quarter.

March 1st - Top of rally.
March 20th - Low of decline. Mch.22nd - Low of quarter just starting.

May 3rd - Low of reaction and low for month of May.
May 8th - Top for reaction to May 14th, from where advance was resumed.

June 14th - Top of rally and high of quarter.
June 22nd - Low of reaction. June 23rd - Low of quarter just starting.

August 12th and 16th - High of rally.
August 24th - Bottom of quick decline.
August 27th - Made bottom. Slightly higher than Aug.20th.

September 3rd - Top of rally; declined to 9th; then went right on up. Sept. 22nd - High of quarter.

October 4th - High for year 94-7/8 and high of quarter.
October 13th - Low of reaction. Oct.15th - Top of quick rally.
October 23rd and 27th - Made bottoms slightly higher than Oct.13th.

November 5th - Top of rally and same top as Oct.15th.
November 30th - Low of reaction and low of quarter. Same low as Oct. 13th.

December 18th - Top of rally. Dec.27th - Low of reaction. Rallied to Dec.30th; high of quarter.

1910

January 7th - First low had three point rally on 8th; then broke low of 7th. Jan.19th - Low of reaction.
January 22nd - Top of quick rally. Just ½ point under Jan.8th top.
January 25th - Low of reaction. Jan.29th - Top of rally.

February 8th - Extreme low of early part of year and of quarter.

March 9th - Top of rally. Never went higher during the year.
March 16th - Low of reaction. March 22nd - Trend turned down.
March 31st - Low of reaction.

April 14th - Top of rally and high of quarter,

May 3rd - Low of reaction. May 21st - Top of rally.

June 6th - Low of reaction and low of quarter.
June 22nd - Top of rally and high of quarter.

July 6th - Low of reaction. July 11th and 15th - Top of small rally.
July 26th - Extreme low of year and of quarter. July 29th - Top of sharp rally.

August 2nd - Low of reaction and low for August. Aug. 17th - High of rally and high for month. Aug.25th - Low of reaction, for rally.

September 14th - Top of rally. Sept.20th - Extreme low of reaction.
September 24th - Low of quarter just starting.

November 4th -Top for quick reaction to 10th. Nov.4th - High of quarter. Nov.19th - Top of rally. Slightly lower than Nov.4th.

December 8th - Low of reaction. Dec.10th, 15th and 19th - Tops of rally. Dec.28th - Low of reaction, extreme low of quarter, but higher than Dec.8th bottom; rallied to Dec.31st.

1911

January 3rd - Low of reaction and low was not broken until late in August.

February 6tb and 10th - Top of rally and high of quarter.

March 4th - Low of reaction. March 21st - Top of rally.

April 24th - Low of reaction and of quarter.

May 1st - Top of rally. May 6th - Low of reaction.
May 18th and 22nd - Top of rally and high of quarter.

June 1st - Low of reaction. June 15th - Top of rally.
June 22nd - Low of reaction.

July 22nd - Top of rally and high of quarter from which big decline followed.

August 5th - Low for small rally to August 7th. Aug.26th - Low for month.

September 6th - Top of rally. Sept.22nd - First low of decline and low of quarter. Sept.25th - Extreme low of month.

October 2nd - Top of rally. Oct.7th - Low for rally to 14th.
October 19th - Low about same as Oct.7th low. Oct.20th and 24th - Last rallies before big break. Oct.27th - Low 50, extreme low for year and of quarter.

November 6th - Top of rally. Nov.8th - Low of reaction, but Nov.3rd was extreme low of month. Nov.27th - Top of rally.

December 8th - Low of reaction. Dec.20th - Top of rally and high of quarter. Dec.29th - Low of reaction.

1912

January 2nd - Top of rally and high of quarter.

February 1st and 13th - Low of reaction and of quarter.

March 25th - Top of rally; declined to 28; then went higher.

April 8th and 30th - Same tops and highest of quarter. From Apr.30th a sharp decline followed.

May 7th - Low of decline and of quarter. May 20th - Top of rally.

June 1st - Low of reaction.

July 2nd - Top of rally. July 11th - Low of reaction and low of quarter.

August 2nd - Top for small reaction. Aug.7th - Low of reaction.
August 21st and 28th - High for month.

September 12th - Low of reaction. Sept.23rd - High of quarter.

October 4th - Top of rally and high for year and quarter.
October 30th - Low of reaction.

November 4th - Low of reaction from Oct.31st. Nov.7th - Top of quick rally and high for month. Nov.12th and 16th - Same lows of reaction. Nov.21st - Last top from which big decline followed.

December 11th and 16th - Low of decline and of quarter.
December 21st and 28th - Top of rally. Dec.30th - Low of reaction.

1913

January 2nd - High for month, quarter and year. Jan.17th and 20th Low for rally. Jan.31st - Top of rally.

February 4th - Top of rally and high for month.
February 25th - Low of reaction.

March 3rd - Top of rally. Mch.10th - First low of reaction and of quarter. Mch.19th - Second low for rally.

April 4th - Top of rally and high of quarter.
April 29th - Low of reaction.

May 5th and 8th - Top of rally. May 12th and 14th - Low of small reaction. May 26th - Top of rally from which big decline started.

June 11th - First low of reaction and of quarter.
June 21st - Second low, slightly higher than June 11th.

July 9th - Low of quarter.

August 13th - Top of rally and high of quarter. Aug.16th and 22nd- Lows of reaction. Aug.29th - Top of rally.

Sept. 4th - Lowof reaction. Sept. 13th - Top of rally, slightly lower than Aug.13th. Sept.22nd - Top of last rally. Big decline followed. Sept.23rd - High of quarter just starting.

October 17th - Low of decline. Oct.27th - Top of rally.

November 10th - Same low as Oct.17th and low of quarter.

December 8th - Top of rally. Dec.15th - Low of reaction.
December 24th - Low of quarter. Dec.26th - Top of rally.

1914

January 3rd - Low of reaction. Jan.31st - High for year and high of quarter.

February 4th and 14th - Tops of small rallies.

March 7th - Low of reaction. March 21st and 24th - Top of rally.
March 25th - Low of quarter.

April 25th - Low of reaction.

May 1st - Low of small reaction. May 28th - Top of rally and high of quarter.

June 25th - Low of reaction.

July 8th - Top of rally and high of quarter. July 16th - Low of reaction. July 22nd - Top of rally. July 30th - Low at 50; extreme low of q uarter. Exchange closed until Dec.15th account War.

December 15th - High 55, of quarter. Decline followed. Dec.22nd-Low of quarter. Dec.26th - Low 48 for small rally.

1915

January 4th - Low of reaction. Jan. 21st - High of rally $53\frac{1}{4}$ and high of quarter; big break followed.

February 1st - Steel passed dividend. The stock sold at 38, made low for the month and extreme low for the year and quarter.
February 13th - Top of rally. Feb.24th - Low of reaction.

March 8th - Top of rally. Mch.18th - Last low of reaction.
March 24th - Low of quarter just starting.

April 19th - Top for reaction. Apr.24th - Low of reaction.

May 3rd - Top of rally for big, quick decline. May 10th - Low of reaction. May 14th - A higher bottom.

June 4th - Top of rally and high of quarter. June 9th - Low of reaction. June 22nd - Top of rally.

July 7th and 9th - Low of reaction and low of quarter but higher than June 9th low.

August 10th - Top of sharp advance. Aug.14th - Low of reaction.
August 18th - Top for month and high for quarter. A quick ten point break followed. Aug.27th - Top of rally.

September 11th and 17th - Low of reaction. Sept.24th - Low of quarter.

October 1st - Top of rally. Oct.6th - Low of reaction; same as Sept. 24th low. Oct.21st - High of rally and high for month. Oct. 29th - Low of reaction.

November 1st and 4th - High of rally. Nov.9th - Low of reaction.
November 12th and 26th - High of rally and of quarter.

December 2nd - Low of reaction. Dec.7th - Top of rally.
December 17th and 21st - Low of reaction. Dec. 27th and 31st -High of rally and of quarter.

1916

January 7th - Low for rally to 8th; then went lower.
January 31st - Low for month and low for quarter.

February 10th - Top of rally.

March 1st - Low of reaction. Mch.17th - High of rally.
March 27th - Low of reaction.

April 4th - Top of rally. Apr.22nd - Low of reaction and low of quarter.

May 1st - Top of rally. May 5th - Low of reaction.

June 12th - Top of rally and high of quarter.
June 23rd and 27th - Low of reaction and of quarter.

July 6th - Top of rally. July 14th - Low of reaction.
July 24th and 26th - Top of rally.

August 5th - Low of reaction; trend turned up strong.
August 23rd - Top of rally.

September 1st - Low of reaction. Sept.22nd - High of quarter just ending. Sept. 25th and 29th - Top of rally.

October 9th and 14th - Same lows from which big advance followed.

November 8th - Top of rally. Nov.14th - Low of reaction.
November 27th - High of year and quarter.

December 21st - Low of big break and low of quarter.

1917

January 4th - Top of rally and high of quarter. Jan.5th and 11th-Low of reaction. Jan.26th - Top of rally. Did not cross top of Jan.4th.

February 1st - Low of big break and of quarter.
February 3rd - Made slightly higher bottom.

March 21st - Top of rally. Mch.27th - Low of reaction.

April 3rd - Top of rally. Apr.10th - Low of reaction and of quarter. Made higher bottom on 17th and 20th. Apr.26th - Top of rally.

May 9th - Low of reaction. May 31st - High of month, quarter and year.

June 1st and 4th - Low of reaction. June 14th - Top of rally.
June 20th - Low of reaction. June 27th - Top of rally and high of quarter.

July 19th - Low of reaction.

August 7th - Top of rally.

September 17t - Low of reaction and of quarter.
September 25th - Top of rally and high of quarter.

October 15th - Low of reaction. Oct.22nd, 27th - Top of rally.

November 8th - Low of reaction. November 26th - Top of rally.

December 20th - Extreme low of decline for sharp quick rally. Low of quarter.

1918

January 3rd - Top of rally. Jan.15th, 18th and 23rd-Lows of reaction.

February 1st - High of rally. Feb.19th and 27th -- high of quarter. slightly lower tops.

March 25th - Low of reaction and of quarter.

April 22nd - Top of rally for small reaction.
April 25th and 27th and 30th - Lows of reaction.

May 16th - High of quarter. Top of rally for sharp decline.

June 1st - Low of reaction. June 27th - Top of rally.

July 15th - Low of reaction and low of quarter.

August 10th - Top for reaction. Aug.15th, 17th and 22nd - Lows of reaction. Aug.28th and Sept.3rd - Last tops before big decline and high of quarter.

September 13th - Low of reaction. Sept.27th - Top of rally.

Oct.9th - Bottom of reaction. Oct.19th - Top of rally and high of quarter.

November 2nd - Bottom for small rally. Nov.7th - Top of rally. Nov.13th - Low of reaction. Nov.21st - Top of rally. Nov.29th- Low of decline and low of quarter.

December 11th - Top of rally. Dec.26th - Low for month.

1919

January 3rd - Top of rally.

February.10th - Extreme low of decline and low of quarter.

March 12th - Top of rally. Mch.19th - Low of reaction. Mch.22nd-Top of rally and high of quarter. Mch.26th - Low of quarter; low of reaction and higher than Mch.19th.

April 23rd - Top of rally.

May 1st - Bottom of reaction. May 5th - A higher bottom.

June 6th - Top of rally and high of quarter. June 16th - Low of reaction.

July 7th - Top of rally and high of quarter. July 11th-Low of reaction
July 14th - Top of rally. Just $\frac{1}{4}$ point higher than July 7th.
July 22nd - Low of reaction. July 28th - Top of rally.

August 8th - Low for small rally. Aug.11th and 13th - Top of rally.
August 21st - Low for big rally. Extreme low of quarter.

September 4th - Top for reaction. Sept.20th - Low of reaction.

October 10th - Top of rally and high of quarter. Oct.25th - Low of reaction.

November 5th - Same top as Oct.10th.
December 12th - Low of reaction and of quarter. Dec.27th - Top for small reaction. Dec.29th - Low of reaction.

1920

January 5th - Top of rally and high of quarter. Jan.6th - Low of reaction. Jan. 10th - Top of small rally. Failed to reach top of Jan.5th. Jan.19th - Low of reaction. Jan.27th - Top of rally.

February 13th - Low of reaction. Feb.18th - Top of rally.
February 27th - Low of decline for big rally; low of quarter.

March 11th - Top of rally. Mch.17th - Low of reaction. Mch.22nd- Top of rally. Mch. 25th - Last low of reaction.

April 8th - Extreme top of rally and high of quarter. Apr.12th- Low of small reaction. Apr.14th - Top of small rally. Apr.23rd- Low of sharp decline. Apr.27th - Top of small rally.

May 3rd - Low of decline. May 8th and 10th - Top of rally.
May 13th - Low of decline. Slightly lower than May 3rd. May 15th- Top of rally. May 19th - Extreme low of decline. May 28th and 29th - Top of rally.

June 1st - Low of small reaction. June 5th - Top of rally.
June 8th - Low of reaction. June 12th - Top of rally. June 20th-Low of quarter. June 23rd - Low of reaction. June 24th - First low of quarter just starting. June 26th - Top of small rally. June 28th - Low of small reaction, higher than 23rd.

July 8th - Top of rally and highest of quarter. July 16th - Low of reaction. July 23rd - Top of rally.

August 9th - Low of reaction and extreme low of quarter. Aug.27th - Top of rally.

September 13th - Low of reaction. Sept.18th - Top of rally.

October 1st - Low of reaction. Oct.5th - Top of rally. Oct.13th-Low of reaction. Oct.25th - Top of rally and high of quarter.
October 28th - Low of reaction.

November 1st - Top of rally. Nov.19th - Low of reaction.
November 23rd - Top of rally.

December 1st - Low of reaction. Slightly lower than Nov.19th.
Dec.2nd and 6th - Top of rally. Big decline followed. Dec.21st and 22nd - Extreme low of month, quarter and year.

1921

January 4th - High of rally. Jan.5th - Small reaction. Jan.11th-Top of rally. Jan.14th - Low of reaction. Jan.19th - Top of rally below top of 11th. Jan.22nd - Low of reaction. Same low as Jan.5th. Jan.28th - Top of rally.

February 4th - Low of reaction; same low as Jan.5th and 22nd. Feb.17th - High of rally and quarter; ¼ above Jan.11th high.

March 14th - Low of reaction. Mch.23rd - Top of rally,

April 14th - Low of reaction. Apr.26th - Top of rally. Apr.28th-Low of small decline.

May 6th - Last top before big decline and high of quarter. May 16th - Low of reaction. May 23rd - Top of rally.

June 21st - Low of quarter just ending. June 23rd - Made extreme low of month and year at 70½ and low of quarter.

July 7th - Top of rally. July 16th - Low of decline.

August 2nd - Top of rally. Aug.24th - Low of reaction.

September 19th high of quarter and 26th- top of rally.

October 17th - Low of reaction and quarter. Oct.29th - Top of rally.

November 2nd and 7th - Last lows before big advance. Nov.28th - Top of rally. Nov.30th - Low of reaction.

December 15th - Top of rally and high of quarter. Dec.23rd - Low of reaction. Dec.28th and 31st - Tops of rally.

1922

January 6th - Low of month and of quarter. Jan.20th - Top of rally. January 31st - Low of reaction.

February 7th - Top of rally. Feb.9th - Low of small reaction. Feb.23rd - Top of sharp advance and high of quarter.

March 6th - Low of reaction. Mch.18th - Top of rally. Mch.24th -Last low and low of quarter; advance followed.

April 10th and 20th - Tops for small reaction.

May 11th - Low of reaction.

June 6th - Top of rally and high of quarter. June 12th and 16th - Low of reaction. June 20th - Top of rally. June 27th - Last low of reaction and of quarter.

July 20th - Top of rally. July 26th - Low of reaction. July 31st - Top of rally and high of quarter.

August 10th and 15th - Low of reaction.

September 11th - Top of rally, Sept.29th - Low of reaction and low of quarter.

October 16th - Top of rally and high of quarter.

November 1st - Low of reaction. Nov.9th - Top of rally. Nov.28th -Low of reaction.

December 18th - High of rally. Dec. 21st and 28th - Low of reaction and of quarter.

1923

January 4th - Top of rally and high of quarter. Jan.17th - Low of reaction. Jan.26th - Top of rally. Jan.31st - Low of reaction and quarter.

February 26th and March 3rd - Top of rally.

March 12th - Low of reaction. Mch.21st - Top of rally and highest of quarter. Mch.26th - Low of reaction.

April 2 nd - Top of rally. Slow and narrow market. Made last top April 18th. Started decline on April 25th.

May 5th - Top of small rally. May 22nd - Low of reaction. May 28th- Top of rally.

June 2nd - Low of reaction. June 7th - High of rally. June 21st- Extreme low of quarter and low for small rally to 23rd. June 30th - Low for month.

July 3rd - Top of rally. July 5th, 11th and 17th - Lows near same level around 89½. July 23rd - Top of small rally. July 31st- Low of reaction and quarter.

August 30th - high of rally and of quarter.

September 4th - Low of small reaction. Sept.6th and 11th- Top of rally but not up to Aug.30th high. Sept.23rd - Low - same low as July 31st. Sept.25th - Low of quarter just starting.

October 4th - Top of small rally. Oct.17th - Low of reaction. October 24th - Top of small rally. Oct.29th - Last low from which big advance started.

November 12th - Top of rally. Nov.17th - Low of reaction. November 27th - Top of rally and high of quarter.

December 19th - Low of reaction. Dec.23rd - Low of quarter. December 31st - Top of rally.

1924

January 4th - Low of reaction and low for month.

February 7th - Top of rally and high of quarter. Feb.27th - Low of reaction. Feb.29th - Top of rally.

March 29th - Low of reaction.

April 5th - Top of rally. Apr.10th, 15th and 22nd - Lows around same level. April 26th - Top of rally and high of quarter. Ap ril 30th - Low of reaction.

May 2nd - Top of small rally. May 20th - Bottom of reaction. May 26th - Top of rally. May 29th - Low of reaction.

June 4th - Top of rally. June 6th - Low of reaction and low of quarter. June 23rd - Low of quarter just starting.

July 10th - Top of rally. Jly.17th - Low of reaction.

August 4th - Top of rally. Aug.12th - Low of reaction. Aug.20th-Top of rally and high of quarter.

September 8th - Low of reaction. Sept. 25th - Top of rally.

October 2nd - Same top as Sept.25th. Oct.14th - Last low from which big advance started and low of quarter.

November 26th - Top for small reaction.

December 11th - Bottom of reaction. Dec.19th - high of quarter. Dec.24th - Low of quarter just starting. Dec.29th - Top of rally. Dec.31st - Low of small reaction.

1925

January 3rd and 5th - Top of rally. Jan.6th - Low of small reaction. January 23rd - Top of rally and high of quarter.

February 3rd - Low of reaction. Feb.5th - Top of small rally. Feb.17th - Low of reaction.

March 6th and 7th - Top of rally. Mch.30th - Extreme low for month and quarter.

April 18th - Top of rally. Apr.30th - Low of reaction. Slightly above Mch.30th low.

May 21st - High of rally and high for quarter.

June 9th - Low of reaction. June 15th and 19th - Top of rally. June 29th - Last low of q uarter and higher than low of Apr.30th and Mch.30th. This was a triple bottom and a big advance followed.

July 29th - High for the month. July 31st - Low of reaction.

August 26th - High of month and of quarter.

September 3rd - Low of reaction. Sept.15th - Top of rally. Slightly lower top than Aug.26th. Sept.28th - Low of reaction and low of quarter. A little higher than Sept.3rd.

October 1st - Low of month. Oct.24th and 26th - High of month. October 29th - Low of small reaction.

November 7th - Top for the year and quarter. Nov.10th-Low of sharp decline. Nov.14th - Top of quick rally but not as high as Nov.7th top. Nov.24th - Low of month.

December 8th - Top of rally. Dec.22nd - Low of reaction. Dec.28th -Top of rally. Dec.31st - Low of reaction.

## 1926

January 4th - Top of rally and high for quarter. Jan.6th - Low of small reaction. Jan.7th - Top of rally. Failed to reach top of Jan.4th. Jan.22nd - Low of month. Jan.25th - Top of rally.

February 1st - Low of small reaction. Feb.4th - Top of small rally. February 26th - Extreme low of month.

March 1st - Top of small rally. Mch.2nd - Low of small reaction and low of quarter. Mch.16th - Top for month. Mch.30th- Extreme low for month.

April 6th - Top of rally. Apr.15th - Low of reaction and low of quarter. Apr.29th - High for month.

May 3rd - Low of reaction. May 6th - Top of small rally. May 17th-Low for month; big advance started.

June 17th - Top of rally and high of quarter. June 18th - Quick decline of five points. June 26th - Low of quarter just started.

July 2nd - Top of rally. July 9th - Low of reaction. July 16th - Top of rally. July 24th - Low of reaction.

August 17th - Extreme high for month, quarter and year. Aug.25th-Low of reaction.

September 8th - Top of rally. Sept.20th - Low of reaction.

October 2nd - Top of sharp rally. Oct.20th - Low of sharp decline and low of quarter. Oct.28th - Top of rally.

November 3rd - Low of reaction. Nov.16th - High of month. Nov.19th- Low of sharp decline. Nov.27th - Top of rally.

December 6th - Low of reaction. Dec.17th - High of quarter - and 27th - high for month and one point above the high of Aug.17,1926.

## 1927

January 4th and 7th - Low of reaction. Jan.11th - Top of rally. January 28th - Extreme low for month, quarter and year on the new stock.

February 24th - High for month. Feb.28 th - Low of small reaction.

March 1st - Top of rally. Mch.8th - Low for month; big advance followed. Mch.17th - High of quarter. Mch.22nd - Low of quarter just starting.

April 11th and 16th - Top of rally.

May 2nd - Low of reaction; then up balance of month.

June 1st - Top of rally and high of quarter. June 30th - Low for month and last low before big advance. Low of quarter.

July 29th - High for month.

August 1st - Low of reaction. Aug.2nd - Top of rally. Aug.12th -Low of reaction.

September 9th - Top of rally. Sept. 12th - Low of reaction. September 16th - Top of rally and high of quarter. Slightly higher than Sept.9th. Sept.29th - Low of month.

October 4th - Top of rally. Oct.29th - Low of month and quarter and last low before big advance started.

November 29th - High for month.

December 9th - Low of reaction. Dec.22nd - High of quarter. December 24th - Top of rally and high of quarter just started.

<u>1928</u>

January 5th - Low of reaction. Jan.7th - Top of rally; declined and broke low of 5th. Jan.17th - Low of reaction. Jan.24th - Top of rally. Jan.25th - Same low as 16th. Jan.27th - Top of rally; lower than 24th.

February 4th - Low of reaction. Feb.9th - Top of rally. Feb.27th-Low of month.

March 1st - Top of small rally. Mch.2nd - Low of reaction and low of quarter; one point lower than Feb.20th. Mch.22nd - Top of rally. Mch. 23rd - low of quick reaction. Mch. 26th - Top of rally; slightly lower than Mch.22nd top.

April 2nd - Low of reaction. April 12th - Top of rally and high of quarter; $1\frac{1}{4}$ points above high of Jan.7th. Apr.24th - Low of reaction.

May 7th - Top of rally. May 9th - Low of reaction. May 11th - Top of rally. May 22nd and 29th - Low of month.

June 1st - Top of rally. June 11th - Low of quarter. June 25th - Low for month and quarter and low of year from which big advance followed.

July 9th - Top of rally. July 17th - Low of reaction. July 28th - Top of rally.

August 3rd and 9th - Low of reactions.

September 17th - Top of rally and high of quarter. Sept. 21st - Low of reaction. Sept.27th - Top of rally and high for month.

October 3rd - Low of reaction and first law of quarter. Oct.4th - Same top as Sept. 27th. Oct.9th - Low of reaction. Oct.24th - High for month. Oct.26th and 31st - Low of reaction.

November 2nd - Top of small rally. Nov.3rd and 8th - Low of reaction. Nov.16th - Top for month and high of quarter. Nov.21st - Low of reaction. Nov.23rd and 26th - Tops of rally; big break followed.

December 17th - Extreme low of quarter; low 149-3/4, last low before big advance. Dec. 24th - Top of rally. Dec.27th - Low of reaction and of quarter.

1929

January 3rd - Top of rally. Jan.8th - Low of reaction, 157$\frac{1}{4}$; advance started and crossed high of Jan.3rd. Jan.25th - High of month. Jan.30th - Low of reaction.

February 2nd - Top of rally. Feb.16th - Low of month.

March 1st - Top of rally and high of quarter. Mch.6th and 11th - Low of reaction. March 15th - Top of rally. Mch.26th - Low of sharp decline.

April 12th - Top of rally and high of quarter. Apr.17th - Low of reaction. Apr.30th - Top of rally.

May 2nd - Broke lows of Apr.9th and 17th; turning trend down. May 3rd - Small rally. May 31st - Low of month, low of quarter and last low before big advance.

June 17th - Top for small reaction. June 20th - Low of reaction. June 25th - Low of quarter just started.

July 20th - Top of rally. July 22nd - Low of reaction. July 24th - Top for month. July 29th - Low of reaction.

August 2 nd - Top for reaction. Aug.6th - Low of reaction. Crossed high of Aug.2nd. Aug. 24th - High for month. Aug.29th - Low of reaction.

September 3rd - High of quarter and final high 261-3/4, up 95 days from last low made May 31st. Sept.13th - Low of sharp decline. Sept. 19th - Last top of quick rally. Sept. 24th - High of quarter just started.

October 4th - Low of sharp decline. Oct.10th - Top of quick rally. Oct.29th - Low of month. Oct.31st - Top of sharp two day rally.

November 7th - Low of reaction. Nov.8th - Top of quick rally. Nov. 13th - Extreme low for month and quarter at 150, down 111-3/4 points in 71 days. Nov.21st - Top of rally.

ecember 2nd - Low of reaction. Dec. 9th - Top of sharp rally. Dec. 23rd - Low of month and quarter and last low before advance started.

1930

January 2nd - Top of rally. Declined same day from 173-3/4 to 166 which was low of month. Jan. 10th - Top of rally. Slightly lower than Jan.2nd top. Jan.18th - Low of reaction.

February 18th - Top of rally and high for the month and quarter. Feb. 25th - Low of reaction.

March 1st and 7th - Top of rally. Mch. 13th - Low of reaction; made higher bottom on March 17th.

April 7th - Extreme high of rally and high for month and high for quarter. April 8th - Low of reaction. April 10th - Top of rally. April 15th - Low of reaction. April 16th - Quick rally. Big break followed.

May 5th - First low of reaction. May 6th - Top of quick rally. May 8th - Low of reaction and extreme low for the month. May 14th Top of rally. May 20th - Low of reaction; slightly higher than low on 8th. May 28th - Top of rally; same high as May 6th and one-half point lower than May 14th top. Then decline to lower levels, breaking support points.

June 25th - Bottom of decline and low for the quarter.

August 5th - Top of rally. August 13th - Bottom of sharp reaction. Then slowly worked higher.

September 8th - High of quarter and near the highs of May 6th, 14th, and 28th. Trend turned down and prices worked lower. September 24th - Last rally; high for that quarter.

October - Broke support points and declined to new low levels.

December 17th - Reached bottom; low of the quarter, Rally followed.

## 1931

February 26th - Top of advance and high of quarter.

March 25th - High for that quarter. Then followed a fast decline.

April - Broke bottom of December 17th, 1930; showed very weak position and indicated much lower prices.

June 2nd - Bottom of decline and low of quarter. Rally followed.

July 3rd - Top of rally and high of the quarter.

September 21st - Low of the quarter. September 23rd - Top of minor rally; high of quarter. Trend continued down.

December 18th - First low of decline; rallied to the 19th.

## 1932

January 4th - Nearly same low as December 18th; low of the quarter. Rally followed.

February 19th Top of rally; high for quarter. Decline followed.

March 22nd - High of the quarter. April - Declined to new lows.

June 10th - Low of the quarter, the lowest close of any quarter since 1907. June 28th - Extreme low of decline, 21¼, and low of quarter. Note the low of October, 1907, was 21-7/8, a double bottom and support point. Advance followed.

September 6th - Top of advance; failed to cross top of February 19th 1932. Also high of quarter. Decline followed. September 20th- Bottom of reaction. September 26th - Last high before decline; high of quarter.

October - Secondary decline continues.

December 22nd - Low of quarter. December 28th - Temporary low,

1933

January 11th - Top of rally; high of quarter.

March 2nd - Low of quarter. Range during the quarter only 8½ points, the shortest range for years on very small volume. Making higher bottom than June 28th, 1932, the stock indicated good support. Trend turned up. March 31st - Low of minor reaction.

June 13th - High of quarter. Trend continued up.

July 18th - Top of advance; high for the quarter. Decline followed.

September 22nd - Low of quarter. September 23rd- High of next quarter.

October 21st - Low point of decline and low of quarter. Trend turned up.

1934

December 27th, 1933 and January 5th, 1934, same low; low of quarter.

February 19th - Top of advance: high of quarter. Trend turned down.

March 26th - High of next quarter.

June 2nd - Low of decline and low of the quarter.

July 11th - High of next quarter.

September 17th - Low of decline and low of quarter.

October 30th- Another low and low of quarter.

December 6th - Top of rally; high of quarter.

1935

January 8th - Top of rally and high of quarter.

March 18th - Last low before the uptrend started; low of the quarter and a still higher bottom than that of March 31st, 1933.

April 3rd - Low of the next quarter. Trend turned up.

# CHAPTER 5

## *NATURAL RESISTANCE LEVELS AND TIME CYCLE POINTS*

Scientific Advice
and Analytical Reports
on Stocks and Commodities
Author of "Truth of the Stock Tape"
"Wall Street Stock Selector"
and "The Tunnel Thru the Air"

W. D. GANN
88 WALL STREET
NEW YORK

Member
American Economic Ass'n
Royal Economic Society
Cable Address
"Ganwade New York"

## NATURAL RESISTANCE LEVELS AND TIME CYCLE POINTS

The resistance levels given below are based upon natural law and can be applied to the measurement of both time and space. Around these points stocks meet resistance going up or down or traveling the same number of points from a top to a bottom. Tops and bottoms of major and minor movements come out on these resistance levels.

When man first began to learn to count, he probably used his fingers, counting 5 on one hand and 5 on the other. Then counting 5 toes on one foot and 5 on the other, which made 10, he added 10 and 10 together, which made 20, adding and multiplying by 5 and 10 all the way through. This basis for figuring led to the decimal system, which works out our 5, 10, 20, 30 and other yearly cycles, as well as other resistance points. Man's basis for figuring is 100, or par, on stocks and $1.00 as a basis of money value. Therefore, the 1/4, 1/8, 1/16 points are all important for tops and bottoms and for buying and selling levels.

Taking the basis of 100, the most important points are 25, 50 and 75, which are 1/4, 1/2 and 3/4. The next most important points are 33⅓ and 66⅔, which are 1/3 and 2/3 points. The next points in importance are the 1/8 points, which are 12½, 37½, 62½ and 87½. The next in importance are the 1/16 points, which are 6¼, 18¾, 31¼, 43¾, 56¼, 68¾, 81¼ and 93¾.

Since 9 is the highest digit, it is very important for resistance levels in time and space. The most important levels according to 9 are: 9, 12, 27, 36, 45, 54, 63, 72, 81, 90, 99, 108, 117, 126, 135 and 144. You will note that many of these points correspond with the other resistance levels, because 12 is simply 9 with 1/3 of 9 added to it.

The second important resistance levels formed by the digit of 9 are the 1/2 points, which are as follows: 4½, 22½, 31½, 40½, 49½, 58½, 67½, 76½, 85½, 94½, 103½, etc. You simply add 1/2 of 9, or 4½, to any even figure, or figure coming out on equal numbers of 9.

The next important resistance levels are those formed by 12 and its multiples. These are very important on account of the 12 months in the year. The points also come out very close to many of the other important resistance points measured on the basis of 100 and 9 and also the points in the division of the circle of 360°. The most important points of resistance according to 12 are: 12, 18, 24, 30, 36, 42, 48, 54, 60, 66, 72, 78, 84, 90, 96, 102, 108, 114, 120, 126, 132, 138, 144 and the other points which you can see on the Master Twelve Chart or Square of 12 x 12. A separate explanation of the Master Twelve Chart gives these other important points. Tops and bottoms of most stocks come out remarkably close to a basis of 12.

The circle of 360°, when divided into its geometrical parts, proves the reason of all resistance levels and measures time and volume as well as space very accurately. It is important to divide the circle by 2, 3, 4, 5, 6, 8, 9 and 12, to get the important resistance levels.

We first divide the circle by 2 and get 180, which is the strongest resistance level because it is the gravity center or 1/2 point. It equals 180 months or 15 years, which is 3/4 of the 20-year cycle and 1/2 of the 30-year cycle, which is very important.

We next divide the circle by 4 and get 90, 180, 270 and 360. These are very important points because they equal 7½ years, 15 years and 22½ years, which is 3/4 of the circle. These points in days, weeks or months mark the beginning and the ending of important Time Cycles, as well as being important resistance levels when the price reaches them, especially when the time is up.

The next important levels we obtain by dividing 360 by 3, getting 120 as 1/3 and 240 as 2/3 points. These equal the 10-year cycle and the 20-year cycle and, of course, the third point, or 360, is the 30-year cycle.

Dividing the circle by 12, we get the following important points, which correspond with other points: 30, 60, 90, 120, 150, 180, 210, 240, 270, 300, 330 and 360. 150 and 210 are very important because 150 is within 30 months of the 180° angle or halfway between 120 and 180. 210 is 1/2 point between 180 and 240.

After dividing the circle by 12, it is next important to divide by 24, because there are 24 hours in a day, and the Earth moves 15° every hour or 360° in 24 hours. Therefore, we get the following points: 15, 30, 45, 60, 75, 90, 105, 120, 135, 150, 165, 180, 195, 210, 225, 240, 255, 270, 285, 300, 315, 330, 345, 360. If we divide 15 by 2, we get 7½. Adding this to any of the other points gives an important point which corresponds to many of the other resistance levels. For example: Adding 7½ to 15 gives 22½, which is 1/16 of a circle. 150 is an important point and if we add 15 to this, we get 165, which is the 1/2 point between 150 and 180, 180 being one of the strongest angles. Get your other important points in the same way by adding 7½ or 15.

Dividing the circle by 8, we also get very important points, which are: 45, 90, 135, 180, 225, 270 and 315. 135 is very important because it is 180° from 45. 315 is very important because it is the opposite of 135 and 90° from 45.

The next important points for resistance and measurement of time are obtained by dividing the circle by 16, which gives 22½, 45, 67½, 90, 112½, 135, 157½, 202½, 225, 247½, 292½, 315 and 337½.

The points obtained by dividing the circle by 32 are also important because they measure out cycles closely in accordance with the Master Twelve Chart and come out closely with the months. These points are 11¼, 33¾, 56¼, 78¾, 101¾, 123¾, etc., just simply adding 11¼ to any of the other figures to get the next figure.

The lowest division of the circle of any importance is 1/64, which is 5⅝ of 1/2 of 11¼. These are of minor importance but tops and bottoms often come out on these points, especially when we are nearing the end of a major cycle. These points are as follows: 5⅝, 16⅞, 28⅛, 39⅜, 50⅝, 61⅞, 73⅛, 84⅜, 95⅝, 106⅞, 118⅛, 129⅜. All of these points are the 1/2 points between the other important points. 22½ is 1/2 of 45, 11¼ is 1/2 of 22½, and 5⅝ is 1/2 of 11¼.

It is very important to divide the circle by 9 because 9 is the highest digit used. Dividing by 9 we get the following important points: 40, 80, 120, 160, 200, 240, 280, 320, 360, all very important resistance levels and corresponding with many of the other resistance levels calculated from the different points.

Dividing these points by 2, we get 20, 40, 60, 80, 100, 120, 140, 160, 180, 200, 220, 240, 260, 280, 300, 320, 340, 360. Many stocks work to these points of a circle in division of time, making tops and bottoms according to price and according to months. I use these points and the Master Twelve points and the other important points obtained through dividing the circle by 2, 4 and 8, as the most important resistance levels in measuring the time cycles.

If you will take the time to go over any stock running back 10 to 30 years, checking all important tops and bottoms, you will see how well these points work out both in time and space. In checking the Weekly High and Low Chart, you will find more of them working out than you can see on the monthly, because there are bottoms and tops made on weekly moves which do not show on the Monthly High and Low Chart. Then checking up on the Daily Chart, you will find minor moves working to these points which do not all show on the Weekly High and Low Chart.

To determine monthly movements, it is important to divide the year by 4, which gives the seasonal changes or the 4 quarters, which equal about 90° in time or 90 days and come to the strong resistance levels. Watch for changes every 3, 6, 9 and 12 months. Most stocks make changes of importance at the end of each 12-month period. The next important thing to do is to divide the year by 3, making 4 months, 8 months and 12 months important points to watch. Dividing 52 weeks or 1 year by 4 gives 13 weeks, 26 weeks, 39 weeks as important points to watch for change in trend. Divide 52 weeks by 3 to get the 1/3 points. On this basis, the 17th to 18th weeks and the 35th to 36th weeks will be important points to watch for a change in trend.

When any important Time Cycle is running out, watch your Daily and Weekly High and Low Charts for an indication that top or bottom is being reached. Keep up your angles closely, as the angles will determine when the trend is changing. One good rule to use after a very extended campaign, which has run 50 points or more in space, is to take the greatest move on the way up or down and then when it exceeds this on a reaction it indicates that the trend is changing. Another way is to take 1/12 of the total movement. Suppose a stock has advanced 144 points, then 1/12 of 144 points is 12 points. As a rule, when a stock has advanced this much and reacts 12 points, especially if reactions have been smaller up to this time, it indicates that the move is coming to an end. Some stocks will go up and never react more than 1/4 of the total distance traveled, others will react 1/3 of the distance and others will react to the 1/2 point. Always calculate from where the move starts the last time and watch the 1/2, 1/4 and 1/3 points from the last bottom or top, as well as your calculations from the major bottoms and tops.

The example given below will show you how we work out the campaigns in U.S. Steel according to time and space movements.

## UNITED STATES STEEL CORPORATION

This company was incorporated February 25, 1901. Trading in the common stock began on the New York Stock Exchange on March 28, 1901, when it opened at 42¾. Now, this being a new stock, which was not listed on the Exchange before, we have no high and low to go by, so the first rule to apply is: If the stock moves down 3 points first, it will indicate still lower; if it advances 3 points, it will indicate that it is going higher. Next, we put on the square of 90°. You will see that I have drawn the angles up from 0 beginning with March, 1901, and drawn the angles down from 90 beginning March, 1901. These angles will show whether the stock is in a strong or weak position after it fluctuates for a short time.

Using the 3-point rule, the stock advanced to 46 from 43, which is 3 points up and would indicate higher, especially as it had crossed 45. But you will note it is below the 8 x 1 angle drawn from 90 which shows a weak position, while from the bottom it is above the 8 x 1 angle and is strong for some kind of a rally. It goes to 55. Now note your resistance levels. 56¼ is the resistance level because it is 45 plus 11¼. 54 is the resistance level on the Nine Square and on the Master Twelve Square. 55 is one of the psychological points where the public buys a stock after it crosses 50 because they think it is going much higher. After the stock has gone up to 55, then take 1/2 from 43 to 55, which is 49. Breaking 49, the halfway point, shows trend down. After breaking this level it broke the low level at 43.

The next way to calculate is to take 1/2 of 55, which is 27½. During the panic of May 9, 1901, U.S. Steel declined to 24. 24 is an exact point on the Master Twelve Chart and 22½ is the support level on the angles. Take the halfway point of the stock, 27½, and the angle of 22½° and get the halfway point between these. It is exactly 25, which indicated around 25 would be a strong support level and a place to buy for a rally.

Next, from the top 55 to the low 24, we get the halfway point which is 39½. If the stock crosses this point, then the next resistance point is the 3/4 point, which is 47. It advances to 48 in July, 1901, and holds for several months without breaking back below 39½. However, it fails to cross the 45° angle from 90 and from 55. In October, 1902, it breaks 39½ and breaks below the 45° angle from the 24 bottom, putting it into a weak position. Notice that in July, 1923, the 45° angles from 0 and from 90 cross at 28 and that 27½ is the halfway point of 55. The stock breaks under the 45° angle from 0 for the first time; then goes straight down to 8⅜ in May, 1904 and rests on the angle of 4 x 1 from 0, the base or beginning point, reaching bottom on the 39th month from March, 1901, and 36 months from the bottom of May, 1901, coming out on an even cycle. Being down 46 points from the top would indicate a strong support level, because 45 points down is equal to the 45° angle and indicates strong support. Nine is 5/6 of 55, a support level and any stock getting down around 9, the digit, always receives good support. This is a strong number for stocks to make bottom on.

In August, 1904, the stock crosses the angle of 2 x 1 from 90 for the first time and gets active in September, crossing the 45° from 55, which shows uptrend. Twenty is 1/4 point from 55 to 8⅜. It crosses this level, which indicates higher. The next point is the 1/3 point which is 23⅝, which level is also crossed. The next point is 1/2 which is 32⅝. In December, 1904, it makes 33, where it hits the angle of 2 x 1 from 55, reacts, then crosses 33 and goes to 38 in April, 1905, which is 5/8 of the distance from 8⅜ to 55. Note that 39 was the last top in February, 1903. The stock declines to 25 in May, rests on the angle of 2 x 1 from 0 March, 1901, and on 2 x 1 from left of 45° angle from 0 May, 1904, showing strong support, also because 23⅛ was 1/2 from 8⅜ to 38. The angles held the stock above the halfway point.

Top reached was 46 in February, 1905. At 45 we naturally expect resistance. Besides, 43¼ is 3/4 from 8⅜ to 55 and it is 60 months, or at the end of a 5-year cycle, and a reaction is due. In July, 1906, it declines to 43. The halfway point from 25 to 46 is 35½, and 33¾ is a strong resistance level. Again, 32⅞ is 1/2 from 55 to 8⅜. The stock is still above the angle of 2 x 1 from 0 in March, 1901, and only 2 points below the 45° angle from the low in May, 1904, making this a strong buying level. The next top is at 50 in October, 1906 and again the same top was reached in January, 1907. There was 4 months' distribution in a 5-point range, holding above 45. January, 1907, the last month that top was reached, was 69 months from the top in April, 1901 and 71 months from the date of incorporation, February, 1901, also 32 months from the low in May, 1904. Going into the 7th year indicated lower prices. The 7th year is always a year for a panicky decline, and failing to go 3 points above the top made in July, 1901, was a sign of weakness. 50 is a resistance level because it is 1/2 of 100; 45 plus 5⅝ equals 50⅝.

In January, 1907, Steel broke the angle of 2 x 1 from 33. In March, 1907, it broke the 45° angle from the bottom of May, 1904, and also got below the 45° angle from 0 in 1904, putting it into a very weak position. It declined to 32, the support level of July, 1906, and 1/2 from 8⅜ to 55. 29¾ is 1/2 from 8⅜ to 50. It made bottom for 3 months around 32. In July, 1907, it rallied to 39. Note the angle of 2 x 1 from 0 in March 1901, and the 45° angle from 0 in May, 1904, crossed at 38, making this a strong resistance level and hard to pass. In August, 1907, Steel declined and broke 32. This was the 4th time at this level and my rules say that when a stock reaches the same level the 4th time it nearly always goes through and makes a higher top or a lower bottom.

In November, 1907, Steel declined to 21⅞. The resistance level is at 22½ and 20 is 3/4 point from 8⅜ to 55; besides 24 is a strong support level, as shown on the Master Twelve Chart. It failed to decline to the angle of 4 x 1 from 0 March, 1901, and 2 x 1 from 0 May, 1904, showing strong support. Bottom was made on the 78th month from the top of April, 1901. Note that 78¾ is a strong resistance level because it is 3/4 of 90. This was 80 months from March, 1901. Note the last low in June, 1904, was on the 40th month, and 40 months later makes bottom again when time had balanced. The reason that 40 is strong is because it is 1/8 of 360 and 1/3 of 120, the 10-year cycle.

In January, 1908, Steel crossed the angle of 2 x 1 from January, 1907, and in March crossed the angle of 2 x 1 from May, 1901, and 3 x 2 angle from 0, 1904, putting the stock into a strong position. Later, the stock crossed 36, the halfway point from 50 to 21⅞, which indicated higher. In August, 1908, which was 90 months from March, 1901, the angle of 2 x 1 from 0 and 90 March, 1901, crossed at 45; also the 2 x 1 from 21⅞ crossed at 45. The stock advanced to 48 in August and reacted to 42 in September. Being now out of the first square of 90°, having moved over 90 months, put it in a strong position. My rule says that stocks always go higher in the 8th and 9th years of a 10-year cycle.

In November, 1908, Steel crossed 50 and advanced to 58¾ on the 90th month from the top in April, 1901, which would indicate top and a strong resistance, but the fact that the stock got 3 points above 55, the high of 1901, indicated higher prices later, especially as it was out of the square of 90. The stock was up 50 points from 1904 low and 1/3 would bring it back to 42, which was the last low made in September, 1908. In February, 1909, Steel declined to 41⅛. The writer predicted the top for 58¾ in November, 1908, and the bottom for 42 in February, 1909. See the Ticker Magazine of December, 1909.

In April, 1909, Steel crossed 1/2 point from 58¾ to 41⅛, regained the angle of 2 x 1 from 0 March, 1901, and in May crossed 58¾, the top, getting above 45° angle from 0, 1904, putting it in a very strong position. Now, the question arises how to figure how far the stock will go when it has gotten into new territory after so many years. If we add 45 to the last important top, which was 50 in 1906 and 1907, we get 95. Steel sold at 94⅞ in October, 1909. Remember my rule says that tops and bottoms become halfway points. 21⅞, the bottom, to 58⅞ equals 37 points. Add this to 58¾ and we get 95¾. The top at 94⅞ made 58½ the halfway point from 1907 to 1909. The writer sold Steel short at 94⅞, stating that it would not go to 95. This is recorded in the Ticker Magazine of December, 1909. When Steel sold at 94⅞ it got slightly above the 45° angle from the top at 50 in January, 1906. This was exactly 73 points from the 1907 low and 86½ points from May, 1904 low. Any time a stock advances 84 to 90 points from the bottom or base, it is in selling territory. While this price was 4⅞ points over 90, it was only 86½ points up from its base; therefore, it would have to cross 99 to be out of the square of 90 from its extreme low in May, 1904. This is figuring according to space movement. The stock was up 53¾ from the low of February, 1909, which was one of the strong resistance points. It made top on the 102nd month. The resistance point is 101¼. It was 24 months from November, 1907, coming out on an exact cycle and 65 months from May, 1904. It started to break when it reached 67½ or the angle of 67½°. This was 104 months from 1901. The 105th month or 8¾ years is an important resistance point.

To determine resistance levels, we first calculate the 1/8, 1/4, 3/8, 1/2, 5/8, 3/4, 7/8, 1/3 and 2/3 points of the space movement. 76⅝ is 1/4 of the movement from 21⅞ to 94⅞. In February, 1910, Steel declined to 75, getting strong support at the 1/4 point. In March, 1910, it advanced to 89, making top 3/4 of the distance from 75 to 94⅞ and just under the 45° angle from 94⅞. In July, 1910, Steel declined to 61⅛ and failed to make 58½, the halfway point from 1907 and 1909, which showed that it was getting strong support. 63¼ was 1/3 of 94⅞, which indicated a support level. The advance started and it worked up to 82 in February, 1911, just under 2/3 point from 94⅞ to 61⅛, hitting the 45° angle from 0 in 1904, and a decline followed.

April, 1911, ended the 10-year cycle from the top in 1901. In August, 1911, Steel broke the 45° angle from 61⅛ and in September, 1911, broke the 45° angle from November, 1907, and in October, 1911, declined to 50. Note this was on the 89th month from the low in May, 1904, working out the 7½-year cycle and reaching the angle of 90°. The bottom at 50 was down 44⅞ points from the top, making this a strong support level because it was down 45 points, and equal to the 45° angle. 50⅝ being a resistance level showed that this was the point to buy Steel again; also 51⅝ was 1/2 from 8⅜ to 94⅞, and 47⅜ was 1/2 of 94⅞, the high point of the stock, all of which shows that this was a very strong support level. The stock was just below the angle of 2 x 1 from May, 1904, which angle the stock soon regained by getting back above it. It was down 2 years or exactly 24 months from the top and was 48 months from November, 1907, bottom, which balanced time and was an indication for another upward move to start. It was the 128th month from March, 1901, which put it out of the hexagon movement. See Hexagon Chart.

In September and October, 1912, Steel made top at 80, which was 3/4 from 94⅞ to 50 and failed to cross the high of May, 1911. Now note top 10 years back, September, 1902, from which a decline followed. In October, 1912, a decline started and in December it broke the angle of 2 x 1 from 50, afterwards getting weaker and breaking all support angles from 1901 to 1904 and 1907 to 1909 bottoms. In June, 1913, again declined to 50, the same resistance level as October, 1911, and 44 months down from the 1909 top, 52 months from February, 1909 bottom, 68 months from 1907 low and 109 months from 1904 low. This was 7 years or 84 months from the 1906 bottom. You can see from this that the stock was still in a strong position according to the space movement or resistance levels, but in a weak position on angles and was running down to complete the 7-year cycle from 1907.

In February, 1914, Steel rallied to 67, just 2 points above the 1/3 point from 94⅞ to 50. Note that it made 67 for 2 months, hitting against the angle of 2 x 1 from May, 1904, and failed to reach the angle of 2 x 1 from October, 1909. To run out a 10-year cycle from low in 1904 would indicate bottom in May and June, 1914, and 7 years from low in November, 1907, would be November, 1914. The Stock Exchange closed at the end of July, 1914, on account of war and U.S. Steel sold around 32 on the New Street Curb in the month of November, 1914. So for the purposes of calculating, November, 1914, should be considered, according to time, the month when Steel reached low. However, this level was lower than it sold after the Exchange opened, so we must also calculate the exact date that Steel made the extreme low. This was in February, 1915, when it sold at 38, just 168 months or 14 years from March, 1901, 64 months, from 1909 top, 72 months from February, 1909 bottom, and on the 88th month from 1907 bottom, all strong time cycles indicating bottom. The stock went below the angle of 4 x 1 from May, 1904, but quickly recovered and stayed above it. This bottom at 38 was just above 2/3 point from 94⅞ to 8⅜, and 3/4 point from 21⅞ to 94⅞ was 40. February, 1909, bottom was at 41⅛. 37½ is a natural resistance level, being 30 plus 7½ or 22½ plus 15, and 7/8 of 45 is 39⅜, all strong resistance points on space movements.

How to forecast from this point according to time: Going back 10 years we see that in 1905, 1906 and in January, 1907, the stock advanced; then in 1915, 1916 and 1917 it should be up trend. We add 7 years to October, 1909 top and get October, 1916. Top was reached in the early part of November, 1916, when the stock sold at 129, and a sharp decline followed to December, 1916, when the stock sold at 101, but final low was not reached until February, 1917, when it sold at 99. This was close enough to the 10-year cycle from March, 1907, when there was a panic, and 7 years from the top of February, 1910. The top at 129 was 21 months from February, 1914, bottom. It broke on the 22nd month, had a small rally in the 23rd month, made bottom 24 months from February, 1915, low. Note strong position on angles at 99, which was 90 or square above the base of 8⅜ and exactly on the angle of 2 x 1 from 80 bottom in April, 1916.

The 180th month or 15-year cycle ended with February, 1916, with the stock holding above the angle of 2 x 1 from May, 1904, low, still below the price of 90. In August, 1916, it crossed the 1909 top at 94⅞, which indicated much higher. Now we want to know what price to expect Steel to advance to, so we look back and see top at 80 in 1909, 1910, 1911 and 1912. In 1916 there was 3 months' bottoms at 80. This being the last low must become an important center or halfway point. Take the 1909 top, 94⅞, and subtract the 1915 low at 38 and get 56⅞. Add this to 80 and get

136⅝. The exact high on May 31, 1917, was 136⅝, the stock being up 95⅝ points from 1914 low, and 128 points from the 1904 low. It is always important to go back 5, 7, 10, 15 and 20 years to bottoms and tops. Taking 1907 low at 21⅞ and 1917 top at 136⅝, we find the halfway point to be 79¼, proving that the starting point at 80 was to become the center of gravity or halfway point for a 10-year cycle.

The 1917 top was 91 months from October, 1909 top, and exact square angle of 90°, being only 1 month over it. It was 193 months or 16 years from 1901 top. Note November, 1908, top was 90 months from April, 1901, top. Sixteen years is 4/5 of the 20-year cycle. Stocks make their best advances in the 8th to 9th years of a cycle. May, 1917, was 16 years and 3 months from March, 1901. There is a cycle of 32 years and 6 months. Steel had worked out 1/2 of this cycle to the top. In view of the fact that top was reached on the 91st month and on the exact space movement was evidence that the stock was top for a further decline. In 1917, top, coming out on the price indicated and on the 91st month, indicated top and a short sale. Besides, the volume of sales was very large, indicating distribution.

We know that 1907 was a panic year and that stocks made low in October and November, 1907; then 1917 must repeat. 1910 was also a bear year and 1917, or 7 years later, indicated a decline. The trend turned down in June, 1917, and in the panic of December, 1917, Steel sold at 80, the halfway point from 1907, getting just below the angle of 2 x 1 from 1907 and getting support 1 point below the angle of 2 x 1 from 0 May, 1904. December, 1917, was 90 months from July, 1910, and 30 months from February, 1914, the exact angle being at 33¾. This was another indication of bottom for a rally. We know that Steel went up in 1908 and 1909. Therefore in 1918 and 1919, 10 years later, we expect it to work like 1908 and 1909. Steel advanced in 1918 and made last top in October and November, 1919, just 10 years from 1909 top. In 1920 and 1921, Steel followed 1901, 1910 and 1911. In June, 1921, made bottom 7 years from the low in July, 1914, nearly 14 years from the 1907 low, 76 months from the 1915 low, 49 months from 1917 top and 242 months from the top in April 1901, working out the 20-year cycle, the most important cycle.

By taking the top at 136⅝, we find that 1/2 of the total value is 68¼. The stock got support above the halfway point of its total value, indicating a good buying price. It was down 66¼ points from the top, another resistance level. The 1/2 point from 8⅜ to 136⅝ was 64. The fact that it held above these halfway points indicated strong support and much higher prices to follow. The next point, 87¼, was 1/2 from 38 to 136⅝. It made bottom in February, 1918, and February, 1919, at this level. In 1920, after Steel broke 87, it never rallied again to 91 until it declined to 70½ in June, 1921. In 1922, Steel crossed 88, the halfway point; went to 111; then declined to 86. It remained 4 months at this same bottom without getting 2 points below the halfway point from 1915 low to 1917 high. This was proof enough that there was strong buying and good support at this main center and that the stock would go much higher later. In May and June, 1924, just 20 years from May, 1904, when Steel made the low, it sold at 95 and has never sold at that price again before the high was made at 261¾, making higher tops and higher bottoms each year.

In November, 1928, Steel made top 20 years from November, 1908, top. In January, February and March, 1929, tops were around the same level, 192 to 193. Steel declined and made the last low in May, 1929, at 162½, a little lower than February and March, 1929, lows.

On September 3, 1929, Steel reached the highest in its history, 261¾. Note that tops were reached in July, 1919, and in October, 1909. This was 1 month sooner than the 1909 top and 1 month later than the 1919 top. The top was reached on the 343rd month from March, 1901. This is a very important number, which marks culminations and indicates tops or bottoms, because it is 7 x 49, and 49 is composed of 7 x 7. The top was reached 98 months from the 1921 low, or 8 years and 2 months, making top early in the 9th year. Note that the top on the old stock before it sold ex-stock dividend, was reached in May, 1927, 10 years from the top of May, 1917. September, 1929, was 175 months from 1915 low and nearing 180 months indicates a big decline. It was 148 months from the 1917 top, 63 months from 1924 low, 71 months from 1923 low, 37 months from August, 1926 top, 24 months from September, 1927 top, and 148 months from May, 1917. This is important because 135 plus 11½ equals 146¼, an important resistance level on the Master 12 x 12 Chart.

From September, 1904, when the trend turned up, to September, 1929, was 300 months, an important cycle, which indicated the end. It is important here to figure the space movement. Figuring from the low of 38 in 1915 to the high of 261¾ in 1929, we get 223¾ points. We know that 225 is one of the very strong resistance levels. Then figuring from the low of 21⅞ in 1907 to the top at 261¾, find the space movement 240 points, another very strong resistance level, because it is 2/3 of the circle of 360°. From the extreme low in May, 1904, Steel was up 253⅜ points. 255 is the halfway point between 240 and 270, therefore a very strong resistance level.

Figuring from the low at 70½ in 1921 to the top in 1929, the space movement equaled 191¼ points. This is exactly 180 plus 11¼, another strong resistance point. The last run on Steel from 162½ in May, 1929, to the top was nearly 100 points. My rule says, when stocks have sharp advances, getting up 90 to 100 points, it is time to watch for top and a change in trend.

I have found, after years of experience, that over a long period of years a stock cannot maintain a gain of more than 1 point per month, or that it cannot do better than to hold the 45° angle. When a stock in its early years goes up too fast and gets ahead of time, sharp reactions have to take place while the stock is squaring itself or adjusting itself to the time period. One of my rules is, when time and space balance, the stock makes top or bottom. This was the most important indication of all that Steel was top at 261¾.

October, 1907, was the next important low level after Steel reached extreme low in May, 1904. From October, 1907, to September, 1929, was 262 points. To be exact, this time was up on August 23, 1929. The top was reached at 261¾ on September 3, 1929, within 1/4 point of the 45° angle from 0 in October, 1907, showing that the stock had made its return to the 45° angle. This indicated that time and space had balanced. Suppose the stock had crossed this angle. So long as it stayed above it, it would have indicated higher prices, but just as soon as it got below it, it would be an indication for lower prices. Analyze other stocks according to this same rule. Allowing 1 point gain per month for the stock to follow the angle of 45°, Steel was behind time in May, 1929. That is why the fast advance of 100 points took place, bringing it up to strike the angle of 45° and make final top when time and space balanced.

I have stated before that important tops and important bottoms become halfway points or main centers. Now, it is very important to know why Steel made low at 150 in November, 1929. We go back to December, 1928, and find the last low on Steel was 149¾, having declined from a top at 172½. There were three weeks' bottoms around this level. After advancing from this level to 192 and 193, it declined to 162½; then advanced to 261¾. From the 149¾ level, Steel advanced to a new high level of its history up to that time. Therefore, 149¾ or 150 must become an important center or halfway point. The last important low level was at 38 in 1915. We subtract 38 from 149¾ and get 111¾. We then add 111¾, which gives us exactly 261½. The stock made top at 261¾, which makes the halfway point from 1915 to 1929 at 149⅞. U.S. Steel declined to 150 in November, 1929, which was a strong buying point, protected with stop at 147.

Figuring the total value of the stock, 261¾, we find the 3/4 point at 196½, therefore a strong resistance level. Then, figuring from the last low, 70½, in June, 1921, to the extreme high of 261¾, we find the 2/3 point at 198. The writer advised selling U.S. Steel short in April, 1930, with stop at 199. On April 7, 1930, Steel sold at 198¾. It was below the angle of 8 x 1 from 261¾, a weak position on angles from the top, but we must always consider the position on angles from the bottom. At this time, Steel was above the 45° angle from 1914 and 1921 lows.

It is important to consider the position of the stock according to the Time Cycle. April, 1930, was 10 years from the high in April, 1920, and the high in 1910, 20 years back, was reached in March and April. Going back 7 years, we find the high in April, 1923, and going back 90 months from April, 1930, we find that Steel made top in October, 1922, and a sharp decline followed in November. All of these time cycles indicated top for Steel in April and when it reached strong resistance levels and the Daily and Weekly Charts showed down, it was a sure sign to go short and pyramid on the way down.

*Looking ahead:* Knowing the date of incorporation of U.S. Steel, February 25, 1901, you would look back to see what happened at the end of the 5, 10, 15, 20 and 30 year cycles.

You would find that in 1901, 1902, 1903 and 1904, Steel was in a bear market and worked lower. Therefore, you would expect at the end of the 30-year cycle very much lower prices, especially after Steel had reached extreme high in 1929, being the third high top in the bull campaign. You would also refer back 20 years to 1911 and 10 years to 1921. These cycles indicated that 1931 should be a bear year. Then you would look for geometrical angles to tell when Steel was getting into a bearish position from the bottom, as it already was in a very bearish position on angles coming down from 1929 top.

May, 1930: When Steel broke below the bottoms of the previous 3 months, getting under 178, it broke under the 45° angle from 0 from the bottom of 1915, and when it was under 174, it broke the 45° angle from the 1921 low, placing it in a very weak position and indicating lower prices.

In December, 1930, Steel declined to 135, on the angle of 2 x 1 from the low of 111¼ from January, 1927. This, being the halfway point of the life fluctuation, was a strong support point.

### 1931

The stock rallied to 152⅝ in February, 1931. This was the end of 360 months or the end of the first 30-year cycle from the date of incorporation. A change in trend of Steel nearly always comes in the month of February. The trend turned down at this time when it went into the new cycle. On this last rally to 152⅝, it failed to reach the 45° angle coming up from 111¼ bottom. Then, declined and broke the 45° degree angle from 0 from May, 1918.

In April, 1931, it broke the 135 bottom; broke the angle of 2 x 1 from 111¼ and the angle of 2 x 1 from 38 low in 1915; then broke the angle of 2 x 1 from the 1921 low, which put it in a very weak position. Dropping below the angle of 45° coming down from the 150 low of November, 1929, and below the 45° angle from 150 of December, 1928, it was in such a weak position behind these 45° angles that it indicated very little rally.

In June, 1931, low was 83¼. The price rested on the 45° angle coming up from 0 from the low of May, 1924, where the bottom was made at 95. Note that the 4 x 1 angle from 1904 and 1915 crossed near these levels, and the 4 x 1 angle coming up from 0 in September, 1929, crossed at 84, making this a strong support point for at least a rally.

In July, 1931, Steel rallied to 105½, still weak on angles from the top and from the bottom.

September, 1931, Steel broke 83, under the 2 x 1 angle from 0 in May, 1924, and under the 2 x 1 angle coming down from the 1929 top. As most all of the strong angles from the bottom were broken, it was in a very weak position.

December, 1931, declined to 36 on a 45° angle from 0 in December, 1928, when the low was 150. At 36 it rested on the 45° angle coming down from the last low of 114 in June, 1925. This was 2 points under the 1915 low of 38 and was 242 months from 1911 low and 60 months from January, 1927 low. The stock held here for a temporary rally to February, 1932, when it sold at 52½.

### 1932

This was 12 months in a new 30-year cycle. Note 1902 top in Janaury was 30 years back, and also 1912 top in January, 20 years back.

The decline continued and in June, 1932, low was reached at 21¼, the same low as October, 1907. This was 34 months from 1929 top. At the time bottom was reached, it was under the 45° angle from the low of March, 1925. Note the 45° angle coming down from June, 1924, reached 0 in June, 1932, an indication for bottom and a change in trend. In view of the fact that Steel made extreme low in May, 1904, we would watch for change in trend in May and June, or when the cycle runs out. June, 1932, was 336 months from May, 1904, low and 26 months from April, 1930, top. Note May and June, 1912, low for a rally.

September, 1932, U.S. Steel had a sharp rally to 52½. This was the same high as the top of February, 1932, which it failed to cross. It was still in a weak position on angles from the top and a decline followed.

### 1933

February, 1933, Steel declined to 23¼. This was a secondary low and a higher bottom than 1932; indicated good support. It was 42 months from September, 1929, or 1/2 a 7-year cycle, and 34 months from April, 1930, top and 24 months in the new 30-year cycle. In 1913, February was low for a small rally; in 1903, February was top for a decline. Steel nearly always makes a change in trend in February. Looking back 7 years to 1926, you will find the low in March and April.

Note the 45° angle from 0 in February, 1931, which was the end of the 30-year cycle, crossed at 24 in February, 1933. Therefore, the stock rested on this angle, which was a strong support angle.

July, 1933, high 67½. Note that in 1923 lows were made in July and August; in 1913, high in August; in 1903, new lows were made in July.

October, 1933: Steel declined to 34½. This was 49 months from September, 1929, top and 42 months from April, 1930, top. October, 1923, was low, 120 months or 10-year cycle. 1913 also low in October. 1903, low in November. Looking back 7 years to October, 1926, we find a low, and looking up the 5-year cycle, in October, 1928, we find a low. Fifteen years back, or 180 months, September, 1918, was high. Therefore, there are many indications for a change in trend and bottom in October, 1933.

### 1934

The stock started up and advanced to February, 1934, when it made a high of 59¾. Again, we find the trend turning down and changing in February. The stock failed to reach the highs of July, 1933, a bearish indication and sign of lower prices. The top at 59¾ was under the 45° angle from the July, 1933, top. Looking ahead, we find that May, 1904, was the extreme low of the stock, therefore we would expect the stock to be down until May, 1934. May, 1934, ended a 30-year cycle from the bottom. Also, look up 1914 and 1924 to tell how Steel should run in 1934.

September, 1934, low 29½. This was 60 months or 5 years from the 1929 top and indicated a change in trend. Note October, 1924, was low, and in 1914 Steel was low in the month of November on the Curb, the New York Stock Exchange being closed. In 1904 Steel started up in September. Look back 7 years to 1927; we find low in October.

### 1935

January: Steel high at 40½, a weak rally and still under the 45° angle from 1932 and 1933 lows. However, it crossed the angle of 2 x 1 coming down from February, 1934, top, but never closed above this angle, indicating a weak position. The trend turned down again in February, breaking the 2 x 1 angle from the bottoms of 1932 and 1933.

March: Low 27½, still higher than the bottoms of 1932 and 1933 and getting higher support indicated that it was in position to rally.

It was under the 4 x 1 angle from 21¼ low, but above the 45° angle from 0 in February, 1933, and on the 2 x 1 angle from July, 1933, high. Note in 1925 the low was made in March; in 1915 the low was made in February; in 1905 April was top. Note that it was 25 months from 1933 low and 33 months from 1932 and 49 months in the second 30-year cycle. Looking back 7 years, we find March, 1928, low. Now, we look at 1905, 1915 and 1925 and find that they were all years of advancing prices for U.S. Steel.

In April, 1935, U.S. Steel started up and crossed the angle of 2 x 1 from February, 1934, top and for the first time held above this angle. In July, 1935, high 44 against the 45° angle from July, 1933, top. In August Steel crossed the 45° angle from 1933 top and got back above the 45° angle from 0 from June, 1932. This indicated that it was in a stronger position. Note the 2 x 1 angle coming up from 0 at the time of the top in February, 1934. It rested on this angle in May and June, 1935; also on the 45° angle from the low of June, 1932, and on a reaction in October, 1935, rested on the 2 x 1 angle from the low of March, 1935, and where the 45° angle from July 1933 coming down crossed the 2 x 1 angle from March, 1935, low. The low price at this time (October, 1935) was 42. This showed that it was getting strong support on these angles.

In November, 1935, it advanced to 50. Note the 45° angle coming down from the last top of 105½ made in July, 1931, will cross at 53½ in November, 1935. Looking back at the previous cycles, we find 1905-high of the year in December; 1915-high of the year in December; 1925-high in November; 1928-low in December. Looking at 1930, 5 years back which was a bear year, however, we find the low in December. In 1935 Steel is following and repeating the bull cycles of 1905, 1915 and 1925.

### Future Forecast: 1936

In order to forecast Steel for the year 1936, you look back at 1906, 1916, 1926, 1921, 1922 and 1929. Note 1906 and 1916 highs were reached in January and the trend turned down, but in both of these years the trend was strong up from July and August to December. In 1926, high in January; low reached in May; high in August; low in October; and then rallied sharply, making high of the year in the month of December.

Apply these same rules to any other stock in forecasting its future trend. Bring up all of the angles from tops and bottoms; look up the resistance levels; study the volume of sales and watch the position on the weekly high and low chart as well as the monthly chart. By applying all the rules and considering all indications, you will be able to get a more accurate forecast.

## TIME AND RESISTANCE POINTS ACCORDING TO SQUARES OF NUMBERS

Every price at which a stock stops on the up or down side is some important mathematical point, which can be determined either by a division of the circle of 360° or by the square of 12, the square of 20, or the square or halfway point of some other number.

There is no top and bottom price which cannot be determined by mathematics. Every market movement is the result of a cause and when once you determine the cause, it is easy enough to know why the effect is as it is.

Everything moves to a gravity center or to a point halfway between some bottom and top or some other important resistance point. For example: We divide the circle of 360° by 2 and get 180. We divide by 4 and get 90; then divide 90 by 2 and get 45; divide 45 by 2 and get 22½; divide 22½ by 2 and get 11¼; divide 11¼ by 2 and get 5⅝; divide 5⅝ by 2 and get $2\frac{13}{16}$, which is the lowest division of the circle that we can use for time periods. Each of these points is 1/2 of one of the other important divisions of the circle.

Stocks work out to the square of different numbers, triangle points of different numbers, the square of their bottoms, the square of their tops, or to a halfway point of the different squares according to the time period. Therefore, it is important for you to study the resistance levels according to these numbers, as outlined below:

**Square of Numbers:**

The squares of each number and the halfway point between the square of one number and the next point are very important. For example:

The square of 2 is 4; the square of 3 is 9. The halfway point between 4 and 9 is 6½.

The square of 4 is 16. The halfway point between the square of 3 and the square of 4 is 12½.

The square of 5 is 25. The halfway point between 16 and 25 is 20½.

The square of 6 is 36. The halfway point between 25 and 36 is 30½.

The square of 7 is 49. The halfway point between 36 and 49 is 42½.

The square of 8 is 64. The halfway point between 49 and 64 is 56½.

The square of 9 is 81. The halfway point between 64 and 81 is 72½.

The square of 10 is 100. The halfway point between 81 and 100 is 90½.

The square of 11 is 121. The halfway point between 100 and 121 is 110½.

The square of 12 is 144. The halfway point between 121 and 144 is 132½.

You can figure out the squares of 13, 14, etc., in the same way.

An important thing to remember is that a stock which makes low on an odd number will work out to the odd squares, that is, a stock that makes a low on 3, 5, 7, 9 or 11 will work out to the odd squares, while a stock which makes a low on 2, 4, 6, 8 or 10 will work out to points in the even squares.

When stocks are selling at low levels, they make bottoms or tops and meet resistance around 2, 4, 6½, 9, 12½, 16, etc. All of these points are also important for time periods, especially on the monthly chart, and should be watched on the weekly chart. When stocks are very active and reach high levels and the time period is a long distance from top or bottom, then these square points should be watched on the daily chart.

Important Numbers for Resistance — 12 to 100

**11 to 12:** This is an important point for resistance, both on time and price, because 12 equals 12 months and 11¼ is 1/32 of a circle of 1/2 of 22½°.

**15 to 16:** The next important resistance point is 16, the square of 4. 15 is important because it is 1¼ years.

**18:** An important number for resistance in time and price because it is twice 9, 1½ times 12, 1/20 of a circle.

**20½:** The halfway point between 16 and 25, therefore important at times.

**22½ and 24:** 22½ is 1/16 of a circle, 1/2 of 45. The reason why stocks often make top or bottom in the 23rd month is because the angle of 22½° comes out at this point.

**24 and 25:** These are very important because 24 is twice 12 and 25 is the square of 5 and 1/4 of 100.

**26:** When you consider the square of 4, which is 16, and the even square of 6, which is 36, the halfway point between them is 26, which is sometimes an important resistance point for time and price.

**27 and 28:** Important tops and bottoms come out around 27 to 28 months, and major or minor campaigns end on this time period. The reason for this is that 4 times 7 is 28 and that 28 is 2⅓ years. Three times 9 is 27 and anything that comes out on multiples of 3 is very important, because it is the first odd number that we can square, as the square of 1 is 1.

**30:** Any halfway point or gravity center is also important. Therefore, 30, which is 2½ years, is an important period for changes in trend. Because 30½ is the halfway point between 25, the square of 5, and 36, the square of 6, it makes this period important.

**34 to 36:** 33¾ is 3/4 of 45. You will recall that the bear campaign which ended in July, 1932, was 34 months from the 1929 top. It is always important to watch for changes in trend around the 34th to 36th months. Thirty-six being the square of 6 makes this a strong resistance point. Three times 12 or the end of the third year is another reason for strong resistance at this point.

**39 and 40:** Forty is a number referred to many times in the Bible. The children of Israel wandered 40 years in the wilderness. The food lasted 40 days. Forty equals 3⅓ years. 7/8 of 45 is 39⅜. Forty is 1/9 of a circle. All of this makes these numbers important for the time periods and resistance levels on price.

**42:** The next important number for resistance in time and price is 42. It is 3½ years of time or 1/2 of a 7-year cycle. Also, 42½ is the halfway point between the square of 6 and the square of 7.

**45:** This is the master of all numbers because it contains all the digits from 1 to 9. The 45° angle divides the 90° angle in half, making it an important gravity center. It is 1/8 of 360 and 5 times 9. Fast moves up or down often occur in the 45th month. On any kind of a chart that you make up with squares, you will find that 45 will come out on a 45° angle or a 90° angle or an angle that is the equivalent of these angles. Notice how 45 comes out on the square of 9, the square of 20 and the square of 12, all proving that 45 is a Master Number. Use 45 in every way possible for measuring price, time, space and volume movements.

**48 and 49:** Strong and important numbers for changes in trend are 48 and 49. Forty-nine is 7 times 7, or the square of 7, and 48 is 4 times 12, or the end of the fourth year. On a decline to 49 to 50, a stock often meets resistance and has a good rally from this point. The same with a stock on an advance to around 49 to 50, meeting resistance around this point and reacting to 45 anyway.

**50:** Important because it is one-half of 100. If we add 5⅝ to 45, we get 50⅝.

**52:** This number has some importance because there are 52 weeks in a year and 51⅜ is 1/7 of a circle of 360°. It is 4⅓ years. 52½ is the halfway point between 45 and 60, which makes this important to watch for resistance.

**56 and 57:** These are very important because 56¼ is 45 plus 11¼ or the halfway point between 45 and 67½. 56½ is the halfway point between 49 and 64.

**60:** This is one of the very important numbers to watch for resistance. It is an important time period because it equals 5 years in time or 1/2 of the 10-year cycle or 1/4 of a 20-year cycle. It is one of the most important time periods after 45 to 49. Sixty is 1/6 of the circle. Here again we use the rule of 3, multiplying 20 by 3, we get 60. Sixty is 1/3 of 180 and the halfway point between 45 and 75. Watch stocks that advance to around 60 or decline to around 60. If they hesitate several days, weeks or months, you will know that they are meeting resistance at this point and a reverse move will occur.

**63 to 64:** 62½ is 5/8 of 100. Sixty-three is 7 times 9. Sixty-four is the square of 8, and is 5⅓ years, and the next important point to watch after 60.

**66 and 67:** Sixty-six is 5½ years or 5½ times 12. 67½ is 45 plus 22½ or 3/16 of a circle.

**70 to 72:** The number 70 is referred to many times in the Bible. It is three score years and ten, the allotted span of the life of man. Seventy is 7 times 10; 3½ times the 20-year cycle. Seventy-two is 6 years and 72½ is the halfway point between the square of 8 and the square of 9. Seventy-two is 1/5 of 360. It is also the square of 12 and a very important time period.

**78 to 80:** These are all important because 78¾ is 7/8 of 90; 80 is 4 times 20 and twice 40. Eighty equals 1/18 of 360° circle and is 4/5 of 100. The square of 9 is 81. Great resistance occurs around these price levels, and the endings and beginnings of cycles take place around these months as you will find by looking them up on your charts.

**84 to 85:** Strong resistance levels because 84⅜ is 15/16 of 90 and 84 is 7 times 12 and equals the 7-year cycle. At this point, the greatest resistance is met before a stock reaches the 90th month or a price of 90. After it breaks under 90, it is the first important resistance level below 90.

**89 and 90:** Ninety is one of the strongest points of all because it equals a vertical angle and represents 1/4 of the circle. 90½ is the halfway point between 81 and 100, the square of 9 and the square of 10. In active markets, moves straight up and straight down occur when the 90th month, 90th week or 90th day is reached. The 90th month is the most important, but the 90th week is also quite important. You should always watch the 89th month for tops and bottoms and important changes in trend. Many important campaigns begin and end in the 89th month; some run to the 91st month. Note U.S. Steel monthly 1915 to 1916 and see what happened around the 89th to 90th months. On the daily chart the change often comes on the 92nd to 93rd day, but a movement often runs to around the 98th day before an important change. It is important to watch this point on a daily chart.

**95 to 96:** This is 8 times 12. 95⅝ is 90 plus 5⅝ and quite a strong resistance level for price and time changes. When an important time period comes out on the 96th to 98th month, you will often find an important change in trend because this is 8 times 12 and starts the 9th year. The 9th year is always important and marks the ending of important campaigns with extreme high or low prices. Stocks often advance to 95 to 97 and fail to make 100; then they often decline to 97 to 95 and meet strong support, rally and cross 100 again.

**99 to 100:** Important because 100 is the square of 10. Ninety-nine is 11 times 9. One hundred is a psychological number for the public to buy and sell, or to hope for prices to reach. Stocks often go to 99 and fail to make 100 and often decline to 99 and then start up again.

Study all of these important squares and gravity centers or halfway points and the squares of numbers above 12, as shown on the 360° Circle Chart. All of these mathematical points will help you to determine changes in trend and resistance points.

November, 1935.

**NAME** **Inc.**

| YEARS | | 19...... to 19...... | 19...... to 19...... | 19...... to 19...... | 19...... to 19...... | 19...... to 19...... | 19...... to 19...... | 19...... to 19...... | 19...... to 19...... | 19...... to 19...... | 19...... to 19...... | 19...... to 19...... | 19...... to 19...... | 19...... to 19...... | 19...... to 19...... | 19...... to 19...... | 19...... to 19...... | 19...... to 19...... | 19...... to 19...... | 19...... to 19...... | 19...... to 19...... | 19...... to 19...... | 19...... to 19...... | 19...... to 19...... | 19...... to 19...... |
|---|---|---|---|---|---|---|---|---|---|---|---|---|---|---|---|---|---|---|---|---|---|---|---|---|---|
| PRICE | HIGH LOW | | | | | | | | | | | | | | | | | | | | | | | | |
| | 1/8 | | | | | | | | | | | | | | | | | | | | | | | | |
| | 1/4 | | | | | | | | | | | | | | | | | | | | | | | | |
| | 1/3 | | | | | | | | | | | | | | | | | | | | | | | | |
| | 3/8 | | | | | | | | | | | | | | | | | | | | | | | | |
| | 1/2 | | | | | | | | | | | | | | | | | | | | | | | | |
| | 5/8 | | | | | | | | | | | | | | | | | | | | | | | | |
| | 2/3 | | | | | | | | | | | | | | | | | | | | | | | | |
| | 3/4 | | | | | | | | | | | | | | | | | | | | | | | | |
| | 7/8 | | | | | | | | | | | | | | | | | | | | | | | | |
| | 0 | | | | | | | | | | | | | | | | | | | | | | | | |
| | | | | | | | | | | | | | | | | | | | | | | | | | |
| | | | | | | | | | | | | | | | | | | | | | | | | | |
| | | | | | | | | | | | | | | | | | | | | | | | | | |
| | | | | | | | | | | | | | | | | | | | | | | | | | |
| | | | | | | | | | | | | | | | | | | | | | | | | | |

# CHAPTER 6

## *HOW TO MAKE PROFITS TRADING IN PUTS AND CALLS*

# HOW
# TO MAKE PROFITS
# TRADING
# IN
# PUTS AND CALLS

# HOW TO MAKE PROFITS TRADING IN PUTS AND CALLS

To make a success trading in stocks every man should learn everything he can about the stock market and the ways to operate in the market in order to make the greatest success. He should learn to take the smallest risk possible and then try to make the greatest profits possible. The more a man studies and learns, the greater success he will have. We quote Proverbs 1: 5— "The wise man will hear and will increase learning." Again, Proverbs 2: 11— "Discretion shall preserve thee; understanding shall keep thee." Proverbs 3: 9— "Give instructions to a wise man and he will become wiser. Teach a just man and he will increase in learning." The "Book of the Lambs" says that the fear of the market is the beginning of knowledge.

Many people do not realize that without preparation and knowledge the stock market is dangerous and that it is easier to make losses than it is to make profits. However, the risks in stock speculation or investment are no greater than in any other line of business if you understand and apply the proper rules to speculative trading, and the profits compared to risks are greater than in any other business.

## WHAT ARE PUTS AND CALLS ON STOCKS

PUTS and CALLS are insurance which provide protection for your profits and permit you to trade in stocks with limited risk. A CALL is a contract between you and the seller whereby he agrees to sell you a stock at a fixed price and deliver it in 30 days. You have the option of calling for delivery at any time during the 30 days. Your loss is limited to the price you pay for the premium, which is the same as buying insurance with a Call. For example:

Suppose a man has a house for sale and agrees to sell it to you for $5,000 and deliver it at that price 60 days later. You pay him $100 for the privilege of buying the house or rejecting it. If at the end of 30 or 60 days you are able to sell the house for $500 profit or for $1,000 profit, then you exercise your option to buy the house for $5,000 and sell it to the man so you can make a profit. But if the option expires and you are unable to sell the house for more than the price, then you lose the $100 and do not have to buy the house.

The same applies in buying Calls on a stock. For example: If you buy a Call when Chrysler is selling around 105, good for 30 days at 110, you pay $142.50, which includes the Federal taxes. Suppose before the 30 days are up, Chrysler advances to 115, which would give you a profit of $500, you can sell Chrysler any time it reaches 115 and demand delivery of the stock at 110. But if Chrysler sells at 115 within 10 days after you bought the option and you believe that the trend is up and Chrysler is going higher, then you hold and do not exercise your option or sell the stock. Just before the end of the 30 days, if Chrysler is selling at 120, you could sell 100 shares of Chrysler at 120 and then call for delivery on your Call at 110, making a profit of $1,000, less your commission and the amount paid for the Call. On the other hand, after you have bought the Call at 110, if at no time it advances above 110 and at the end of 30 days Chrysler is selling below 110, you, of course, make no profit and are only out the amount of money that you paid for the Call.

A PUT is an option or an agreement with a man from whom you buy the Put that you can deliver to him the stock at a fixed price any time within 30 days after you buy the Put. A Put costs you $137.50 per 100 shares. We will take this example: When Chrysler is selling at 105, say, you believe it is going down and buy a Put for 30 days at 100, for which you pay $137.50. This means that when Chrysler declines below 100, it puts you in a position of being short 100 shares at that price, because the man from whom you bought must take from you 100 shares of Chrysler at 100 any time that you deliver it to him within the 30-day period. We will assume that Chrysler goes below 100 and declines to 95. You can buy 100 shares when it goes to 95 and then hold it to the end of the 30 days. In the meantime if Chrysler advances to 105 giving you 10 points' profit, you could sell it out. Then at the end of the time the option expired if Chrysler was still selling above 100, you would have made the profit on the stock that you bought against the Put and would simply let the option expire and only be out the price you paid for it. But, on the other hand, if you do not trade against the Put and the stock declines and, we will say, at the end of 30 days is selling around 90, you then buy 100 shares of Chrysler and your broker delivers 100 shares to the man that you bought the Put from, giving you the profit of $1,000, less the money you paid for the option and your commission.

PUTS and CALLS are perfectly safe because every Put and Call sold by a reliable Put and Call broker is endorsed by a member of the New York Stock Exchange who is thoroughly reliable and will deliver you the stock that he agrees to deliver on which he sold an option or will receive from you any stock that he agrees to buy on an option.

Again, to make it plainer, when you buy a Call on a stock you are long of the market if it goes above the price at which you bought it, just the same as if you had the stock bought, except that your risk is limited. Again, when you buy a Put on a stock, it means that you are short at the price at which you bought the Put, but you do not have to put up any margin or have to stand any loss except the price you paid for the Put. Then as it declines below the price at which you bought the Put, you are making money just the same as if you made a short sale.

## SPREAD OR STRADDLE

When you buy a Put and a Call on the same stock it is called a Spread. For example: Suppose Chrysler is selling at 100 and you are in doubt whether it will go up or down but you want to take advantage of a move when it gets under way. Therefore we will say that you buy a Put at 96 and a Call at 104. Let us assume that the market starts to react and declines to 95, then hesitates and looks like making bottom. Then you buy 100 shares of Chrysler, knowing that if it continues to decline you cannot lose anything because you have a Put at 96. Let us assume that you are right and the market starts to advance. It continues to advance and before the end of the 30 days Chrysler advances to 110 and there are 6 points' profit in the Call that you bought at 104. You also still have the stock that you bought against the Put at 96. Now, you can sell out 200 shares of stock and call for the 100 shares at 104, which gives you a profit on the Call and your Put expires because it is of no value.

Often Spreads can be bought very close to the market when you are buying a Put and a Call from the same man. On some stocks you can often buy Spreads at the market by paying an additional premium. As a rule, it would not pay to buy a Spread except on very active stocks which have a very wide fluctuation during the 30 days, giving you a chance to operate against both the Put and the Call during the month. At least when you buy a Spread if the stock moves 10 or 15 points or more in either direction, you are sure to make some money. However, it is not always advisable to spend as much as it costs to buy Spreads unless the market looks like it is going to be very active and you are trading in high-priced stocks.

Put and Call brokers, give these definitions: "A PUT is a negotiable contract by which the taker may put —to the maker a certain lot of securities at a specified price on/or before a fixed date. A CALL is the opposite. A SPREAD is one PUT and one CALL. PREMIUM is the money paid for a PUT, CALL or SPREAD. MAKER is he who writes or sells PUTS, CALLS and SPREADS. ENDORSER is a N. Y. Stock Exchange firm which guarantees a PUT, CALL or SPREAD contract by endorsing it like a check. The insurance feature provided by these privileges is considered valuable.

## HOW PUTS AND CALLS ARE SOLD

Puts and Calls are sold by traders and large operators who make it a business trading in and out of the market and selling Puts or Calls on the stocks that they have bought or sold, but Puts and Calls are always endorsed by members of the New York Stock Exchange. As a rule, Puts and Calls are sold so many points away from the market, that is, a Call costs you $142.50 and the price that it is away from the market depends upon the activity of the stock and the condition of the market. A Put is the reverse, so many points below the price at which the market is selling that day, depending upon the price of the stock and the activity of the market. However, often traders who make it a business of selling Puts and Calls, sell them at the market price for an additional premium. For example, Douglas Aircraft might be selling at 56 and by paying a premium of $300 to the seller you could buy a Call or a Put on Douglas for 30 days at 56, therefore when it moved 3 points up or down from the price at which you bought the Call or the Put, you would have made the money back or the price of the stock would show you a profit for the money you paid out; then when it went more than 3 points in your favor, you would have a net profit above the price you paid for the privilege, either Put or Call, that you bought at the market.

As a rule, I favor buying Puts and Calls with risk limited to the price of $142.50 per 100 shares for a Call or $137.50 per 100 shares for a Put, and buying Puts or Calls a number of points away from the price at which the stock is selling.

## WHY PUTS AND CALLS ARE SOLD

The question might be asked, If there is a chance to make large profits on a small risk in buying Puts and Calls, why do traders and wealthy speculators sell them?

Often a trader who is out of the market is willing to buy stocks if they decline 4 or 5 points, therefore he will sell you a Put on a stock 3 or 5 points away and you pay him the premium of $137.50; then if the stock declines to the level at which he is willing to buy and even though it goes lower, you deliver it to him, he is satisfied to buy it at that level. On the other hand, often these big traders have accumulated a large line of stock and already have profits in them, so they are willing to sell all or part of their line should the market advance 5 or 10 points more, therefore they are willing to sell you Calls on the stocks they hold or part of what they hold 5 or 10 points above the market, as the case may be, and are perfectly willing to deliver you the stock and permit you to have the profit above that price for the premium that you pay. Another reason they sell them is that they know they can always protect themselves. If the market is very strong and you are going to make profits on the Call they sold to you or you are going to call the stock, they can buy more. On the other hand, suppose they sell you Puts: The market starts declining fast and looks like going lower, where you will have a profit on the Put you bought, they can sell short, put up the margin and carry the stock until you deliver it to them against the Put. It is a perfectly legitimate business just the same as insurance business and is fair to both buyer and seller.

## LENGTH OF TIME PUTS AND CALLS ARE SOLD

As a rule, you can buy Puts and Calls good 7 days, two weeks, and 30 days, and sometimes you can buy them good 60 or 90 days, but most traders who make it a business of selling Puts and Calls do not write them for more than 30 days. However, you can always ask your broker or the Put and Call broker to make an inquiry and get you a quote on what you can buy Puts and Calls for good 30, 60 or 90 days; then if the price looks right, you can buy them.

My advice is that you will make more money buying Puts and Calls good 30 days than you will buying them good 7 days or two weeks because the shorter periods of time, except when markets are extremely active, do not give you an opportunity for a wide enough range to make profits. However, when you buy Puts or Calls good 7 days or 14 days, you pay less premium than for those good 30 days. The premium, as a rule, for 7 days is $62.50; two weeks is $87.50.

## HOW TO BUY PUTS AND CALLS

If you live outside New York City, you can give an order to your local broker and he will buy Puts and Calls for your account that are endorsed by a New York Stock Exchange firm and place them to your credit with your broker in New York City or the correspondent of the house you trade with in your own city. Then when you want to make a trade against your Puts or Calls, or want to buy or sell and call the stock or put it and take profits, the broker will take care of the transaction for you. Always deal with brokers who are members of the New York Stock Exchange when you buy or sell stocks.

The unit for Puts and Calls is 100 shares, but at times you may be able to buy odd-lots or 50-share lots of Puts and Calls, but when you buy Puts or Calls be sure that they are endorsed by a New York Stock Exchange firm. There are often bucketshops that will sell you Puts and Calls on 10 shares, 25 shares or anything else, but there is no Stock Exchange firm behind them, and you have no assurance of getting your profits if you make them.

## PUT AND CALL BROKERS

There are many brokers in Puts and Calls in New York City who buy and sell Puts and Calls for a commission and have the Puts and Calls endorsed by a New York Stock Exchange house and deliver them to you or to your broker. Any honest broker can stand investigation and for your own protection you should ascertain whether the Put and Call broker whom you buy Puts and Calls from is reliable and will have the Puts and Calls guaranteed by a firm that is a member of the New York Stock Exchange.

## ADVANTAGE OF BUYING PUTS AND CALLS DIRECT

Should you want to send orders direct to buy Puts and Calls, you can send your check or money order direct to a Put and Call broker in New York and he will buy Puts and Calls for your account on your order and mail them direct to you or deliver them to your bank or your broker, as you request.

The advantage in sending your order direct to a Put and Call broker instead of over a broker's private wire is that you often get quicker service by using the Postal Telegraph or Western Union because all orders over brokers' private wires to buy and sell stocks have precedence over all messages pertaining to off-the-floor business. This would naturally delay the transmission of your order to buy a Put or a Call and if the market is very active, it might result in a point or more against you, whereas if your order went direct to the Put and Call broker by Western Union or Postal Telegraph, you would get a quicker execution. For example: Suppose you decided to buy a Put on Chrysler and you thought that Chrysler was about top and wanted to get it in a hurry, if you sent your order to a Put and Call broker, your telegram would read as follows:

BUY A PUT 100 CHRYSLER CLOSEST OBTAINABLE 30 DAYS

On receipt of this order the Put and Call broker would immediately buy a Put on Chrysler to the best advantage and would wire you the price at which he bought it. You, of course, would have to have your money on deposit with the Put and Call broker before you sent the order because he will not fill orders until the money is in hand. However, you could wire the money with your telegram. You would wire him $137.50 with the above message. On the other hand, if you wanted to buy a Call on Chrysler, then your order would read as follows:

BUY A CALL 100 CHRYSLER CLOSEST OBTAINABLE 30 DAYS

and with this message to buy a Call, if you did not have the money on deposit with the broker, you would wire $142.50 to pay for the Call.

If you were not in a hurry, you could send a telegram to the Put and Call broker and ask him to quote you Puts and Calls on Chrysler, General Motors, U. S. Steel or any other stocks, good 30 days. He would then wire the price at which he could buy, this price being subject to change any hour or any minute. After receiving the telegram from him, if you thought the price was close enough to the market that you could make money in 30 days, you could then wire your order to buy.

## THE ADVANTAGES OF PUTS AND CALLS TO THE BUYER

The great advantage to the man who buys Puts and Calls is that his risk is always limited. Another advantage is that he saves payment of interest. For instance, if you buy a Call and the stock moves up in your favor, for 30 days you do not have to pay any interest until you have called the stock and it has been delivered into your account.

Since the Securities Exchange Commission has raised margin requirements to where it requires 55% margin to buy stocks, it makes it a great advantage to buy Puts and Calls. For example: If you wanted to buy 100 shares of a stock selling at $100 per share, you would have to put up $5,500 margin and would expect it to go up more than 5 points if you bought it, therefore instead of putting up $5,500 to buy the stock and carry it and besides pay interest, you buy a Call, we will say, 5 points away for 30 days, which costs you $142.50. Then if the stock advances during the 30 day-period to where you have a profit of $1,000, you have made nearly 100% on your money. On the other hand, if you put up $5,500 and the stock advances so you have a profit of $1,000, your net return on your capital would be less than 20%,while at the same time if you bought 100 shares of stock on margin, it might decline 10 or 20 points and your loss would be 10 or 20 points according to whether you held it or used a stop loss order and limited your risk.

## HOW TO USE PUTS AND CALLS IN PLACE OF STOP LOSS ORDERS

Another advantage in buying Puts and Calls is to protect the stock that you already have bought or to protect the stock that you are already short of. When markets are very wild and active and unexpected events take place that cause stocks to open up or down several points, as has happened many times in the past and will happen again in the future, you want to be protected against losses. You can always use a stop loss order, but if the stock should open off 3, 4, or 5 points under your stop loss order, then your stock will be sold at the market. On the other hand, if you had 100 shares of Chrysler bought at 100 and it declined and closed some night at 97 and you had a stop loss order at 95 and something unexpected happened overnight and the next morning the stock opened at 90, your stock would be sold on stop at 90 at the market and you would lose 5 points more than you expected to lose by placing a stop loss order. If instead of placing a stop loss order when Chrysler was selling around 100, you bought a Put at 95, then when the stock opened off at 90 and continued to 80, your stock would be protected at 95 or you could deliver it at 95 on the Put and would not lose anything by the overnight drop, the Put having protected you against the unexpected.

Reverse the position. Suppose you are short of Chrysler at 100 and have a stop loss order on it at 105. If the unexpected happened and Chrysler opened at 110, then your stop loss order would be executed 5 points higher than you expected and you would lose

$500 or 5 points more than you had figured on. On the other hand, if you had a Call bought on Chrysler to protect your short sale and Chrysler opened 5 points above your stop loss order some morning, then the Call would protect you because you would have a contract to buy the stock at a price on the Call and you could call it and deliver it against your short sale.

Thus, you see that you can use Puts or Calls for insurance or for protection when you are long or short of the market just the same as you can use them to limit your risk in getting in and out of the market, limiting your loss to the amount you pay for a Put or a Call, when you want to take advantage of a stock that you think may have a fast move one way or the other.

## WHEN TO BUY PUTS AND CALLS

The time to buy Puts and Calls is when stocks are very active or just before activity starts. You can determine when to buy Puts and Calls and on what stocks to buy Puts or Calls by reading, studying and applying the rules in my books, Truth of the Stock Tape, Wall Street Stock Selector, and New Stock Trend Detector.

I will give you a few rules that will help you to determine the time to buy Puts or Calls:

RULE 1 - Buy Calls around double bottoms or triple bottoms, or buy the stock around double or triple bottoms and buy Puts, which will protect you should the stock break the old bottom. By this I mean, if a stock has held at a low level, then advances; then reacts to that same low level months later and makes a bottom, this would be a double bottom. Then if it advances and reacts the third time to around the same level, this would be a triple bottom.

Reverse this rule at tops. Buy Puts around double or triple tops, or sell the stock short and buy Calls for protection in case the stock should cross the old tops.

It is always well even when stocks are moving very fast and are very active to wait several weeks or several months if a stock holds around a bottom or top before you buy Calls or Puts, giving the stock time to complete accumulation or distribution because this has to take place before there is a reverse move of a large number of points. You can easily see this by a study of past action of stocks on charts.

RULE 2 - Buy Calls when old levels are crossed. If a stock stays for several weeks, several months, or even several years in a narrow trading range around top levels, as referred to in my books, then when it breaks over the previous tops, it certainly will indicate activity. That is the time to buy a Call, as I will prove in examples later.

Reverse this rule. When a stock holds for a long time around low levels, then breaks the first support point, buy Puts or sell the stock short and buy Calls for protection.

RULE 3 - If a stock advances to a top that it has made many months previous or many years previous and fails to go thru, then has a reaction; then rallies and makes a lower top, that is, a third top and fails to go thru, this would be the place to sell the stock short and buy a Call for protection in case the stock went higher. It would also be the place to buy a Put for 30 days, because if this top is a final top and the stock is starting on a long decline, you would make money on the Put and could also be short of the stock at the same time by putting up margin.

Reverse this rule after a prolonged decline. If a stock makes a second or third higher bottom several weeks or months apart, then shows activity on the upside, it is the time to buy Calls or buy the stock and buy Puts for protection.

RULE 4 - When a stock holds for several months around the same level and fails to break the first support point, buy a Put and buy the stock when it begins to show activity, or buy a Call as soon as activity starts on the upside. (See example of Chrysler February 3, 1936 to June 5, 1936)

Reverse this rule when a stock holds for several months around top levels and fails to cross the first top. Buy a Put when activity starts on the downside or buy a Call and go short.

RULE 5 - After a stock advances thru an old top where it has held for several weeks or several months, and advances several points above this top, then reacts to the old top, buy Puts and buy the stock, or buy Calls.

Reverse this rule in a bear market. When a stock breaks thru an old bottom and goes several points below it, then rallies back to the old bottom, buy Calls and sell short against them, or buy Puts.

RULE 6 - In a Bull Market when trend is up wait for reaction of 5, 10 or 12 points, then buy Calls, or buy the stock and buy Puts to protect the purchase.

In a Bear Market wait for rallies of 5, 7, 10 or 12 points, then buy Puts, or sell short and buy Calls to protect the trade.

RULE 7 - Buy a Call when a stock reacts 40 to 50% of the last advance or buy the stock and buy Puts to protect it.

Reverse this rule in bear market: Buy Puts when a stock rallies 40 to 50% of last move or buy Calls when it rallies to protect short sales. For example: Suppose a stock advances from 100 to 120. A decline to 110 would be one-half or 50% of the advance. If all indications point to a bear market with the main trend down, then you would buy Puts when the stock rallied 40 to 50%. Example: U. S. Steel, March 6 to 11, 1937, made top at 126½. After an advance of over 50 points, a big reaction could be expected and it was time to buy a Put. March 22, U. S. Steel declined to 112½, down 14 points from the top. A 50% rally would be 7 points or to 119½, where you would buy Puts. Steel advanced to 123½ on March 31, better than 50%, giving a good opportunity to buy Puts for 30 days, which made good as Steel declined 24 points in 30 days.

## WHEN TO BUY MORE PUTS AND CALLS ON THE SAME STOCK

Suppose a stock breaks out on the upside, moves up fast and shows uptrend. You have bought Calls and have profits in them the first month. The trend still shows up and when it crosses previous tops or Resistance Levels, then you buy Calls the next month and can protect the profits that you have on the first Calls by buying Puts under the market and still carry your original stock. Many traders do this when a move of 50 or 60 points takes place in two or three months. They continue to buy Calls every month and continue to carry their stock and then often buy Puts to protect their profits instead of placing stop loss orders, thus making a large amount of profit on a very small risk.

## HOW TO TRADE AGAINST PUTS AND CALLS

Suppose you buy a Call on General Motors at 50. At the time you buy the Call, General Motors is selling at 47. You have bought a Call at 50, good 30 days. When General Motors advances to 50, holds for several days and doesn't look like going thru, you could then sell short 50 shares of General Motors; then no matter which way General Motors went, up or down, you would make money. If it advanced to 55, you would still have a profit of 5 points on your Call, and on the stock that you sold short at 50, you would have a loss of 5 points, but this would be made up because you could call 100 shares. After you sold short at 50, if you were right and General Motors declined to 45 or to 40, then when your Call expired it would be of no value but the stock that you sold short would be down 5 points or more and you could close your short trade with a profit.

Example of trading against a Put: Suppose Douglas Aircraft is selling around 50 and you buy a Put on 100 shares, good 30 days, at 46. Douglas declines to 46 or to 45 and holds for several days and looks like making bottom and not going any lower, but you are not certain which way it will go for the remainder of the time for which your Put is good, so you buy 50 shares of Douglas at 46 against your Put, then if it goes up 5 points you are making profit on the stock you bought and you cannot lose because you have a Put. Then, if it should decline 5 points, you would have a profit of 5 points on your Put and could deliver 100 shares against what you bought and have no loss except the cost of the commission and the premium paid for your Put.

Many shrewd traders who buy Puts and Calls make money trading against them and at the end of the time the Put or Call expires there is no profit in it but they have made a profit because they traded on the fluctuations of the market. Often you can sell against a Put or buy against a Call several times during the month and scalp anywhere from 2 to 5 points or more and possibly make 10 points' profit and be protected all the time and yet at the end of the Put there would be no profit in it.

Some traders handle Puts and Calls in this way: Suppose they have bought a Call on a stock at 100 and it advances to 110; then they buy a Call for 30 days longer at a higher level, and when the first Call expires on which they have profit, they call the stock in and do not sell it out; then buy a Put to protect their profit and continue to buy Calls and buy Puts, pyramiding all the way up, not selling out their stock until they think the time has come for a change in the main trend.

This way of trading is reversed on the downside of the market. Buying a Put and getting short; buying more Puts on the way down; staying short; then buying a Call to protect the short stock, following the main trend for several months or as long as it indicates that it is down.

## KIND OF STOCKS TO BUY PUTS AND CALLS ON

Stocks always move faster at higher levels than they do at low levels, therefore, as a general rule, you can make the most money by buying Puts and Calls on stocks selling between $75 and $150 per share, but there are times when you can buy Calls on stocks selling between $5 and $10 and make a large percentage on the risk.

The next range of price is between $20 and $36. In this range you can often buy Puts and Calls at the market or within one or two points of the price at which the stock is selling. After stocks cross $36 to $40 per share they move much faster, therefore you will make more money by buying Puts and Calls on stocks after they are above $36 to $40 and from there up to $60 to $75 per share than you will buying options on stocks in the lower class.

In the same way, by buying Calls or Puts on stocks selling at 100 or higher you will make more money as they will decline faster until they get down to around 50 to 40; then in most cases they will decline slower. Therefore your chances of making profits are less in buying Puts or Calls on lower-priced stocks. I will give examples later and you can see by watching and studying charts when there are often opportunities for very large profits when a low-priced stock gets out of the zone of accumulation. In the same way, when a stock is in a congested area at high levels and remains in a narrow trading range for a long time, then breaks out, you can then make money buying Puts just as a big decline is ready to start.

## EXAMPLES OF TRADING WITH PUTS AND CALLS

### CHRYSLER MOTORS

1932 - July 30, note Chrysler on the Weekly Chart had remained in a narrow trading range for 8 weeks after it had made bottom at 5. When it crossed 8 it was over the top of the previous weeks and indicated higher. At that time you could probably have bought a Call on Chrysler around 10. It advanced to 16 in 30 days and was up to 21¾ in 6 weeks, giving a possible profit of 10 to 12 points. This trade would have been made by watching the chart and seeing a long period of congestion in a narrow trading range and then not anticipating anything but waiting until the stock showed itself by advancing above the tops of the previous weeks; then you would buy the Call.

1933 - April 25, again Chrysler crossed 8 weeks' tops. You could probably have bought a Call at this time around 15 good for 30 days. It advanced to 21½ and the trend did not turn down, the stock continuing up until it reached 39½, showing a possible profit of around 20 points. After the stock advanced to where you had a profit of 10 points or more, you could have bought a Put which would have protected the profits, or followed it up with a stop loss order after you had called the stock which you bought lower.

1934 - February 3 to March 1, Chrysler made tops around 60, showing that it was meeting great resistance. Around March 1st you could probably have bought a Put at 55. The stock started a downward move and declined to 49 in 30 days; then rallied to 56 and you could probably have bought a Call around 55 before the rally took place, which would have protected your short sales; then you could have stayed short. The stock declined on May 19 to 36½; then rallied to 44 and continued on down to 29¼ on August 7, giving another possibility for a profit of 20 to 25 points on Puts and a limited risk of not more than $280 if you bought a Put and then bought a Call, after it went down, to protect your profits.

1935 - March 12, Chrysler reached a low of 31. It had made a bottom at $29\frac{1}{4}$ in August, 1934, and made a double bottom at 29-3/8 in September, 1934. This decline to 31 was a third bottom at a higher level and would have been a place at which to buy the stock with a stop under $29\frac{1}{4}$ or to buy Calls because this was a double and triple bottom. Around that time you could probably have bought a Call around 34 or 35 because the stock had been narrow for a long time. In 4 weeks it advanced to 37 and the trend continued up until May 25, when it reached $49\frac{1}{2}$, giving an opportunity for a profit of at least 10 points' net. Then the stock reacted to $41\frac{1}{2}$, which was an old top and a place to again buy a Call or to buy a Put and trade against it.

In July and August, 1935, Chrysler crossed 60, the old top of 1934, and held for 4 weeks without breaking back under 57, which according to the rules in my books, was a place to buy with a stop at 57. Having crossed the top of 1934, it indicated higher. After holding for 4 weeks in a narrow trading range, around September 10 you could probably have bought a Call at 65. In 30 days it was up to $74\frac{1}{2}$ with the main trend strong up. You could have bought another Call and also bought a Put and held your stock after calling it at the time the first option expired.

In November, 1935, Chrysler advanced to 90 and at no time had it reacted 5 points after it crossed 60. This was another opportunity for making 25 to 30 points' net profit on an original risk of $142.50 and you might have bought more Calls on the way up after you had profits and started handling a pyramid and made much larger profits.

Always watch a stock if it makes a top or a bottom and holds for several months without breaking the first support level; then when it begins to show activity by breaking to new lows or advancing to new highs, it is the time to buy a Put or a Call. (Refer to Rule 4)

1936 - February 3, Chrysler declined about 10 points, making low at $91\frac{1}{2}$; then advanced on April 13 to 103-7/8; then again declined on April 30 to 91-5/8 and held in this range until June 5, when it was again down to 91-5/8. From February to early June, nearly 5 months, it held in a narrow range without breaking the low level of $91\frac{1}{2}$, and making bottom for so many months around this level indicated that it was due for a big move one way or the other. In the early part of June you could probably have bought a Call on Chrysler around 97, good 30 days, but if you waited until it crossed several weeks' tops at 98, you would have bought a Call in the early part of July good 30 days, which you could probably have bought around 100 to 101. In 30 days it was up to 116, when you would have a profit of 12 to 16 points. It went right on up to 124-7/8 on July 27, advancing 32 points from the low of June 5 without ever reacting 5 points. If you had bought stock when it was near the low or bought a Call, you could have called the stock; then bought a Put to protect it and kept it right on thru, or you could have put a stop loss order on it and carried it thru. In the second month you could have bought another Call. This move certainly gave you an opportunity to make 25 points or more on a Call.

After a sharp advance of 32 points in less than two months, you could naturally expect a reaction. After these fast moves, as a general rule, the reaction runs one-half or 50%. (See rule 7) When Chrysler was around 124, you could probably have bought a Put at 119 to 117. On August 21 Chrysler declined to 108-5/8, down 16 points, giving you a chance to make a profit of 6 to 7 points, anyway, on a Put. Then it held for 5 weeks between 108-5/8 and 117; then started up. When it started up you could have again bought a Call. It advanced 18 points in 30 days, advancing to 130½, affording another excellent opportunity for profits on Calls.

On November 12, 1936, Chrysler made the high of its move at 138¾. This was an important point because the top made on October 6, 1928 was 140½. You would sell out long stock around these levels and go short with a stop above 140½. This was also the level at which to buy Puts or Calls. You could buy Calls and then go short or buy Puts expecting that it would not go to a new high. You could probably have bought a Put at 130 or higher. In 30 days Chrysler was down to 121; then continued down to 110¾, which price it reached on January 4, 1937, down 28 points. You certainly would have an opportunity on this decline to make 15 or 20 points on Puts, or after you bought the first Put and it declined, you could have bought a Call for protection and carried the stock on down.

1937 - Around January 4 would be a time to buy a Call or a Put because the stock was down near the low levels of 108-5/8 made on August 21, 1936. You could have bought a Put at this time and then bought the stock, figuring that it would not break the old low levels before a good rally, or when it reached 110¾ or anywhere around that level, you could have bought a Call, probably at 117, good 30 days. Before the 30 days was up Chrysler was up to 124, and on February 11 advanced to 135¼, giving a possible profit of 15 points. This would be another place to buy a Call and go short figuring the stock would not cross the old top at 138¾, or after you saw it hold and not go thru, you could buy a Put. Chrysler first declined to 124; then rallied to 134-7/8 on March 3. This was the third top around the same level, 135¼ being a lower top than 138¾, and 134-7/8 being slightly lower than the other top. This was an excellent time to go short of the stock with a stop above old tops and also a good time to buy Puts because the old tops were so close. It declined in 30 days to 120; then you could have bought a Call to protect your profits on the Put and could have bought another Put good 30 days. By May 13 the stock declined to 106½, down 29 points from the top, giving an opportunity for a profit of 20 points or more on Puts. Then Chrysler rallied on May 24 to 115, a rally of 8½ points, which was a fair-sized rally in a weak market. On May 24, when Chrysler was selling around 114-5/8, Puts were offered at 110, good for 30 days, at a cost of $137.50.

## U. S. STEEL

We will give you some examples as to where Puts and Calls could have been bought on U. S. STEEL to advantage:

1932 - May 7 to June 28, high and low on U. S. Steel during this period was 31½ and 21¼. When Steel declined to around 22 you would buy Calls because the low of 1927 was at 21-7/8. You could propably have bought a Call at that time at 25 or lower, or you could have bought a Put and bought the stock against it. Another way to trade would have been to wait until U. S. Steel crossed the top of 32, which was above 7 or 8 weeks' tops, then bought Calls. In 30 days it advanced to 44 and by September 6 advanced to 52½, giving a possible profit of 25 to 30 points on Calls.

1933 - July 18, U. S. Steel advanced to 67½ and by July 21 declined to 49, down 18½ points in three days. A Put good 7 days or two weeks at that time would have made good. However, when it was around the high levels, if you had bought a Put good 30 days, you could have made profits because the stock declined again to 49 on August 16 and never rallied above 58 until it declined to 34¾ on October 21, 1933.

1935 - January 8, U. S. Steel made high at 40. March 18, declined to 27½. This would have been a place to buy Puts or Calls because it was a double bottom against a low made September 17, 1934, when Steel sold at 29¼. You could have bought the stock and bought Puts as protection, or you could have bought Calls, or you could have waited until after U. S. Steel crossed 40, the high of January, and then bought Calls. After it crossed 40, it never sold at 40 again until it advanced to 72 on April 9, 1936. Thus, you can see that if you had bought stock and bought Puts or bought Calls and once had profits in them, you could have moved up the stop loss order or bought a Put to protect the profits and carried it for big profits.

1936 - April—You could probably have bought Puts on U. S. Steel good 30 days around 66. Within 30 days it declined to 54¼, giving an opportunity to make a profit of 10 to 12 points in 30 days.

October 3 to January 9, 1937, U. S. Steel held in a range from 72 to 80, or four months in an 8-point range. When Steel narrows down for several months like this, it is getting ready for a big move one way or the other.

On November 23 when it declined to 72, it was at the old top of April 9, 1936, a buying point, or a place to buy Puts and buy the stock or to buy Calls, but a better time and the surest place to buy Calls was when it crossed 80 on January 7, 1937. You could probably have bought Calls at that time at 85 good for 30 days. The last low was made at 79 on January 12 and in 30 days or February 11 U. S. Steel sold at 109½, giving a possible profit of 24 points. With the trend still up you could probably have bought Puts 5 points down to protect your profit and held your stock. You could also have bought Calls good 30 days.

1937 - March 11, U. S. Steel advanced to 126½, up 57½ points in 60 days. Thus, after the long period of dullness in an 8-point range, you had an opportunity in 60 days to make profits of over 50 points by buying Calls. Then, after this rapid advance you could have bought a Put. On March 22 U. S. Steel declined to 112½, off 14½ points. On March 31 it rallied, making a top at 123½, lower than the first top. This would have been the time to buy Calls and go short because it was near the old top, or to buy Puts. You could probably have bought Puts at this time around 117. Thirty days later U. S. Steel was down to 99. Then, if you were short on Puts, you could have bought a Call to protect your profits or placed a stop loss order to protect profits. On May 18 U. S. Steel declined to 91-5/8, down 32 points in 48 days. This shows you that when activity follows a long period of dullness there are big opportunities for making large profits on small risks trading in Puts and Calls.

## RULES FOR BUYING PUTS AND CALLS ON LOW-PRICED STOCKS

Many low-priced stocks remain in a narrow trading range for many years and do not offer any opportunity for making profits buying Puts and Calls. Therefore, if you bought too often without waiting for definite indications on low-priced stocks, you would just lose the money you paid out for Puts and Calls.

You must have a rule to determine when to buy Puts and Calls on low-priced stocks because at times there are really big opportunities for making profits if you study and watch stocks when they start to move from low levels. You either have to wait until a stock holds in a narrow trading range from 4 to 6 months or until it holds in a narrow trading range for several years and then crosses the old top levels and shows activity; that is when you can buy Calls. For example:

JOHNS MANVILLE—

1929 - February, Johns Manville advanced to a high of 242. There is no use talking about how much money could have been made buying Puts even 20, 30 or 50 points away on high-priced stocks in 1929 or buying Puts to protect stocks that people were long of. The opportunities were certainly there. But I want to be conservative and point out how profits can be made trading in Puts and Calls in normal markets.

1932 - During April, May, June and July Johns Manville made a low each month at 10 and the high during that period was 16. It started up around the middle of July, 1932, after the general market had made bottom. Of course, after it stayed several months around 10, you could have bought a Put probably one point down and could have bought the stock, but the safest and best time was in August when it crossed 16; then you could probably have bought a Call at 19 or 20. It was then above a four-months' range and showed that it was going to move up. In 30 days it advanced to 29 and in the early part of September sold at 33. There was certainly an opportunity to make 10 to 12 points' profit buying Calls on a low-priced stock after it gave a signal to advance.

1933 - March, Johns Manville declined to 13, 3 points above the old low level of 1932 and a place to buy with a stop under 10 or a place to buy Puts and buy the stock; also a place to buy Calls.

In May the stock crossed 33, the high of September, 1932, which indicated activity and higher prices. You could have bought a Call after it crossed 33, which would have made you at least 15 points' profit in 30 days. In July Johns Manville sold at 60.

1935 - In July Johns Manville crossed a series of tops at 57. This was the time to buy Calls. In August, 1935, it crossed 67, the top of February, 1934, another time to buy Calls because it indicated a definite trend up. It never reacted over 10 points until it sold at 129 in February, 1936. You could have bought Calls right along all the way up or bought Puts to protect your profits on Calls and made large profits.

BOEING AIRCRAFT—

September, 1934, to July, 1935, this stock had a range between $11\frac{1}{4}$ and $6\frac{1}{4}$, or a range of 5 points. From March, 1935 to June, 1935, it moved in a range of 2 points between $6\frac{1}{4}$ and $8\frac{1}{4}$. In July, 1935, it advanced to 9, crossing the tops of the previous three months. This was a place to buy Calls. However, if you had waited until it crossed 12 in August and bought Calls when it was above all these high levels, you could have made big profits because it never sold below 12 until it advanced to $26\frac{1}{2}$ in January, 1936. Notice how much faster the stock moved up after it reached high levels. I have told you that when stocks get above 36 to 40, they move much faster. In March, 1937, Boeing advanced to $49\frac{1}{2}$, up 13 points in 13 days.

DOUGLAS AIRCRAFT—

1935 - March, low $17\frac{1}{2}$. October and November, high 35. December, low 34. Then it crossed the old high levels and advanced to 59 in the same month, making a range of 25 points, the first month after it got above 36. Of course, there was big money in buying Calls good for 30 days.

1936 - January, Douglas made a low of $50\frac{1}{2}$ and the same month advanced to $75\frac{1}{2}$, making a 25-point range in 30 days, again proving how much faster stocks move after they get above 50 and the greater opportunities for profits as they move into high levels.

November, 1936, Douglas high 77. December high $77\frac{3}{4}$.

1937 - January, high 77. Three months with tops around the same level. This would have been a time to buy Calls and go short because the high level of the stock was 82, made in October, 1936. It was also a time to buy Puts because they could probably have been bought 5 points down or you could have waited until the stock broke 68, the low of December, 1936, and then bought Puts good 30 days. The stock declined fast and after you had profits on Puts, you could have bought a Call and carried it on down.

In May, 1937, Douglas declined to $47\frac{1}{2}$, down 30 points from the January high, affording excellent opportunities for pyramiding on the way down and selling the stock short or for staying short after you once had a profit in a Put and a chance to protect it with a Call. The percentage of profits compared to the risk would have been enormous.

---

The above examples show you the advantages and opportunities of using Puts and Calls at critical times and when stocks are active. No one can expect to make a great success in any line of business unless they study it constantly and learn more and more about it. There is no business in the world that will return greater profit on the risk and the capital than speculation, using Puts and Calls, provided you keep up monthly and weekly high and low charts on quite a few stocks and study them. Follow the rules laid down in my books, Truth of the Stock Tape, Wall Street Stock Selector, and New Stock Trend Detector, and you will learn how to trade successfully in Puts and Calls.

The more you study the market and the more you study Puts and Calls and learn how to operate, the more advantages you will see in using them.

W. D. G A N N

May 26, 1937

## *Cosmological Economics*

# The Masters Of Technical Analysis Series

The Masters of Technical Analysis Series brings together a collection of the most important classical and modern works on technical analysis and financial market forecasting. These classic works from the Golden Age of Technical Analysis were carefully selected by the late Dr. Jerome Baumring of the Investment Centre Bookstore in the 1980's, as representing the most valuable and important works in technical analysis ever written. They were included as the foundational source texts for his program in advanced financial market analysis and forecasting, and serve as the ideal foundation for any analyst seeking a thorough education in market theory and technical trading.

The Golden Age of technical analysis was a period from the early 1900's through the 1960's where the foundational theories of modern financial analysis were initially developed. The ideas and technologies developed during this fruitful period have formed the basis for most modern technical market theory, which is considered to be mostly a repetition or reworking of these past ideas and techniques developed by the Old Masters of the Golden Age. In these historical works can be found the timeless trading wisdom which has laid the foundation for all modern investment theory and literature. These techniques are as useful in today's markets as they were in the past, providing rare and valuable insights, tools and strategies that give the modern trader an edge over traders and investors that are unaware of these time honored tools.

Each quality reprint of these classical texts has been reproduced as an exact facsimile of the original text, maintaining the original layout, typeset, charts, and style of the author and time period, helping to preserve and communicate a sense of the feeling of the original work that a reproduction in modern format does not capture. Many of these rare works and courses were originally printed in only very small private editions or as correspondence courses, so that the originals were easily lost or destroyed over time. Our reproductions of these important source works have been printed on acid free paper and bound in a quality hardcover format that will compliment any trading library and help to preserve this important resource for generations to come.

The series is also currently being digitized and archived for permanent digital preservation by the Institute of Cosmological Economics, creating a searchable reference library of market wisdom accessible globally and available in new digital formats to keep the knowledge fresh and accessible through new devices and technology as we advance further into the information revolution. To see our full catalog of hardcover reprints, new publications, and digital editions please visit our website at www.CosmoEconomics.com.

- **Samuel Benner, An Ohio Farmer** - Benner's Prophecies - *Of Future Ups and Downs in Prices* - (1879)
- **Geo. W. Cole, La Marquette** - Graphs & Their Application to Speculation - (1936)
- **Frank Tubbs** - Tubbs' Stock Market Correspondence Course - (1944)
- **R. N. Elliot** - Collected Works of R. N. Elliot - *The Wave Principle. Nature`s Law: The Secret of the Universe. "The Wave Principle": A Series of Articles Published in 1939.* - (1946)
- **Joseph A. Wyler** - Wyler Series on Stock Market Speculation - *Vol.1, The Application Of Scientific Principles To Stock Speculation. Vol.2, Trading And Trending* - (1960)
- **Edward Dewey** - How to Make a Cycles Analysis - *Correspondence Course in Advanced Cycle Analysis*- (1955)
- **Nikolai D. Kondratieff** - Long Waves In Economic Life - (1935)
- **Pickell & Daniel** - Pickell-Daniel Extension Course of Market Analysis - (1937)
- **Franklin Paul Jackson** - The I-S Method - *Individual Stock - Intermediate Swing* - (1972)
- **Richard Schabacker** - Technical Analysis & Stock Market Profits - (1930)
- **Richard Schabacker** - Stock Market Profits - (1934)
- **M. V. Woods** - Seven Studies In Stock Market Trading - (1943)
- **William Dunnigan** - Collected Works of William Dunnigan - *Gains in Grains. New Blueprints for Gains in Stocks & Grains; Barometers for Forecasting Stocks. One-Way Formula for Trading In Stocks & Commodities* - (1957)
- **Henry Ludwell Moore** - Collected Works of Henry Ludwell Moore - *Economic Cycles Their Law & Cause. Generating Economic Cycles. Forecasting The Yield of Cotton* - (1923)
- **Edwin S. Quinn** - Action - Reaction Signals - (1950)
- **Emil Schultheis** - Basic Trend Barometer - *A Long Term Stock Trend Study* - (1946)
- **Payson Todd** - The "Todd Theory" of Market Measurement & Price Projection - (1953)
- **Dr. Alexander Goulden** - Behind The Veil - (2010)
- **C. S. Johnson, C. P. A.** - A New Technique of Stock Market Forecasting - (1931)
- **William D. Gann** - The Collected Writings of W. D. Gann, Volume I - *Marketing Brochures, Interviews, Annual Forecasts & Trading Records* - (1909-1954)
- **William D. Gann** - The Collected Writings of W. D. Gann, Volume II - *The Master Time Factor: No. 3 Master Forecasting Method & Stock Market Forecasting Courses* - (1921-1954)
- **William D. Gann** - Collected Writings of W. D. Gann, Volume III - *Master Mathematical Formula & Calculators* - (1955)
- **William D. Gann** - Collected Writings of W. D. Gann, Volume IV - *The Complete Commodity Courses* - (1940)
- **William D. Gann** - Collected Writings of W. D. Gann, Volume V - *Introductory Stock Market Courses, Mechanical Methods, & Trend Indicators Courses* - (1935-1950)
- **William D. Gann** - Complete Collected Writings of W. D. Gann - In 6 Volumes - (1955)
- **Timothy Walker** - How To Trade Like W. D. Gann - *An Exploration of the Mechanical Trading Lesson on U. S. Steel* - (2014)
- **James P. Morton** - When to Sell to Assure Profits - (1926)
- **Daniele Prandelli** - The Polarity Factor System - *An Integrated Forecasting & Trading Strategy Inspired By W. D. Gann's Master Time Factor* - (2012)
- **Daniele Prandelli** - The Law Of Cause And Effect - *Creating A Planetary Price/Time Map Of Market Action Through Sympathetic Resonance* - (2010)
- **Perspectives, National Graphic Co.** - The Great Bull Market & Collapse - (1932)
- **Richard Martin** - An Introduction to Trend - Action - *A Scientific Method of Forecasting* - (1943)

- **George Bayer** - Money Investing In Stocks, Trading In Commodities, Or The Time Factors In The Stock Market - *The Art of Scientifically Detecting Direction & Distance of Swings* - (1937)
- **George Bayer** - The Egg of Columbus - (1942)
- **George Bayer** - Stock & Commodity Traders Hand-Book of Trend Determination - *Secrets of Forecasting Values, Especially Commodities, Including Stocks* - (1940)
- **George Bayer** - Gold Nuggets for Stock & Commodity Traders - (1941)
- **George Bayer** - Preview of Markets - *VOL. I, NOS. 1-10* - (1939)
- **George Bayer** - George Wollsten - Expert Stock & Grain Trader - (1946)
- **George Bayer** - The Collected Works of George Bayer - *9 Books In 2 Hardcover Volumes* - (1939)
- **Cliff Stewart** - Magic of Making Money in The Stock Market - (1951)
- **Dickson F. Watts** - Speculation as a Fine Art - *& Thoughts On Life* - (1865)
- **Henry Ansley** - I Like the Depression - (1932)
- **Henry Hall** - How Money is Made in Security Investment - *Or A Fortune At Fifty-Five* - (1908)
- **Dr. Jerome Baumring & Julius J. Nirenstein** - Gann Harmony: The Law of Vibration: The Complete Course Manuals & Lecture Notes - *The Complete Gann 1-9 Course Manuals. Compiled By Dr. Jerome Baumring With Notes On W. D. Gann's Hidden Material: The Complete Gann 1-9 Lecture Notes* - (1989)
- **Dr. Jerome Baumring** - Gann Harmony: The Law of Vibration. The Complete Course Manuals - *Course Manuals For Gann 1 Through Gann 9* - (1989)
- **Julius J. Nirenstein & Dr. Jerome Baumring** - Notes on W. D. Gann's Hidden Material: The Complete Lecture Notes - *Lecture Notes for Gann 1 through Gann 9* - (1989)
- **Alfred Friedman** - Lecture Notes from Baumring's Investment Centre Series - (1987)
- **B. Edlin** - Minor Swings of the Stock Market and their indications - (1924)
- **Henry Howard Harper** - The Psychology of Speculation - *The Human Element In Market Transactions* - (1926)
- **S. A. Nelson** - The ABC of Options & Arbitrage - (1904)
- **Daniel T. Ferrera** - The Gann Pyramid - *Square of Nine Essentials* - (2001)
- **Daniel T. Ferrera** - The Mysteries of Gann Analysis Unveiled! - *A Detailed Presentation of W. D. Gann's Technical Trading Principles* - (2001)
- **Daniel T. Ferrera** - Wheels Within Wheels – *The Art of Forecasting Financial Market Cycles* - (2002)
- **Daniel T. Ferrera** - W. D. Gann's Mass Pressure Forecasting Charts - (2004)
- **Daniel T. Ferrera** - The Keys to Successful Speculation - (2004)
- **Daniel T. Ferrera** - Spirals of Growth and Decay - *Exposing the Underlying Structure of Financial Markets* (2005)
- **Daniel T. Ferrera** – Gann for the Active Trader - *New Methods For Today's Markets* (2006)
- **Daniel T Ferrera** – Economic & Stock Market Forecasting – *W.D. Gann's Science of Cyclical Periodicity Sequencing* (2013)
- **Daniel T. Ferrera -** The Path of Least Resistance - *The Underlying Wisdom & Philosophy of W. D. Gann Elegantly Encoded in the Master Charts* - (2014)
- **Warren Hickernell** - What Makes Stock Market Prices - (1932)
- **William C. Moore (Market Expert)** - Wall Street - *Its Mysteries Revealed, Its Secrets Exposed.* - (1932)

www.ingramcontent.com/pod-product-compliance
Lightning Source LLC
LaVergne TN
LVHW081949200926
848484LV00009B/2530